FORGOTTEN REGIMENTS

For My Parents

FORGOTTEN REGIMENTS

REGULAR AND VOLUNTEER UNITS
OF THE BRITISH FAR EAST

WITH A
HISTORY OF SOUTH PACIFIC FORMATIONS

Barry Renfrew

Terrier Press

First published in 2009 by Terrier Press,
15 Hollow Way Lane, Amersham,
Bucks HP6 6JP, UK

ISBN 978-0-9563175-0-6

Printed and bound in Great Britain by T J International Ltd, Padstow

Contents

Acknowledgements

This book is a small attempt to tell something of the hundreds of thousands of men from many races who served in Britain's Far Eastern military forces. With the exception of the Hong Kong Volunteers and some early work on the Malay Regiment, their endeavours have gone virtually unnoticed despite the many books written on British colonial military history. Regimental history, it has been said, is no history at all. Histories of military units often are inspired by members and veterans with an understandable desire to show a unit in the most positive terms. That tendency has not prompted this book to focus on the faults, if any, of the formations it covers: rather the aim is to give some idea of the whole story. A particular effort has been made to cover the overlooked Asian and mixed-race soldiers who made up most of the Far Eastern units. If there was a single inspiration behind the book, it was admiration and fascination for all of the men of these diverse formations. That regard has increased many times over in the course of researching and writing. I am aware of the book's shortcomings. Survivors and others, doubtless, will find errors and unintentional oversights. Nonetheless, it is hoped the book is a start on telling a story neglected for far too long.

Only writing a book makes you understand why authors start off by thanking those who helped in its birth. My thanks for permission to use materials in their collections to The National Archives at Kew, whose staff's professionalism and cheerfulness are a national treasure; Roderick Suddaby and the peerless staff of the reading room at the Imperial War Museum, in particular Sabrina Rowlatt: Alastair Massie and the equally excellent staff at the National Army Museum; and the wonderful staff and library of the Royal Artillery Museum. The book draw on some early histories of Volunteer units, particularly I. I. Kounin's *Eighty-Five Years of the Shanghai Volunteer Corps.* I have been unable to trace any copyright holders for these works, and will be pleased to acknowledge any such copyrights in any future editions. I am indebted to an eclectic group devoted to the pursuit of historical and military knowledge: Geoff Newman, Rod Flood, Dixon

Pickup, Julian Russell, Les Stillman, Alan Pullen, Mike Lukich and Vincenzo Sidone. I owe much to two men who are not only steeped in the military history of the British Empire, but served through its closing stages: Sir John Chapple and Bill Cranston. My deepest thanks to three friends, Steven and Sally Bosley and Bernard Pass. A particular thrill during my work was to meet Tom Evans, one of the last of the Singapore Volunteers, who fought in the doomed battle of 1942, and was as cheery and insightful as if still 25. Donald Sommerville's editing was subtle and skilled. Hugh Allan did an excellent job in seeing the book through publication.

My deepest thanks to two close friends of many years, Jim Donna and David Parker. Also to Sarah, Bethany and Glen for their good-natured toleration of a father who spends his days at the dawn of the 21st century immersed in the pursuit of forgotten colonial regiments. To my wife, Margaret, no words can possibly recount what I owe. And finally, this book is dedicated to my parents, who made it all possible.

Illustrations

Chapter 1
GUARDIANS OF EMPIRE
Britain's Far Eastern Formations

EXHAUSTED AND FILTHY SURVIVORS of Hong Kong's Volunteer Defence Corps crouched in foxholes and shattered buildings at the start of the most joyless Christmas Day they would ever see. Japanese artillery and infantry attacks had pushed the garrison of regular and part-time soldiers into rapidly dwindling pockets. The days since Japan had invaded the British colony were a nightmare far beyond the darkest imaginings of Hong Kong's colonial rulers. Most of the amateur soldiers of the Volunteer units were businessmen or civil servants, serving along with lawyers, engineers and other professionals. Such men had been serenely confident of what to expect in life. Comfort and privilege were their birthright. Most enjoyed careers with regular and predictable moves up the promotion ladder. Each step brought more authority, greater privileges and a higher perch in the social hierarchy. Retirement in London, Edinburgh or a pretty village in the shires stood at the end of their tidy plans. All that changed when Japanese troops poured over the virtually undefended border on 8 December 1941.

*

The Hong Kong Volunteer Defence Corps was an important part of the colony's meagre defences. It was shoved into the fighting along with regular British and Indian troops and last-minute Canadian reinforcements. Pre-war plans about front lines and holding the enemy until reinforcements arrived proved to be illusions. Every effort to halt the invaders was a bloody failure. Volunteers, as they were called, and regular troops were hurled, often a few dozen at a time, in hopeless attacks against Japanese regiments of a thousand men or more. Scores of Volunteers had been killed in anonymous encounters on the scrubby hillsides or amid the wreckage of homes and offices. Nothing in their casual peace-time training – an hour or two of weekly marching and comfortable evenings in the regimental bar – prepared the Volunteers for the sights and experiences of the battle. Some of the military amateurs were slashed and skewered with swords in hand-to-hand fighting. Captured Volunteers and regulars had been tied up and then shot or stabbed to death. Others were bayoneted in hospital beds where they lay helpless from earlier wounds. Teenagers and elderly men were killed or wounded with equal impartiality.

Men from other Hong Kong units were also holding positions on that sombre Christmas morning. Indian gunners of the Hong Kong–Singapore Royal Artillery, who had lost most of their guns or run out of shells, fought on as infantry. One officer strode towards the enemy with a machine gun and a bucket of grenades to die fighting. Survivors said it was as if he was setting off for a round on the golf course. A small unit of Chinese, raised at the last minute to defend a colony whose rulers despised them, suffered one of the highest casualty rates of any army in the war. And it had all been in vain as orders to surrender trickled around what was left of the garrison.

Similar scenes of stunned defeat were replayed in the coming weeks and months across Britain's Far Eastern empire. An edifice that seemed invincible just a few weeks before collapsed almost overnight. British administrators and residents, haughty even by the arrogant standards of empire, had run for their lives or fallen apart with the shame of defeat. Many survivors of the Straits Settlements Volunteer Forces calmly resigned themselves to dying in the ruins of Singapore. British forces had been hounded down the Malay Peninsula by a Japanese army whose men were derided at pre-war colonial dinner parties as freaks and incompetents. Many of Singapore's Volunteers were willing, some even eager, to die if it meant they could stop running away. Very few Volunteers had seen a Japanese soldier after two months of war. Determination turned to dismay as word spread there would be no brave last stand: just another British surrender. Men of the Volunteers and other British units were marched into a captivity that took the lives of many and irredeemably scarred the men who survived.

Malay and Chinese soldiers were singled out by the Japanese for the harshest retribution. Fighting for Britain was an inexcusable crime in the eyes of Singapore's new rulers. Scores of Asian soldiers were executed on Singapore's beaches, their blood mixing with the warm brown sea water. It was cruelly ironic that the British had often been ambivalent about accepting the services of these men.

A few weeks later the remnants of the Burma Army stumbled through the jungle-choked hills leading to the Indian frontier. Burma's little force of regular and volunteer units had been formed barely five years earlier. Its formations were devastated in the fighting or collapsed before even seeing action. Many regiments had been reduced to one or two officers and a handful of men. A survivor recalled seeing a forlorn group of five infantry colonels who had all lost their battalions. Men who escaped from the wreckage of Hong Kong, Singapore and Burma sometimes ran into new torments when they reached friendly lines after journeys over thousands of miles. British staff officers castigated or spurned them for not fighting or for running away. Some survivors of those early battles, who wanted to go on fighting, were rejected or used as virtual coolies.

*

This is an account of the forgotten regiments and units of the Far East that fought the wars of Empire, guarded its outposts and embodied its racial and cultural diversity. It encompasses a wide range of formations and men, from professional native soldiers such as the Burma Rifles to mostly white part-time reservists like the Singapore Volunteer Corps. They symbolised the Empire's might and its creed of many races loyally serving the Crown. Hundreds of thousands of Europeans, Chinese, Malays, Eurasians, Burmese, Indians and others soldiered in their ranks over the years. Local formations played a critical role in the defence and policing of the British Far East. Units like the Malay States Guides or the Hong Kong Volunteer Defence Corps were part of the daily fabric of colonial life. White Volunteers parading on the monarch's birthday and native soldiers standing guard at government buildings were an essential facet of colonial iconography.

The history of these formations is a remarkably rich and complex story: many were disparaged by rivals and critics as upstarts and amateurs. Historians' preoccupation with the British and Indian Armies has overlooked the importance of local units in the military and social history of the Far East. British forces in the Far East encompassed dozens of regular, volunteer and para-military formations. Only the more prominent units have been followed in this book. Not all of the units described here were part of the British military establishment. Shanghai's and other volunteer corps in China were multi-national forces; Sarawak's Rangers were the private army of a British rajah. Britain insisted the Chinese Labour Corps was not a military unit even as its men were killed and maimed on the Western Front in the First World War. And yet Britain counted all of them, officially or informally, as part of its imperial bulwark.

Some of these units were undisputed successes in war and peace. Others left legacies of disappointment and failure. Some formations only existed for a year or two; one or two survived for just a few weeks. Several units went on to become part of the regular forces of independent nations. Determined British and local leaders and officials had to overcome prejudice and bureaucratic indifference to show that Chinese and Malays could make superb soldiers. It helped that the British Empire produced officers who excelled at leading unorthodox and irregular formations. More than a few found their calling in units such as the British Army's only regular Chinese regiment or Burmese tribal levies. Many of these formations led precarious existences. It was not always easy to find suitable recruits. Most units were starved of funds and equipment by an imperial exchequer keen to police the Empire on the cheap. Local colonial administrations could be just as adept at shirking their share of military costs. Colonial taxpayers also resented having to help to pay for local defence. However, shortages of modern weapons and other essentials did not mean these units were spared from front-line duty when the need arose.

*

Captain T. M. Winsley recounted in his 1938 *History of the Singapore Volunteer Corps* how he once saved some of the unit's early records as they were about to be tossed onto a bonfire with old crates and packing material. Little has been written about most of these regiments and units. Records for many are scanty, incomplete and sometimes contradictory. Many units never thought to keep records; some never saw the need to leave accounts or imagined the Empire would go on forever and there would be time enough to write their histories. A great deal of information was lost in the fall of Singapore and other colonies. A three-page typed report is virtually all that remains of the Hong Kong Chinese Regiment. Little effort was made to capture the experiences and reminiscences of veterans of these units as was done with British and Indian Army formations.

   This account aims to provide brief histories of the principal Far Eastern colonial units. A section or addendum on Fiji and its sister colonies reflects how a great deal of the Asian experience was repeated in the South Pacific. I hope this book provides some sense of who these men were and what inspired them. An attempt has been made to view each regiment against the historical context of its times. Particular attention has been paid, when possible, to non-white regular and volunteer troops; these men have gone almost unnoticed despite their central role in British colonial forces. Very little exists in surviving records and other sources to say who these Asian soldiers were. Most first-hand testimony is in the recollections of white officers and men.

*

Broadly these regiments fit into two quite different categories: native professional or regular troops and, in the early years, mostly white, part-time volunteers that were a colonial version of the Reserve and Territorial formations in Britain. The two groups had little official contact beyond occasional joint training and, when war or civil unrest came, serving alongside each other. Volunteers, the ubiquitous name of reservists in all the colonies, frequently came from the upper ranks of white colonial society. Some Volunteer units in Malaya boasted of their men having more university degrees than any other military formations in the British Empire. Their administrators, professors and engineers could not have been more different from the peasants and tribesmen who made up the rank-and-file of native regular units. And yet there were numerous points where the worlds of the Volunteers and the regulars overlapped. Both groups generally called the various colonies where they lived home, at least temporarily, and shared a common interest in its protection and welfare. Each group had a basic understanding of the make-up and workings of colonial society. Volunteers in their civilian roles usually oversaw or worked with Asians. Many whites could at least get by in the local language and knew something about indigenous culture and attitudes. Large numbers of Volunteers were drafted as officers for native units on the eve of the Second World War because of their local knowledge. Volunteers and regulars were part of local life, unlike British and Indian Army units, which tended to live apart when on eastern garrison duty.

*

One of Britain's greatest imperial achievements was the creation of native armies to guard what poets described as her far flung domains. Millions of Indians, Africans, West Indians and others served and fought for Britain throughout the Empire's history. If India was the jewel in the imperial crown, India's army was its most brilliant facet. African soldiers held vast swathes of territory that rarely ever saw British troops. Only ancient Rome matched the immense scale and diversity of Britain's imperial legions.

It took a surprisingly long time to develop regular forces in the Far East despite this British talent for raising indigenous troops. It was felt for many years that such units were not needed. The British and Indian Armies generally provided garrison troops throughout the colonial period. It was a lucrative sideline for their own exchequers. Civil servants in the Malay States and elsewhere frequently complained about the exorbitant charges for such services. India was notorious for sending other colonies bills for unbudgeted and often unexplained extras.

There were bigger obstacles to the use of local regular troops than the availability of imperial units. Early colonial officials undermined local martial traditions to eradicate threats to British rule and dispersed the local sources of soldiers. It was also fashionable to insist the defeats inflicted by Britain on native states proved they could not fight: a view which blithely ignored huge disparities in weaponry and military organisation. Such policies and attitudes hardened into self-perpetuating myths that Malays, Burmese and others could not fight. Changes in attitude had to be forced by British officials and soldiers who were eager to boost the standing of the colonies they ran and saw the military potential of the local people.

Further pressure came from various levels of local society. Malaya's traditional rulers pushed for years to raise regular troops as a matter of local pride. Providing troops was seen by such elites as bolstering ties with Britain and advancing embryonic national interests. Poorer Malays, with less lofty designs, saw a military career as a way out of rural poverty. British officials had to balance their desire to placate local allies against the risks of arming people who might use the weapons against the colonial regime. Nations such as the Burmans, who clamoured for their own troops and had a taste for rebellion, generally were not recruited. A few Far Eastern units were purely mercenary formations that neither knew nor cared much about the British Empire. Men of the 1st Chinese Regiment were willing to serve and fight until something better came along. When it did they deserted by the hundreds. Government officials and accountants, for their part, were glad to get what they saw as cheap material that could be unceremoniously discarded when no longer needed.

British India's storied Army was a major influence in the development of Far Eastern units. An early tendency was to send agents to India to recruit men instead of enlisting the indigenous peoples. The manpower, methods and traditions of the Indian Army were faithfully duplicated in formations like the Hong Kong Regiment. It was as if a regiment was ordered off the shelf complete with officers and men, even if it had to be trained or assembled on arrival. Hong Kong residents grumbled because their preference for Sikhs was rejected because of low stocks in India. Malaya's states followed suit with the all-Indian Malay States Guides. Colonial strategists saw the Indians, outsiders dependent on the British, as more loyal and pliable. Indian soldiers dominated the armed forces of Burma, imperial units such as the Hong Kong–Singapore Royal Artillery, and even played a role in the rajah's private army in Sarawak. Alarmed at the success of such units, which were outside its control, the Indian Army raised battalions for Far Eastern duty and thereafter made sure it kept a near monopoly on the country's valuable military franchise. Preference for Indian soldiers diminished in the early 20th century as Far Eastern colonies became more confident and clamoured for their own regular units. Only Burma clung to Indian soldiers but it had to begin recruiting 'local' Gurkhas and Sikhs, descendants of men who had settled in the colony, after India cut off the supply of recruits in the 1930s. Purists grumbled that the locally grown varieties were poor imitations of the originals from Nepal and the Punjab.

Outright racial prejudice and pseudo-scientific notions about warrior or martial races at times hindered or blocked the enlistment of some races. This was most extreme in the use of the Chinese as soldiers. Chinese soldiers in the British forces were vilified by their own people and many British with equal venom. Suggestions from some seasoned officers that Chinese soldiers could play as big a role as the Indian Army never found support. Whitehall was never comfortable with the idea, although it struggled to find plausible objections. India's powerful military establishment resisted any challenge to its Asian hegemony. 'Of the Chinese as a soldier, there is little to say, except that he is utterly useless compared with Western standards', stated an official Indian Army handbook.[1] British settlers, who generally feared and loathed Chinese, insisted that arming them would be suicidal folly. Western residents openly insulted Chinese troops of the British Army who helped save them from the Boxers in 1900. Lonely advocates of the China school were left suggesting Chinese troops could be used to garrison Canada's west coast. Attempts to reach out to the Chinese on the eve of the Second World War made little difference, even though many men were willing to serve against the Japanese.

*

Volunteer soldiering was a prominent feature of colonial life in the Far East. Units first appeared in the middle of the 19th century when Hong Kong and other colonies were lightly defended outposts. These early part-time forces were small, ramshackle outfits that could do little more than form ranks and loose off a volley or two. What the early settlers lacked in numbers and military skill was balanced by their sense of heaven-ordained superiority. A handful of Shanghai's British and American merchants and clerks blithely marched out with a few sailors and marines to see off a Chinese army in 1854.

It took repeated attempts to form lasting Volunteer forces in the Far East. Many early units collapsed or withered away because they could not keep up their numbers. Enlistees found that marching up and down in Victorian attire in the tropical humidity or the monotony of rifle drills were nothing like their initial dreams of military glory. Many men simply stopped showing up.

Organisational flaws, uncertain funding and personality clashes added to the problems. Most early Volunteer corps were private and self-financing and lacked the resources and foundations to endure. It took intervention and support from local administrations to give most Volunteer units a permanent basis. Keeping up numbers was a perennial headache as the turbulence of the early years gave way to peace. Young men saw little point in sacrificing leisure time when there were far more agreeable diversions. Recruiting jumped when there was a war or some other threat only to slump after normality returned. Volunteers who spent evenings and weekends charging around with swords and guns were a favourite target for local wits. Cynics ridiculed them as overgrown schoolboys or self-important little men strutting about in sweaty tunics and baggy khaki shorts. Opponents of colonialism derided the Volunteers in later years as whisky-swilling reactionaries. Stock images of bumbling amateurs or bigoted settlers, then and now, often obscure the high quality and dedication of many Volunteer units.

Colonial Volunteers were very different from the working men and shopkeepers who made up most Territorial units in Britain. White units were often made up of well-educated, largely upper-class men who held important posts in local government and business. Many Volunteers possessed public school backgrounds, were good at sport and had served in school cadet corps or the regular forces. Such stock yielded serious and talented soldiers. Far Eastern Volunteer units provided hundreds of officers for the regular British and Indian forces in the two world wars. Many of these lieutenants, captains and even colonels from the First World War came back eager to serve in the Volunteers. Most were happy to join as privates if there were no openings for officers. Regular army generals inspecting Volunteer units would demand to know why half the privates were sporting medals reserved for officers. Volunteer forces were seriously weakened by being stripped of scores of their best men to serve as officers in regular units in the Second World War.

Peacetime soldiering in the Volunteers was remembered by many veterans as great fun. Volunteers' reminiscences are filled with happy memories of camaraderie. It was all fairly light-hearted with a chance of an occasional adventure. Some men saw serving in the Volunteers as part of their duty or loved soldiering. To most it was just another aspect of the

Compass Group UK & Ireland
COSTA COFFEE
UNIT NO: 76890
GENERAL MANAGER: Sharon Forster
VAT NO: 466 4777 01

Customer Copy

AMERICANO 16OZ   2.20

SUBTOTAL   2.20
Cash/Chq   5.20C
CHANGE   3.00

20.0%SALES   1.83
VAT@20.00%   0.37

Kerry
#002-037-0282-0001 11/10/2012 16:01-R

Great People..Great service..Great Results
Great Service
Great Results

weekly routine they were expected to follow along with tennis and horse riding. Military rank meant little and officers and men would sit together to drink and talk after parades. Regular army inspectors complained bitterly about such disdain for military etiquette and pushed to stop officers mixing with the men. Such efforts were laughed off by the Volunteers, who never tired of pointing out that their officers were frequently subordinate to some of the privates in civilian life.

Training was not taken too seriously in most units, although most men were proficient in basic military skills. Chronic shortages of modern weapons and equipment made it difficult to attain high standards. Improvisation was celebrated as a great virtue because there was no other way to equip many units. Armoured cars were cobbled together in the inter-war period with iron sheets mounted on trucks borrowed from the local municipality. The trucks had to be returned to the local harbour board or public works department during working hours. Even the keenest Volunteers usually only spent an hour or two a week training, with annual camps of a week or two. Enlistment dipped so low in the early 1930s that some units reduced the annual training requirement to 18 weekly drills.

Little of real military use could be learned in a few hours a year. Most men learned to shoot, march and look after their kit – although some young gentlemen brought their 'boys' or servants along to do the latter chore. Few had any real knowledge of tactics. Inspectors complained that volunteers did not know how to jump out of trucks under fire and warned they would be wiped out in a war because of strong individualist traits. The workings of large units or cooperation with the regular army were usually a mystery. All of these deficiencies were exposed ruthlessly in late 1941.

*

Race influenced or shaded almost every facet of colonial life. It played a major role in the identity and effectiveness of local military forces. Regular units made up of native troops and mostly white officers were usually recruited from a particular ethnic group or a precisely measured mix of races. This supposedly produced the best fighters and the most reliable. British recruiters in the Far East imitated the Indian Army's fetish for paler, taller men by recruiting northern Chinese or Burmese hill men. Particular groups were extolled as physically and morally superior. Policies of divide and rule and exploiting ethnic divisions to ensure the loyalty of native units were a significant, if often tacit, part of fixing units' make-up. Few regular units recruited impartially from all Asian races. Military officials argued that different languages, cultures and diets made it necessary to base companies and battalions on a single ethnic group. Mixed Asian units formed during the Second World War, however, showed the effectiveness of such units.

Race was a troublesome issue throughout the history of the Volunteer forces because of the colour bar that rigidly divided colonial life. Most whites wanted to keep Asians out of Volunteer units just as they were excluded from European social clubs. Standing next to an Asian in the ranks, in the bigoted view of most whites, was as distasteful or unnatural as sitting with one in the club. Barriers to Asian recruiting began to crack with the rise of Westernised Asians. It was hard to exclude men who had been to Oxford or Cambridge and were barristers or members of the local aristocracy. Asian elites in Singapore and Hong Kong saw entry into the Volunteers as a way to challenge second-class status. Wealthy and privileged Asians also had an interest in supporting the Volunteers' primary role of maintaining law and order and extending its umbrella to their own affairs. Volunteer service could help boost Asian political influence. Joining the Volunteers was not always a matter of self-interest. An increasing number of non-whites saw themselves as loyal British subjects: 'King's Chinese' was the term used to describe Chinese members of the Straits Settlement Volunteers. Service in the Volunteers was a way for such groups to show their fidelity.

Asian Volunteer units were often of very high standards because local communities hand-picked recruits to ensure their success. Asian leaders sought help from London after attempts to break the colour bar in some Volunteer forces were rebuffed by local officials. London was far more enthusiastic about Asians in Volunteer ranks as proof that the Empire existed to raise up 'lesser races'. It also saw Asian enlistment as the best way to strengthen the local defences and tackle chronic white recruiting problems. The spread of Christianity in some colonies added to the pool of Asians who wanted to join the Volunteers. Other Asians, particularly the less well-off, saw Volunteer duty as a way to improve their chances of getting a job or a promotion. The poorest needed the paltry allowances that Volunteers were sometimes paid for attending exercises.

Singapore was the first colony to admit Asian Volunteers. Other forces remained bastions of white exclusivity for many years. Hong Kong shunned recruiting large numbers of Chinese until the 1930s. Units that took Asians early on were also quicker to advance them. Chinese and Malays became officers in the Singapore and Malay forces fairly early on, although they rarely had authority over white troops. White Volunteers generally remained uncomfortable at serving with non-whites up to the Second

World War. Most units remained segregated with different races in separate companies or platoons. There was virtually no mixing outside of official duties and many units had segregated training facilities. Whites who served in the Straits Settlements forces in the inter-war era knew little or nothing about Chinese and Malay Volunteers in the same battalions. Elite units like the artillery frequently remained all-white. Asian recruiting for the local regular and Volunteer forces jumped across the Far East as part of last-minute attempts to boost local defences in the late 1930s. Most units were still segregated when war came, however, and this impaired military effectiveness. Still, units such as the Straits Settlements Volunteer Forces saw a greater mingling of races than many colonial institutions.

Eurasians were a separate, quite distinct group in the history of volunteering in the Far East. Mixed-race recruits were accepted early on in the ranks of most forces. They were often pushed aside or segregated later as the number of white residents rose and racial barriers hardened. Eurasians invariably saw themselves as Europeans – even if they were generally shunned by whites. Joining the Volunteers was an obvious way for Eurasians to demonstrate both their European identity and almost desperate sense of loyalty.

Mixed-race Volunteers appeared to fall into two distinct categories in the history of the Volunteers. One group was described as Portuguese and traced its roots to Macao. Portuguese units appear fairly early on in some forces and had an important role even if their members were rarely treated as social equals. Eurasians with British ancestry appear to have constituted a separate group. They were far less welcome in the Volunteers or elsewhere because of taboos on British intermarriage or sexual relations with non-whites. More than one force had separate 'Portuguese' and 'Eurasian' units. Eurasians continued to face prejudice and opposition even as barriers to Asian recruiting broke down. Eurasian officers in the Burma reserve forces faced being snubbed by white colleagues. It is particularly difficult to follow the experience of Eurasian Volunteers. Very few records survive and Eurasians were reticent about anything that might suggest they had a separate identity.

*

Social class was a significant factor in the make-up of white volunteer forces. Most units, especially in later years, tended to draw recruits from higher-class backgrounds. Senior civil servants and businessmen in the Volunteers did not want to mingle with the white foremen from the local sanitary department. London repeatedly lectured the Volunteer forces on the need to recruit only gentlemen to maintain high military standards. Volunteer privates joked in the Second World War about how regular soldiers mistook them for officers because of their accents. Some Volunteers were shocked and ashamed to learn of the realities of working-class life in Britain when they lived alongside regular soldiers in prison camps. Most had grown up with no conception of the grinding poverty of daily life in their own country.

*

Volunteer and regular units had two key roles: territorial defence and maintaining internal security. Paramilitary policing was the Volunteers' main function for much of their history. Colonial Volunteers were part of the apparatus to maintain the control of an occupying power: unlike their Territorial counterparts in Britain. Maintaining that control became increasingly difficult after the First World War as British rule was challenged by nationalists, communists and other groups. Volunteers were summoned with increasing frequency from their offices and homes to help the police deal with demonstrations and strikes. Volunteer and regular units occasionally marched through native quarters in shows of force aimed at intimidating the local population. Turning out to help the civil powers, while an exciting change for the Volunteers, could be a strain on local businesses and government departments. Business leaders complained about losses incurred by the frequent absences of their employees on emergency duty. Local government officials were often sympathetic and argued that security was the responsibility of the regular forces. Local Volunteer forces in China, on the other hand, were often the main defence for isolated expatriate communities. They sometimes had to hold off the troops of the local warlord or nationalist mobs until a gunboat or regular Western troops arrived.

Nobody enjoyed the British reputation for colonial eccentricity more than the Empire's rulers. Colonial soldiering seemed to encourage curious or comic behaviour. A young officer in Burma had a superior who went on exercises with a mule loaded with a case of whisky on one side and a case of gin on the other. Malay planters and Singapore businessmen took their 'boys' on exercises to clean and carry their kit. Other Volunteers did not want 'natives' doing anything that seemed like real soldiering. Hong Kong's white Volunteer gunners insisted on hauling their own cannons despite the armies of local coolies. Bemused officials in London suggested such enthusiasm was laudable if misplaced and should not be encouraged. One crusty colonel lectured his men on the tactics of shooting tigers as the best way to prepare them for dealing with human opponents. A love of military finery inspired many of these units. Officers of the Burma forces were still wearing ceremonial cavalry uniforms in the late 1930s. Regulars like the Hong Kong Regiment preened like peacocks in dashing red tunics and rainbow-hued turbans despite the colony's oppressive humidity.

Many Far Eastern regular and Volunteer regiments were decimated in unequal battles with overwhelming Japanese forces in the first few disastrous months of the Second World War in Asia. Critics questioned the courage and dedication of many units by claiming they should have done more to stop the Japanese. The stain of defeat obscured the fact that Europeans and Asians had united to fight as best they could against a common enemy. Disastrous defence polices and decades of penny-pinching were behind many of the military shortcomings. Abysmal treatment continued after the war for some survivors. Bureaucrats argued over paying compensation to Volunteers' widows and orphans. Post-war thoughts of reviving some regular and Volunteer formations floundered as calls for independence swept away the eastern Empire. India refused to provide men to uphold British rule in other countries. Units that were resurrected mostly helped build the armies of soon-to-be-independent nations. Volunteer forces reappeared in Hong Kong and Malaya to help deal with the new threats of the Cold War, but Asians played ever bigger roles as whites were nudged towards the exit.

Britain's Far Eastern colonial army has received little attention or recognition in later years. It is an unfortunate omission. The story of these regiments is a significant strand in the story of British rule in Asia. These formations played a crucial and intricate role in the guarding and workings of empire. Rarely have men from so many races and cultures been melded into such an enduring and capable force despite so many differences and obstacles. It was a remarkable and unique military saga.

Chapter 2

IN ORIENTE PRIMUS

The Singapore and Malay Volunteers

Singapore's volunteer corps was immensely proud of its claim to be the first such unit in the history of the British Empire. The formation of the Shanghai Volunteer Corps a year earlier was airily dismissed by the Singapore corps' historian because it contained 'various nationalities'.[1] The motto *'In Oriente Primus'* was later inscribed on the badge of the Singapore Volunteer Corps (SVC) in case anyone doubted its primacy. Oldest or not, the Singapore and Malay units became the largest British Volunteer military force in the Far East and played a significant part in the doomed battle for Singapore.[2]

*

It actually took the handful of British officials and traders who first settled Singapore several years to form a volunteer defence force. A local force was first proposed in 1846 when Chinese riots tore through parts of the island but it was not until 1854 that a meeting was held to form a unit after new clashes between recent Chinese immigrants and the existing Chinese community. Rival mobs had attacked and plundered houses and businesses in the city's Chinese quarter. Regular British troops, police, and sailors from ships in the harbour guarded the European parts of the city. A wave of killings swept surrounding rural areas, as a British official reported:

> 'While in town the [Chinese] people are comparatively civilised, the mass of the population in the jungle consists of men who have never for any length of time come in contact with Europeans or with the more orderly part of the town residents, with little or no idea of what law or order is. When, therefore the disturbances spread among them, they naturally plunged at once into far greater excesses than had characterised the town population, and the consequences was, that for a series of days the rural districts were the scene of the most lamentable outrages.'[3]

Although Europeans were unscathed by the rioting, it was decided to form a Volunteer unit to be called the Singapore Volunteer Rifle Corps. A resolution passed at the meeting stated the force would 'be of manifest advantage to the Settlement'.[4] Captain Ronald Macpherson, an officer of the Madras Artillery, was the corps' first commandant. Thirty-two men enlisted right away and the force's strength rose to 61 within a few days. Although some of the Volunteers did not show up regularly for drills, a newspaper noted that the force 'as far as the unprofessional eye could judge' appeared to march fairly well. 'We have no doubt that they will highly distinguish themselves whenever they may be called upon to take the field,' the report added.[5] Directors of the East India Company, who oversaw Singapore and the British enclaves in Malaya that made up the Straits Settlements, congratulated the Volunteers and hoped their example would be followed in India.

The first Singapore force was a purely private organisation, administered and funded by its members. It was run like an affable gentlemen's club on distinctly egalitarian lines. The applicants had to be of 'British descent'. Officers and NCOs were elected by the unit members; an elected management committee had representatives of the officers, NCOs and men; and new recruits had to be approved by the committee and three-quarters of the corps. Life in the corps was not very demanding. Training sessions were held once a month with the timing set by what was 'most generally convenient to the members'. Drills were generally held at 5 a.m. or in the evening to escape the worst heat. Members who missed a drill without a good excuse were fined 5 straits dollars.

Article VI of the unit regulations spelled out its primary function:

> 'The Corps shall not be liable to any call for actual service except in cases of emergency, such as an attack on the Town from without by foreign enemies, or a disturbance on the part of our population, when the Police Force may be found insufficient to secure the maintenance of the Public Peace.'[6]

The rank of sergeant was changed to 'sub officer' to raise the unit's social standards and avoid comparisons with the ruffians of the regular army. Green uniforms were worn on formal occasions, with white jackets and trousers for drilling and other activities. The East India Company passed an ordinance in 1857 giving the force official status, an event later marked as the creation of the settlement's second Volunteer corps although it was no different from the original formation. A set of regimental colours was presented to the force in February 1857. W. H. Read, the first Volunteer to command the corps, accepted the colours at a special parade. He made a little speech stressing that the Volunteers were sober, unpretentious businessmen and traders rather than blood-thirsty adventurers:

> 'We seek not the glory of the battlefield, nor to embroider the names of victories on these colours. Ours are less martial, more practical aims. Our object is to assist in protecting the lives and property of the public, and to show the evil-disposed how readily Europeans will come forward in the maintenance of order and tranquillity.'[7]

Read's men soon got a chance to prove him right when they mobilised in 1858 alongside regular troops to handle renewed Chinese rioting. The colony's governor said after reviewing the Volunteers in 1860 that the small European community was surrounded by dangers and 'no dependence could be placed on the duration of peace'. He praised non-British residents who joined the corps. All Europeans, and presumably Americans, were eligible. Eurasians were welcome in the early days when the settlement was still small. Eurasian enrolment trailed off in the 1880s, however, as the increasing number of European residents saw the rise of racial and social barriers.

Despite fears of local uprisings, membership in the Volunteers was small in the early decades. Recruiting was discouraged by work, the colony's growing distractions and the tedium of drilling in tropical temperatures. There was embarrassment when just three officers and 47 NCOs and men turned out for the Queen's birthday parade in 1867.

Two howitzers were issued to the corps in 1868 to form a small battery. Officers and NCOs were required to pay for horses and ponies to pull the guns and ammunition wagons. Interest in the new battery soon dwindled, though, because there were no shells for gunnery practice. The guns were reassigned in 1875 to help suppress unrest in the Malay state of Perak. A corps band was formed in the late 1860s to try to boost recruiting. It had to borrow musical instruments from an Indian Army regiment after the colony refused to equip the band. It collapsed when the Indian regiment left Singapore and took its instruments. Interest in the force rose briefly in 1869 when new rifles were issued. Drills were held at the city racecourse where snipe abounded 'and rifle practice was profitably intermixed with pleasure'.

Support for the corps rose whenever there was trouble and a chance of active service. The Volunteers were called out again in 1871 to deal with Chinese rioters. A report said some of the men became so excited at seeing looters sacking shops 'that they broke ranks and started belabouring the rioters until the Commanding Officer managed to get them to fall in again'.[8] Membership trailed off when local conditions were calm and the corps seemed to offer nothing but drilling. An 1873 proposal to replace the Volunteers, who had shrunk to a few men, with a compulsory militia was angrily rejected by local residents 'on the grounds of Prussianism'. Anything that smacked of forced service was adamantly opposed by most Englishmen as an infringement of their traditional liberties.

A Volunteer unit was formed for the first time in Malaya with the raising in 1861 of the Penang Volunteer Corps. Initial enthusiasm soon faltered for the same reasons that undermined the Singapore force and it was disbanded in 1879 after being virtually moribund for three or four years.

Singapore's Volunteer force staggered on for a few more years as enthusiasm and numbers steadily declined. Its end came in 1887 when just a handful of men turned up for a parade. Corps commander Major W. R. Grey, a former regular officer and now superintendent of the local jail, told the settlement there was no future for the force.

*

A vigorous new spirit was ready to save Volunteer soldiering in Singapore. W. G. St. Clair, the editor of the *Singapore Free Press*, was one of those swashbuckling journalists who lived and espoused the cause of Empire. St. Clair had no doubts about the divine inevitably of British rule and his own small part in spreading its dominion. St. Clair led a delegation of prominent citizens to see Governor Sir Cecil Clementi Smith. St. Clair had been campaigning in his paper to end the embarrassing disintegration of a British military force in front of the natives. The solution, he told the governor, was to replace the Volunteers with an artillery unit made up of men from the right social backgrounds. A unit of gunners would also be a far more useful supplement to the regular garrison. Major-General W. G. Cameron, the garrison commander, who attended the meeting, said its success depended on Volunteers being held to the highest standards and the swift removal of any incompetents. 'In matters Military ... nothing is so mischievous or fruitful of dangerous delusions as playing at soldiers,' the general warned.[9] Smith accepted the plan and the Singapore Volunteer Rifle Corps was dissolved in December 1887.

The Singapore Volunteer Artillery (SVA), the settlement's third Volunteer force, was embodied by official proclamation on 22 February 1888. It was successful from the very beginning with 96 'gentlemen' enrolling. Defence officials in London frequently lectured the colonies on the need to recruit men from superior social backgrounds for their Volunteer forces. The workmen and former common soldiers who might have been acceptable in the early years were increasingly less welcome as colonies prospered and more upper-class settlers arrived. Most gentlemen were not willing to enlist if it meant rubbing shoulders with prison warders or sanitation foremen. Applicants for the new force had to be approved by a committee, and just eight men from the old corps were accepted. Civil servants, businessmen, bankers, teachers and journalists dominated the new artillery. Europeans from other nations were welcome if they had the right social standing. Foreign residents were assured that helping local defence was not disloyal to their own nations.

As a garrison artillery unit the new Volunteers trained initially in the colony's outlying fortifications. A boat took Volunteers to the forts after work for evening drill. A gun was later moved to the city for practice after Volunteers said they could not spare time for the long voyages. There was also a rueful admission that the gentlemen, who spent their days at their desks, 'are only able to take active bodily exercise for a few hours per day'. The corps' first training camp was held at one of the forts during Easter 1888. Launches carried Volunteers' 'boys' out to the fort with the baggage. Scores of guests were ferried over on Easter Sunday, the last day, for an 'at home' and to witness the force's first practice shoot. A passing steamer was lit up with the fort's electric searchlight as the Volunteers pounded away with blank shells. Boisterous celebrations followed with singing, a display of whistling and some spirited Scottish dancing around a bonfire. Volunteers wore khaki uniforms and khaki sun helmets with a blue pugaree and a badge. White uniforms and helmets were worn on ceremonial occasions. Higher professional standards were adopted in the new force, and officers had to pass exams for the first time to ensure adequate leadership. St. Clair modestly declined a commission and initially served as a sergeant.

The SVA took on a new role as field artillery in 1897. Six 2.5-inch RML mountain guns with 'jungle transport' were issued to the unit. Realistic exercises were staged with the men dragging guns for six miles across rough country. Local contractors were unwilling to hire out good ponies for such work. Four Maxim machine guns were purchased by public subscription. Most of the money came from the colony's Chinese residents with the Malay, Arab and Chetty (ethnic Indian) communities also contributing. A Chinese newspaper, appealing for donations, sought to counter the traditional Chinese view of soldiering as dishonourable, writing: 'The Volunteers are not lawless vagrants who are fond of fighting and quarrelling, but are all merchants or gentlemen of reputation.'[10] The new corps flourished and had 104 members by 1890. Since the Royal Artillery had only 211 men in the colony, the new unit was a powerful addition to the defences. A cyclist section was added in 1894. A drill hall was erected in 1890 so the Volunteers no longer had to borrow the town hall. Intended as a temporary structure, the wood, iron and zinc building lasted until 1933.

Social activity was a major part of corps life and helped to ensure its success by providing members with inexpensive and pleasant entertainment. Camp-fire evenings with sing-songs for the ladies and other guests were a regular event. Monday and Thursday evenings were club nights at the new drill hall. The rather unmilitary nature of the force was caught by an evening route march in 1891. Volunteers wore white dress uniforms and halted at a private residence for a formal dinner at tables set up on the tennis lawn before completing the march. Sporting events were also a regular attraction.

Volunteering in Penang was revived in 1899. An infantry corps of Europeans and Eurasians had 158 members by the end of the year. Evaluations gave the force mixed ratings. A practice alert was held in 1902 to test the unit's ability to respond to emergencies. Sixteen rockets were fired as a pre-arranged signal from local police stations to summon the force. About half of the men turned up within the prescribed 45 minutes. Absentees were 'not sufficiently impressed with the absolute necessity of obeying such a summons regardless of all personal convenience', the inspecting officer wrote. Inspectors suggested the Penang unit use more realistic training methods: 'Swords should be dispensed with on manoeuvres: field glasses would be more suitable.' Volunteer units still provided their own uniforms and equipment, and it was noted that the unit's Eurasian members were too poor to buy ammunition for target practice.[11]

The Singapore Volunteer Artillery got its first taste of war in 1891 – albeit on the most tenuous basis. A Malay chief in the state of Pahang rebelled against changes imposed by British administrators. Rebels ambushed several small groups of Sikh and Malay military police. British forces were sent to ferret the rebels out of the jungle. Two SVA members took part in the subsequent campaign. Major H. E. McCallum, the SVA commander, happened to be wearing his Volunteer uniform when he was sent up to Pahang in his role as the Straits Settlements' chief engineer. The indefatigable St. Clair also found his way to the front, enabling the journalist in him to claim the Volunteers had served in the campaign. He went to Pahang on his own, probably to report on events, and was asked to join a detachment of the Perak Sikhs. 'I did in SVA khaki naturally,' he later wrote. St. Clair spent five months on garrison duty in the bush without seeing action.

Singapore was a major commercial centre by the start of the 20th century. Its European population expanded as business flourished and local trading firms brought out young men from Britain to serve as managers and clerks. European society flourished as the full colonial panoply of clubs, sports and a few modest cultural amenities sprung up. New arrivals with the right social qualifications were welcome in the Volunteers. Applications jumped when the outbreak of the Boer War inflamed patriotic souls across the Empire. There were calls to expand the Volunteers after the regular British Army battalion was withdrawn for active service. British residents of all social classes wanted to show their patriotic devotion. A new European infantry unit, the Singapore Volunteer Rifles, was formed in 1900 as an alternative to the snooty SVA. It was probably not a coincidence that the new unit was first suggested by Arnot Reid, a newspaper editor and likely rival of St. Clair. The Rifles quickly attracted enough men to form two companies, but fell apart soon after the South African war ended. A 1903 report complained of poor discipline in the force. Absenteeism was rife with all four sergeants missing the annual inspection parade. Twenty percent of the unit was rated inefficient, including the colour sergeant. It was disbanded a few months later.

A far more historic development was the raising of the first Volunteer Chinese unit. Singapore now had a Westernised Chinese elite who supported British rule. Some of its members wanted to join the Volunteers as a demonstration of loyalty and to help safeguard their growing wealth and influence. The powerful Straits Chinese British Association offered the services of 'Straits-born Chinese' for local defence during the Boer War. A mass grimace of disdain jolted the British community. Most British residents still saw the Chinese as the main reason to have a local defence force. Chinese leaders refused to give up when their offer to serve was rebuffed. Tan Jiak Kam, a senior Chinese community leader, travelled to London to appeal to Lord Onslow at the Colonial Office. Tan's idea of Britain's loyal Chinese sons serving the Empire was enthusiastically received. In London's eyes it validated the view that British colonialism was intended to 'raise up' the native peoples. Orders flew to Singapore to accept the Chinese offer.

London could coerce the Singapore government into accepting Chinese, but it could not force Europeans to serve alongside them. A separate force, the Singapore Volunteer Infantry, was formed in November 1901 with separate Chinese and Eurasian companies. Separate drill halls were constructed for the Chinese and Eurasian companies. Some of the settlement's leading Chinese businessmen and professionals joined the unit. Early evaluations of the Chinese company by regular officers praised its enthusiasm and dedication. Chinese Volunteers were held up as an example to the less energetic European members.

Having reluctantly accepted Asians, Singapore was far ahead of other Far Eastern colonies in appointing Asian officers. Song Ong Siang became the first Chinese officer when he was promoted to lieutenant in April 1907. He eventually rose to the rank of major. Chinese support for the Volunteers was strong. A 1907 waiting list for the Chinese company had more than 80 names. Not everyone admired the eager Chinese recruits. A scathing 1909 evaluation by a regular army inspector complained the men wore putties of different colours and talked on parade!

The Singapore Volunteer Corps (SVC), the fourth of the settlement's Volunteer forces, was formed in 1901 with the European and Asian units forming separate wings. It was largely a restructuring to meld the various groups. Additional units were formed to flesh out the corps. A European engineer company was raised in December 1901, becoming the Singapore Royal Engineers (Volunteers) in May 1902. A multi-racial stretcher-bearer section formed in 1901 later evolved into a medical company. Remnants of the defunct all-white Singapore Volunteer Rifles formed a European machine-gun section. It borrowed the artillery's machine guns and became the SVA Maxim Company. Relations were strained because the gunners resented losing the machine guns, and regularly reminded the new unit they could be reclaimed at any time.

The new corps still maintained a fairly casual atmosphere that was more like a club or sporting organisation than a military unit. A special corps meeting to air complaints or anything else could be summoned at any time if 50 men signed a motion. Members could keep their rifles at home if they paid a $50 deposit. But poor European recruiting was becoming a persistent problem. Peace and prosperity meant many settlers no longer saw a need for a volunteer defence force, and even those who did join often were dilatory about attending drills. A cutting 1909 report said the Singapore artillery could only mobilise 40 per cent of its strength. It also complained that out of 1,500 eligible white Britons in the city just 157 belonged to the Volunteer force.

A lack of any evident threat and growing diversions meant that many young men saw no point in sacrificing leisure time. European units also struggled with constant turnover. Businesses and the settlement's government frequently transferred staff, making it difficult for many Volunteers to complete the three-year terms of enrolment. It did not help that most Europeans got six months of leave to return to Britain every few years. Such factors meant the Singapore artillery was at half strength in 1913.

Despite the recruiting problems, it again took intervention from London to admit Malays to the ranks of the SVC. In 1910 General Sir John French noted that Malays were a fighting race and questioned why the Volunteers did not recruit them. French's view flouted the general view in the Straits Settlements that Malays were lazy and weak. 'The Malays have fought well against both the Dutch and English, and used to be considered manly and brave. They do not, however, appear now to command the same confidence as soldiers,' commented a government handbook on British colonial forces. Despite this a senior general like French could not be ignored, even by entrenched local prejudice. A meeting was held with the Malay Football Association, a local athletic group, to discuss creating a unit. Noor Mohamed Hashim, one of the association's leaders, visited each of the group's 42 teams to urge young men to enrol in the SVC. He stressed the right and duty of Malays to take part in their own defence as a step toward greater rights.

Reluctant local European officials would only accept 60 Malays at first. Additional Malay recruits were admitted in 1911 and a Malay company was finally added to the Singapore Volunteer Infantry. Malay Volunteers were consistently among the keenest and smartest SVC members with many more eager to join than could be accepted. Poverty was widespread among Malays and most appreciated the modest payments Volunteers received for travel to drills and camps. Some hoped service in the Volunteers would help them get jobs or advancement if they already had government posts. But most simply wanted to be soldiers, debunking the old colonial conceit that Malays lacked the will to fight.

Things did not go as well in the Eurasian company. Local Eurasians, many of Portuguese descent, had increasingly been pushed into a social limbo as more whites poured into the colony. A feeling that their patriotism and service was not appreciated crippled morale in the company. Its numbers plummeted and the unit was disbanded in 1909. A few keen members were kept on as part of the headquarters section. It was probably not a coincidence that most were excellent shots who helped the SVC to do well in shooting contests with other Far Eastern Volunteer forces.

Smaller states in the Straits Settlements that wanted to raise Volunteer forces sometimes formed multi-racial units because of their small white populations. An attempt to raise a multi-racial unit of British, Chinese,

Malay and Eurasian men in Malacca in 1902 attracted 47 Volunteers. It was designated as the SVC's Malacca Company. The experiment did not work and the unit was disbanded in 1906. Imperial defence officials in London repeatedly warned that units had to be racially segregated to attract 'the better class of European residents'. An attempt to mix Europeans and Eurasians in a single unit in Penang was abandoned in 1909. The Colonial Defence Committee applauded the decision, commenting, 'This change will tend to encourage persons of good social status to give their personal service to the corps.'[12]

Only Europeans were recruited for the first Volunteer military units after the states of Perak, Selangor, Pahang and Negri Sembilan were formed into the Federated Malay States (FMS) in 1896. At first there was just a single European company with five officers and 80 NCOs and other ranks. A regular army NCO on loan served as instructor. There was talk of using the Volunteers as scouts because most worked outdoors as planters and were said to be good shots. Training was difficult because the men lived on remote plantations and could not get to drills. The force developed into the all-European Malay States Volunteer Rifles by 1911 with 554 men. Most of the members were well-educated planters, officials and estate managers. An evaluation praised the unit, while noting that many of the men resented having to march and drill: such activities were 'somewhat irksome to men of superior intelligence', the report conceded, but essential to 'true discipline'. War games did not go well because most of the men were strong characters who tried to fight independently. The force would be quickly wiped out in a war because it had no idea of how to fight as a unit, the report added.[13]

A Volunteer unit in the backcountry could face unusual problems. Training on the corps' rifle range had to be reduced after it was overgrown by jungle. Enthusiasm varied in later years. FMS Volunteers living in remote locations, with little to do after work, regularly attended drills. Volunteers who lived in towns were rebuked for allowing 'the attractions of games and amusements to interfere with the regular weekly parades'.[14] Men from towns and outstations responded enthusiastically when the force was called out for the first time to help police deal with disturbances in Kuala Lumpur during Chinese New Year celebrations in February 1912. Two companies were called in from across Selangor state to patrol the capital's streets. Volunteer commander Lieutenant-Colonel A. B. Hubback reported, 'I think I am correct in saying that the moral effect of any armed European force on the streets of Kuala Lumpur was very considerable on those who had been causing trouble.'[15]

Volunteer strength and morale soared with the patriotic surge unleashed by the First World War. Men rushed to join Volunteer units in Singapore and Malaya. New forces were formed in the Malay states. The SVC was mobilised in 1914 to help guard Singapore after the regular garrison was cut. It saw fighting of a quite unexpected kind in 1915 when an Indian Army battalion mutinied. The 5th Light Infantry was told it was being transferred to Hong Kong but rumours swept the unit that it really was going to France, where other Indian units had suffered heavy losses. Poor leadership from the British officers and quarrels between some of the Indian officers had wrecked the regiment's discipline and Britain's war with Turkey, then the leading Islamic nation, pitted the loyalty of some of the Muslim soldiers against their faith. Half of the regiment revolted, attacking the bungalow where their colonel and some officers had barricaded themselves inside.

Malcolm Bond Shelley, a young officer with a Malay States Volunteer detachment in Singapore for training, had earlier heard the first shooting when trouble broke out at the nearby barracks of the 5th Light Infantry. Ignoring the noise, he wandered into town to post a letter, narrowly missing the roaming mutineers who randomly gunned down whites. Shelley returned to find two officers from the 5th Light Infantry who said their men had mutinied. Shelley tried to wake his commander, who rolled over and went to sleep with the words 'tell them to go to hell'.[16] A detachment from Shelley's force joined the besieged British officers and held out during the night. Singapore's Volunteer forces were mobilised along with regular troops and sailors as word of the revolt spread. There was fear and confusion that first night as alarms and rumours hurtled around the colony. Two machine-gun sections of the SVC occupied a lookout point on Cemetery Hill. Several times the men opened fire after noises in the dark made them think the mutineers were creeping up on them. A search of the bushes below the position next morning found the bullet-riddled carcasses of a herd of pigs.

The besieged Malay Volunteers and the 5th Light Infantry officers were relieved by Singapore Volunteers and Royal Navy sailors from a warship in the harbour. Sent out with a Navy patrol, Shelley struggled to stop the sailors gunning down every native they met:

> 'To these gallant naval men every Tamil coolie and Bengali bullock-cart driver was a potential enemy and it was with difficulty that they were restrained from training their machine guns on these inoffensive citizens.'[17]

Sent to Johore to collect some captured mutineers, Shelley was horrified to meet a group of Singapore civilians who had armed themselves to go looking for mutineers. None of the men knew how to handle weapons properly. Shelley recounted how they carelessly pointed their rifles at each other as they tried to load the weapons.

Swift trials and sentences followed for the hapless mutineers. It was decided that units which lost men in the fighting would provide firing squads to execute publicly the 47 mutineers sentenced to death. Shelley was given command of a firing squad from his regiment. Neither Shelley nor his sergeant had any idea of what to do. They spent hours scanning military handbooks on musketry, ceremonial drill and other subjects, but found nothing on firing squads and executions. Shelley recalled schoolboy tales of how only one man was issued with a bullet, and the rest of a firing squad with blanks, so that nobody knew who killed the victim:

> 'It was a pretty piece of sentiment in the case of white men, who were firing at one of their own race: but I was taking no risks in this case. Unless I received instructions to the contrary, each man was going to load his rifle with a clip of five ball cartridge.'[18]

The executions were grotesque, agonisingly prolonged spectacles. The Singapore Volunteers sent an absurdly large firing squad of 110 men to execute 23 mutineers in front of the city jail. The condemned men stood tied to stakes as the long sentences were tediously read out in different languages. Large crowds of ogling European civilians looked on. Shelley and his squad were assigned to execute two mutineers. Some of the squad were nervous, fumbling as they tried to load their rifles. One of the mutineers was still standing after the squad fired a ragged volley. 'The expression on his face was one of such terrible agony that will forever remain impressed on my memory,' Shelley wrote. A second volley was fired, knocking the man to the ground. A doctor inspected the body. Turning away, he told Shelley that the man had been killed by the first volley, but his clothes had stuck to the stake and kept the body standing upright.[19]

*

The First World War saw major developments in Volunteer forces across Malaya. New units were formed in both the Federated Malay States and the newly formed Unfederated Malay States. Most units were small, such as the 18 Europeans who formed the Kedah Volunteers the day after war was declared. Its strength never rose above 25 men and it was led by the local police commander. Even smaller was the defence detachment of 12 men on Labuan Island. Tiny units in the remoter states struggled to train men and acquire equipment. Free passes were sometimes provided by the railway companies so that men could get to training sessions, and some officers paid for equipment for the units out of their own pockets. Members of the new Province Wellesley Volunteer Rifles in the Federated Malay States complained that the local trains did not run late enough to get them home after evening drills.

Singapore's mutiny helped boost recruiting as worried Europeans looked for protection. A rifle company formed in Malacca 'had the immediate effect of allaying the fears of the European population'. All but two of Malacca's eligible Europeans joined the force, which practised with old rifles from the local school cadet corps. A row over dress dominated the corps' first months until the men eventually decided to wear riding breeches rather than shorts.

A Singapore ordinance passed in August 1915 required all European residents between the ages of 18 and 55 to do compulsory military training and to mobilise in an emergency. Small groups of Singapore and Malay Volunteers took part in suppressing the 1915 Kelantan Rebellion. Americans living in Singapore joined the Volunteers when their country entered the war in 1917.

Asian units were formed in the Federated Malay States in 1915 and became the Malayan Volunteer Infantry with Malay, Chinese, Indian and Eurasian members. The unit was kept separate from the European-only Malay States Volunteer Rifles. Singapore's Eurasians, who no longer had their own unit, made repeated requests to re-form a company in the SVC. Officials did not agree until 1918, and then the members were 'carefully selected'.

Halcyon Years

The inter-war years were a golden era for the British in Malaya and Singapore. Their rule and all the privileges that went with it seemed destined to go on indefinitely. Few Europeans seemed even aware of the nationalism and other powerful forces that were beginning to transform Asia. Business suffered badly in the Great Depression only to boom in other years as global industry demanded all of the tin and rubber that Malaya could produce. Singapore flourished as one of the world's great ports. Most settlers just wanted to have a good time, make money and build comfortable lives. Turning out to march up and down in the local Volunteers was not part of that cosy goal for most young men. But the British government's finances had been devastated by the recent world conflict. London wanted the colonies to take greater responsibility for their own defence. That meant more reliance on local forces and the colonies paying a major share of the costs. It was the last thing local officials and settlers wanted to hear. Defence and its cost, they insisted, were the central government's responsibility. Was it not enough that they were upholding the cause of Empire by living in these forlorn backwaters despite untold discomforts?

Things seemed fairly promising for the Volunteers right after the war. Military matters were fashionable, the settlements were full of returned veterans, and the Volunteers were keen to keep up the expanded role they had assumed during the war. A general inspecting a Volunteer unit in Singapore after the war was startled when he saw a private wearing the ribbon for the Military Cross on his tunic. 'You have no right to wear that. It's for officers,' the general snapped. The Volunteer replied he had won the medal as an officer at Ypres in the world war. Going a little further down the rank, the general spotted a private with the ribbon of the Distinguished Service Order. 'I suppose you're going to tell me you were a colonel as well?' the general sarcastically asked. 'Yes, sir.' the private replied.

A 1921 reorganisation grouped the various Straits Settlements units – Singapore, Penang, Province Wellesley and Malacca – into a new single formation: the Straits Settlements Volunteer Force (SSVF). All existing commissions were rescinded and a new officer corps selected. Older, less able officers were weeded out to improve standards: those who lost commissions had a choice of resigning or re-enlisting as ordinary soldiers. Some accepted the changes with notable loyalty. D. T. Thomas, a top civil servant who had commanded the Singapore Artillery with the rank of major, became a private after he was refused a commission and served in the ranks until he left the colony in 1928.

Recruiting for the new SSVF began on 1 January 1921. There was an encouraging response. Enlistment was staggered along racial lines with Europeans enrolling on the first day. Induction took about 10 minutes, and included filling in an application, medical exam, swearing in and being issued with a rifle and equipment. Men were given vouchers for local tailors to purchase uniforms. There were 413 European Volunteers in Singapore by the end of 1921. Their ranks included 178 men from the old Volunteer force. Civil servants, merchants and businessmen along with bankers, lawyers, journalists, engineers, accountants and teachers filled out the white ranks. Regular army officers and NCOs were lent to the new force on temporary assignment. They oversaw training and ran the corps headquarters. Recruits were told their training would focus on handling civil unrest. Brigadier-General F. E. Spencer, a regular officer who took

Straits Settlements Volunteer Force, 1921

Singapore Volunteer Corps
  Singapore Volunteer Artillery
  Singapore Royal Engineers (V) *with signal section*
  Machine Gun Platoon
  A Company (European)
  B Company (European)
  C Company (Scottish)
  Eurasian Company and band
  Chinese Company
  Malay Company
  Field Ambulance Company
  Labuan Detachment

Malacca Volunteer Rifles
  A European Company
  B Chinese Company
  C Malay Company
  Machine Gun Platoon

Penang and Province Wellesley Volunteer Corps
  A European Company, Penang Volunteer Infantry
  B Eurasian Company, Penang Volunteer Infantry
  C Malay Company, Penang Volunteer Infantry
  D Chinese Company, Penang Volunteer Infantry
  European Company, Province Wellesley Volunteer Infantry

Field Reserve

Each corps also had reserve and auxiliary personnel, the latter to carry out technical and support tasks in an emergency.

Straits Settlements Volunteer Force, 1928
Further changes in 1928 saw the SSVF organised into a brigade with four battalions:

1st Battalion	*Singapore Volunteer Corps*
2nd Battalion	*Singapore Volunteer Corps*
3rd Battalion	*Penang and Province Wellesley Volunteer Corps*
4th Battalion	*Malacca Volunteer Corps*

Source: PRO CAB 9/19/54.

command of the new corps, told the community, 'Parades may occasionally interfere with recreation or pleasure. But a man can surely give something in return for the benefits of Empire.'[20]

The SSVF was fleshed out with Chinese, Eurasian and Malay companies. Some Asian Volunteers joined to show their loyalty, and underline their right to imperial citizenship and its benefits. 'Those of us who are Straits-born of British nationality must not forget nor shirk our duty to our Empire,' the Penang Chinese company stated.[21] Malay companies had the biggest turn-out and turned away applicants. Unemployment and poverty were still widespread in the Malay community; some recruits again hoped that joining the Volunteers would help them find jobs. Most also needed the modest allowances paid for attending weekend and annual camps

Volunteer forces in the Federated Malay States were also reorganised in 1921. The Malay States Volunteer Regiment, an all-European unit that had been the Malay States Volunteer Rifles, was grouped with the all-Asian Malay Volunteer Infantry in the new multi-racial Federated Malay States Volunteer Force (FMSVF). Significant numbers of Indian Volunteers were enlisted for the first time. An artillery unit was created in 1928 with four 3.7-inch mountain howitzers. It was named the Federated Malay States Light Battery in 1929. Further changes in 1937 aimed at improving efficiency by grouping the various companies into battalions in each of the four FMS states. Europeans, Chinese, Indians, Malays and Eurasians generally served in separate companies or platoons in the new battalions.

Volunteer units in the Unfederated Malay States made less progress. Kedah's local defence unit, which was disbanded at the end of the First World War, was revived in 1933 as the Kedah Volunteer Force. It became the largest of the UMS forces, fielding a weak battalion by 1941. Johore's small European rifle unit was transformed into the Johore Volunteer Engineers in 1928 because there no sapper units on the mainland. Johore's sultan had a personal force of an infantry battalion and an artillery section that were assigned to the UMS forces in an emergency. The Kelantan Volunteer Rifles became the Kelantan Volunteer Force with one European platoon and two Malay platoons. Terengganu & Perlis was the only Malay state without Volunteer forces.

The post-war flush of enthusiasm for volunteering began to fade after a few years. Volunteer units by the mid-1920s were struggling to attract and retain men – above all from the British community. Annual reviews of the units are a catalogue of complaints about supine young British men refusing to do their duty. Singapore asked London to persuade big companies with branches in Singapore and Malaya to pressure their white employees to enlist. Similar pressure was applied to young civil servants. Disgruntled military bureaucrats complained about what they saw as the poor quality of modern youth. 'This reluctance seems to be associated with a general lack of athletic powers,' one official wrote.[22] Others blamed the

Federated Malay States Volunteer Force, 1925

Unit	Officers	OR	Race
Perak Volunteer Corps	***1st Battalion FMSVF***		
Malay States Volunteer Regiment *2 companies*	20	598	European
Malayan Volunteer Infantry *7 platoons*	13	572	Chinese, Malay, Indian
Selangor Volunteer Force	***2nd Battalion FMSVF***		
Malay States Volunteer Regiment *2 companies*	21	665	European
Malayan Volunteer Infantry *8 platoons*	20	680	Malay, Chinese
Medical Unit			Eurasian, Tamil
Negri-Sembilan Volunteer Corps	***3rd Battalion FMSVF***		
Malay States Volunteer Regiment *1 company*	10	299	European
Malayan Volunteer Infantry *4 platoons*			Malay
Pahang Volunteer Corps	***4th Battalion FMSVF***		
Malay States Volunteer Regiment *No unit in existence*	–	–	–
Malayan Volunteer Infantry *3 platoons*	7	300	Malay

Source: PRO CAB 9/19/54.

many amusements and other distractions available to Europeans in the big towns. Local newspapers were praised by officials for running campaigns exhorting young Europeans to enlist in the Volunteers. Singapore's *Straits Times* sneered in 1924 at 'pampered lap dogs' who went to tea dances rather than serving in the defence force.[23] Newspapers reminded readers that it was their patriotic duty to serve and a very small return for all the benefits of Empire. 'Make the colony a Xmas present of your services,' suggested one appeal.[24] Some exasperated editorial writers called for compulsory military service. Modest material inducements were offered when patriotic appeals and pressure at work failed to yield enough recruits. Volunteers and their families were given 50 per cent discounts at government hospitals, while officers and NCOs were exempted from jury duty. It made little difference: recruiting figures continued to drop. London said local officials could do more to solve the problem. Army officials dropped disparaging hints about how few senior Malay Civil Service officials had served in the recent conflict.

A 1925 evaluation of the Straits Settlements Volunteer Force reported it was 35 per cent below its authorised strength. It was highly embarrassing that the biggest shortage was in European units with a shortfall of 43 per cent. Eurasian units were 37 per cent below strength and Chinese units 32 per cent below strength. Malay units were the only bright spot, although the report found even they were 11 per cent below strength. Penang and Province Wellesley's unit had just 197 Europeans in 1926. Penang's Eurasian company could only muster 63 men out of an authorised strength of 136 in 1928. Some units would do well for a year or two when a drive was made to boost recruiting, only to see their numbers plunge as men got tired of drilling and doing little else. A tin and rubber boom in the 1920s hurt recruiting because most businessmen were too busy at work. Economic hard times did not mean more time for volunteering. Recruiting struggled during the Great Depression as many businesses sharply cut the number of young men sent out from Britain. No matter how the local economy fared, however, the number of young Europeans willing to serve in the Volunteers was low.

Enlistment of suitable foreigners was legalised in 1931 to try to boost recruiting, including: 'foreigners of European descent (which, of course, includes Americans). They are enlisted for dealing with internal disturbances only, and are released from their obligations in case of war with a foreign power,' the colony reported.[25] It made the corps more cosmopolitan without doing much for its numbers: the SVC 1931 intake comprised 38 whites from 13 nations.

Those who did join were exhorted to encourage friends and colleagues to follow them, as the SSVF year book stated as late as 1939:

> 'It is earnestly hoped that individual members of the units will use their most persuasive arguments to encourage the younger men coming to the Colony to take an active interest in what cannot be denied is a very important essential service.'[26]

These were the years when Singapore was supposedly being turned into a great naval base to defend the eastern Empire. Construction of the base was as fitful as progress in building up the Volunteers. Building was frequently halted or scaled back because of fluctuations in government policy and finances. London nonetheless expected the local territorial forces to be expanded as part of the base's defences. Exhortations from the imperial capital stated that Volunteer forces must be ready to respond to a major emergency at any time. 'It is, in fact, during the opening phases of a campaign, before Imperial troops can arrive to assist the local forces, that the greatest strain is likely to be imposed on the latter,' the Imperial Defence Committee gravely intoned.[27] London was furious when Singapore cut defence spending by 50 per cent in 1931 because of the economic slump. Bureaucrats in London saw no contradiction in their decision at the same time to cut the number of regular instructors loaned to the Volunteer forces to save money. Deteriorating finances were behind a decision in 1933 to cut each Asian company to 100 men: 204 Asian Volunteers were dismissed in spite of the general shortage of men.

A favourite Volunteer anecdote of the 1930s recounts how a European company was getting some advice from a grizzled drill sergeant of the regular army. There are, he said, two types of Volunteers. 'Good Volunteers always do their best,' the instructor continued, 'and then there are the other sort ...' At that moment two planters, well known for propping up the bar at the local club, tottered unsteadily onto the parade ground. Servants followed the planters, helping them to don their webbing as others carried their rifles. 'Here they come now,' the sergeant dryly concluded.

Volunteering remained a fairly undemanding affair for those who did enlist in the 1920s and 1930s. Many men saw it as just another pleasant social activity. Charles Kinahan of the Singapore Engineers recalled:

'It was all fairly light hearted. You played tennis on Monday, swam on Tuesday, played soldiers on Wednesday, golf on Thursdays etc. ... the atmosphere was one of a club with a gathering of all ranks in the bar after parade.'[28]

Volunteer commanders had to ensure there were plenty of social activities to keep the men happy. Singapore Volunteer HQ 'boasted a very fine large Hall where we could hold Dances, Dinners and suchlike jollifications, and of course a very useful Bar where many of us congregated after parades,' said W. M. Innes-Ker.[29] Tom Evans, a young member of the Singapore Volunteer Artillery, said it was all very easy and relaxed. 'It was so cushy some people took their Chinese boys to camp with them to sort out their clothes.'[30]

Training was minimal and most men learned little about fighting wars in the few hours they spent on the parade ground. Volunteers in Singapore were only asked to do one hour of drill or training every fortnight in the mid-1920s. This was later cut to 18 drills a year. Pragmatic commanders tried to exclude 'eyewash' or ceremonial drill and focus on practical skills. Some of the men did not care for the change. Parades, when the Volunteers marched in front of the admiring European community, were seen as one of the few benefits of enlistment. Standards declined even more as the number of drills fell off. Many Volunteers were not physically fit. Machine-gun crews on an exercise were too exhausted to fire accurately after carrying their weapons a few hundred yards. Inspectors complained that some European Volunteers, with their superior social backgrounds, thought that basic training was only for the working-class privates of the regular army. Some gentlemen privates on an exercise 'failed to grasp the principle of dismounting from lorries in sufficient time to engage the enemy on foot or to appreciate that such an occasion had arisen,' an army inspector complained.[31]

Calls during this period to improve the skills and strength of the Volunteers with modern training and weapons frequently floundered on a lack of money and resources. Progress, when it came, was often improvised and amateurish. Singapore's first armoured car was a home-made contraption, for example. It was constructed in 1931 by the Singapore Harbour Board from a commercial truck chassis with surplus armour plate. A second vehicle produced in 1933 had to double as a municipal truck. Its chassis was used by the Public Works Department during the days when the armour body was stored at the Harbour Board.

Support and logistics units were, however, formed to supplement the SSVF's infantry units. Motorcycle, intelligence, fortress engineer, and provost sections joined the Singapore battalions. Trained Indian post office operators formed the new Asiatic Signal Unit as part of the artillery. Asians also formed the new Defence Electric Light Unit.

Flashes of active service enlivened the Volunteers' normal humdrum routine. Machine-gun and artillery sections were mobilised in Singapore in 1922 after police surrounded some 20 armed robbers in a house. A brisk pistol battle ensued. A Volunteer machine-gun section arrived just as the robbers were surrendering after a four-hour siege. Word reached the artillery that they would not be needed as the gunners were hooking their weapons up to trucks. Even the gunners admitted their intervention could have been very costly for the surrounding area. Singapore provided armed Volunteers in 1928 and 1929 to guard ships against Chinese pirates on the Hong Kong route. Guards were recruited from men who wanted a free sea voyage and could get time off work. They were replaced by regular soldiers after officials feared the colony could be held liable if any of the Volunteers were hurt. Still, few believed there was any threat of war even when the Volunteers staged anti-invasion exercises with the regular forces. Volunteer publications in the late 1930s are notable for the lack of virtually any reference to a possible Japanese threat.

Most units remained racially segregated during the inter-war era although some technical and medical units were integrated. Commanders of segregated units tried to use racial pride to spur recruiting and unit efficiency. A Chinese unit whose recruiting was lagging might be told it faced being replaced by Malays. All units were commanded by Europeans when the SSVF was first formed. This policy was relaxed, with Asians commanding companies in the mid-1930s in Singapore, but Asian officers seem to have only commanded fellow Chinese or Malays. No Asian was given direct command of a white unit, although some held posts in headquarters units. Several Asian officers were promoted to the rank of major for the first time in the mid-1930s.

War

The Volunteers were ill-prepared even by the lamentable local standards of the British Army when war engulfed the region. It was not the fault of the Volunteers in the ranks. Men who were essentially civilians in uniform could hardly excel when regular units failed so badly. Most Volunteer units were relegated to rear-echelon duties where they saw little fighting. It saved them from likely slaughter. More than a few Volunteers got their first glimpse of a Japanese soldier as they marched into captivity.

In later years many Volunteers wrote of their experiences in the campaign. An abiding anger colours much of what they wrote. Culprits singled out by many survivors are the blind British strategy, lack of preparation, inept generals and the poor performance of their own officers. Lieutenant C. Thornton of the FMSVF Selangor Battalion said Britain had tried to bluff Japan by pretending Singapore was an impregnable fortress.[32] It had failed and the colony was completely unprepared despite years of warning signs. He accused the government of criminal negligence, insisting it had only fooled its own people by fostering complacency. Some Volunteers thought their own commanders had failed to do any serious planning or preparation for war. Thornton echoed such views when he wrote: 'The fault lay in the past: our administrative officers had paper schemes to play with only and when reality came chaos came with it.' It was sardonically observed that the army had orderly chaos and the Volunteers disorderly chaos. Some later said the defeat showed how British Malaya was rotten to the core after decades of arrogant complacency. Many of the survivors admit they never thought that mere 'Asiatics' would even dare attack the British Empire. There had been almost universal contempt before the war for the Japanese, who were lampooned as myopic morons. 'We had an immense contempt for the Japs ... couldn't build ships that did not turn turtle, and as for aeroplanes!' recalled R. A. Middleton, a corporal in the Johore Volunteer Engineers.[33]

Singapore and Malaya responded enthusiastically to the outbreak of war in Europe in 1939. Young men pushed to be released from jobs to return home and fight. Loyal Asians raised millions of pounds to purchase aircraft for the defence of Britain. Very few thought that war would touch Asia. It was going to be a European show, most believed, like the last world war. Some Army officers, worried that Japan might use Britain's distraction in Europe to attack, wanted to improve local defences. It was not a message the local government wanted to hear. Relations between the military and the colony's government had never been good. Demands from the Army for increased training for the Volunteers and even conscription were opposed by the governor, Sir Shenton Thomas, and his aides. A shortage of European manpower made it extremely difficult to meet civil and military needs. Conflicting instructions from the imperial government encouraged both sides. London said the local forces must be expanded to free regular troops for service in Europe and Africa. At the same time it agreed that Malaya's main role was to keep up vital production of tin and rubber for the war effort. This encouraged Thomas to insist that the economy's needs must come first, and he resisted diverting men to the Volunteers.

There were just 31,000 Europeans and 19,000 Eurasians in British Malaya alongside more than 5 million Asians at the start of the war. Almost every male European had an important post in the economy, government and local infrastructure. Taking them from their civilian roles for military duty would damage the war effort by hurting economic production. A need to form civil defence organisations added to the general manpower shortage. Balancing the conflicting demands of the economy and the colony's defence was almost impossible. It was made far worse by often bitter personal differences between civilian officials and the military. Local government officials opposed the Army's proposals to build more defences to deal with a possible invasion. They argued the sight of soldiers building trenches and gun emplacements would be taken as a sign of weakness by the native population and tarnish British prestige. Britain must give the appearance, it was said, of invincibility whatever the reality.

A few steps were taken to increase Volunteer training without hindering the economy. Men had to do 50 parades a year compared to the previous requirement of 18 sessions. A 1940 ordinance gave the government power to call up men for compulsory service but Thomas diluted and delayed the measure until it was largely ineffective. Even if it had been adopted, it was all far too little to prepare for the impending deluge bearing down on the colony.

Recruiting for the Volunteers rose, although many Europeans still believed there would never be war with Japan. That view was not shared by Chinese recruits, who had been watching Japan ravage their ancestral land for years. Some Chinese units soon had waiting lists. A depot company was formed in Singapore to handle the influx of recruits from all races. New men trained twice a week to learn the basics of weapons and tactics. Some Volunteers were mobilised for up to two months in early 1941 for exercises. Singapore was still not inclined to take things too seriously: training was suspended during the 1940 Christmas holidays. Some Volunteers claimed Malays in their units had lost civilian jobs because employers would not release them for compulsory training.

Many Volunteers complained that little thought was given to how they would be used if war came despite supposed years of planning. 'We were seen as a lot of whisky swillers who didn't know anything,' Evans recalled.[34] Some admitted they were little more than a part-time militarised police force fit only to handle small-scale civil unrest. Others complained that their talents and skills were wasted by an incompetent and insensitive military bureaucracy. G. E. D. Lewis said his company, made up mostly of lawyers, engineers and civil servants, probably had more university degrees than any company in the British Army.[35] Yet it was given no meaningful role. Wasting such brainpower, he complained, was a criminal mistake. A mining engineer, who was a reserve captain in the Australian Army, Lewis spent most of the campaign as a private waiting on tables in an officers' mess and digging latrines. Repeated requests for transfer to a technical unit, at a time when the Army was desperate for demolition experts, were rejected. I. A. McDonald, of the Johore Volunteer Engineers, had a similar experience when his unit of highly skilled and educated professionals was put to work loading cement blocks on to trucks.[36] This was at a time when regular formations were desperate for experts with knowledge of local conditions and languages. No one complained, he said, because they had learned that there was no point in arguing with the Army chain of command.

Some Volunteers were given roles for which they had not received any preparation or training. R. M. Hoops of the Penang Battalion was made commander of an armoured car at the last minute. He did not know how to fire the vehicle's weapons and never managed to load them.[37] Some of the men complained the food was inedible because it was cooked by

European Volunteers who had never prepared a meal before. Few Europeans cooked in a country where legions of servants catered to their domestic needs. Kinahan's Singapore Engineer company was retrained before the war to deal with unexploded bombs. Japanese planes bombed the city on the first day of war. 'So next day off we went to deal with our first lot of unexploded aerial bombs – not having a clue what a Japanese bomb looked like!' They had spent the previous two years practising on German bombs.[38]

News of the Japanese attack stunned and confused many Volunteers. Some learned of the war when mobilisation orders arrived at homes and offices. Most blithely assumed it would be a short war culminating in a swift Japanese defeat. McDonald, of the Johore Volunteer Engineers, and his friends imagined it would be a holiday and they would all be home in two or three weeks.[39] Numerous Volunteers went to barracks in their own cars after being called up.

Some had a vague sense that their world was about to disappear. For some that meant the loss of comfortable, privileged lifestyles. 'I wondered what was going to happen to my belongings in the house, thinking of my gramophone that I had recently received from my mother at home, and my two lovely cameras and new suits,' recalled S. J. Littledyke of the FMSVF 2nd Battalion.[40] Many men never saw their homes again. Some who did return in the following weeks found only burned-out wrecks destroyed during the British retreat.

Others grasped that far more than possessions were at stake. Evans, the prescient artilleryman, realised the entire colonial edifice might disintegrate: 'Ours was no jingoistic fervour of patriotism, but a blatant realisation that no one could have a better conception of the important issues at stake, nor a better stake in those issues than we Malayans.'[41] Other Europeans were plagued with guilt because they believed they had abandoned native employees and servants. It seemed, they thought, as if the British Empire was breaking all of its age-old promises.

Military commanders rated the Volunteers as second-class units fit mostly for guard duty and other static chores. Nonetheless they formed a major part of the British force. Malay States Volunteer units were assigned mainly to lines of communications work with the FMSVF under the command of Brigadier-General M. R. Moir, except for the 4th FMS Battalion which was assigned to the 9th Indian Division.[42] Volunteer units had far too few men to cover the hundreds of miles of jungle and coastline they were assigned to watch over. Tasks included guarding air bases, bridges, supply dumps and controlling traffic. Two companies of the 3rd FMSVF

Battalion guarded interned Japanese civilians. Some companies spent much of the campaign guarding virtually empty airfields. They rarely saw any British aircraft, but were regularly bombed by Japanese planes. At least a few Volunteers claimed the planes that quickly defeated the Royal Air Force were actually German with Nazi pilots because no Japanese aircraft could perform so ably. Volunteers had been trained in anti-paratroop defence in case Japanese airborne forces rained down on key targets. Though white puffs of anti-aircraft fire over airfields were frequently mistaken for parachutes, the Volunteers were never called upon to face paratroopers. Volunteers instead confiscated and destroyed thousands of bicycles to ensure the Japanese could not use them.

Volunteers assigned to maintain civil order and aid emergency services saw some of the worst aspects of the campaign. Penang's Volunteer battalion collected and buried scores of civilians killed in air raids. Other tasks involved disarming the terrified civil police, dealing with looters and feeding the torrent of refugees. Hoops, the neophyte armoured car commander, remembers roaring through bombed and shattered streets to stop looting.[43] An infantry squad followed him on one trip, rounding up suspects to take back to Volunteer headquarters to be caned.

Life in the early weeks of the war was far quieter in Singapore. Volunteers manned beach defences on the island's south coast. Gunners and infantrymen sat in concrete emplacements with little to do. Life was not unpleasant with a local boarding house providing meals. Residents of the boarding house stayed on even though Japanese troops were expected to land on the beach. Men complained of boredom and fretted that they would not see any action. Middleton spent his days erecting barbed wire at an air base and the evenings at Singapore's Tanglin Club.[44]

A few Volunteer units were given combat roles in the early days of the campaign. The FMSVF artillery battery was part of a regular force earmarked to advance into Siam (Thailand) to forestall any Japanese attack. It missed the doomed venture because the gunners could not be released from their civilian jobs in time. An FMSVF infantry unit helped blunt a Japanese advance at Grik in the first days of the war. Kelantan's tiny defence force defended Kota Bahru town after Japanese landings on the east coast.

Armoured cars from Malay Volunteer units were combined in a regiment with 18 vehicles in two squadrons. Some of the armoured cars had allegedly been used in Palestine during the First World War. C. H. Lee, an NCO in the Perak Battalion FMSVF, recalled the crews getting a pep talk from a cheerful regular officer who said the vehicles were expendable because they were outdated.[45] Lee said the bemused crews thought it was rather heartless, although the men were willing to sacrifice themselves in vehicles he described as antediluvian. Four of the cars were lost in a rearguard action in Johore. Volunteer engineers demolished bridges and key installations to try to stall the enemy advance. Most units spent weeks preparing defensive positions, only to abandon them without firing a shot as the army fell back.

Most Volunteers who saw any fighting were severely shaken. Nothing in their training had prepared them for combat. H. A. Porter, a sapper in Singapore, wrote his first taste of shelling 'left me shaking like a jelly, quite unreliably. I was in a blue funk.'[46] Senior army officials reported the Volunteers were badly affected by Japanese air attacks; so were many of the regular troops. FMSVF units fought in scattered actions to block Japanese landings on the west coast. In one rare success Volunteer artillery help beat off a Japanese landing at Kuala Selangor, scoring several hits on landing craft. Coastal defence was a hopeless task. A few hundred troops, some artillery and six armoured cars guarded one section of 170 miles of coastline. Each of the Malay states was abandoned as the British forces fell back. Successive defence lines collapsed without blunting the Japanese advance. Remnants of the Volunteer forces that fought in Malaya shuffled across the causeway to Singapore with the regulars for the final battle.

Abandoning the Malay states one by one during the retreat created a special problem for the Volunteer forces. Many Asian Volunteers did not want to leave their homes and families behind. There were growing fears that Asians who fought for the British, and their dependents, would face Japanese retribution. Men began to desert to stay with their families as the British pulled out. British authorities made matters worse by only evacuating European civilians. Families of Asian Volunteers were excluded when white women and children were evacuated from Penang. British commanders later gave Asian Volunteers the choice of leaving or fighting when their home states were abandoned. Men who left were required to turn in their weapons. There was no hint of animosity from many of the European Volunteers. Thornton said Malays in his unit, who fought well at first, were demoralised at seeing their families left behind.:

> 'Their fighting spirit had been pretty well extinguished by the knowledge that neither the government nor the military authorities had done anything whatsoever to assist their relations in getting away from the Japs or providing means of subsistence. Officials who should have stayed at their posts had fled and the Kampong [village] Malays were left to the mercy of the Japs.'[47]

Perhaps European Volunteers, many of whose families had been evacuated, felt some shame.

British scorched-earth policies further dismayed Asians. They saw British attempts to delay the Japanese by destroying food stocks and fuel supplies as more likely to threaten their own peoples' survival. Malay Volunteers were most likely to abscond. Chinese and Eurasian Volunteers tended to stay with the retreating British forces. General Moir expressed sympathy, albeit in typically paternalistic tones, for the men who left: 'It is somewhat difficult to condemn altogether the attitude of the Malays as they had their homes and women in the Federated Malay States and the Malay is a very home-loving and family man.'[48] Moir criticised the Volunteers' training as utterly inadequate 'to instil into them that pride of regiment and *esprit de corps* which is so essential to hold together a unit in spite of all diversity.' Donald Webber, an FMSVF sergeant, refused to criticise the mostly young Malay Volunteers. 'The Malays showed up very badly . . . and during the last week we had a lot of desertions. The reason of course was obvious – you simply cannot make a soldier out of anybody on about 24 hours of parades per year.'[49]

Volunteers of all races generally believed they were fighting for common goals and usually got on well together in the field. That did not mean a relaxation of peace-time barriers. Volunteer units remained largely segregated during the campaign. Colonel C. W. S. Seed, paymaster of the FMSVF, stayed with his Asian clerks in an almost empty civilian hospital during the retreat. He put the men in a third-class ward for Asians while he slept in a first-class whites-only ward.[50] Europeans slept in the grand-stand and the Asians in the stables when Penang's Volunteers were quartered at the local race course at the start of the war. European and Malay Volunteers were assigned to escort interned Japanese civilians by ship to Singapore. Cabins were set aside for Europeans of all ranks while the Malays slept on the decks or wherever they could find room. The few European Volunteers who served under Asians were often unhappy with what they saw as an unnatural reversal of authority. J. R. Hodgson, 1st Battalion SSVF, was furious when assigned to a squad under a Malay corporal. He claimed Europeans always had to take over whenever there was an emergency. At the same time Hodgson praised the work of some nearby searchlight crews even though, as he noted, they were mostly Asiatics.[51] Evans, of the Singapore Artillery, said younger whites had some pre-war social contact with Eurasians within strict boundaries. 'You didn't go to Raffles Hotel to dance with a Eurasian girl,' he recalled.[52] In fact, according to Evans, Eurasian Volunteers excelled during the war; many insisted on going into prison camp when they could easily have slipped away. Most of the white Volunteers knew nothing about the Chinese and Malay Volunteers. 'We hardly ever came across them. I suppose in a way we were snobs,' Evans said.[53]

Many Volunteers still steadfastly believed Singapore was impregnable as the army pulled back to the island fortress. There was widespread incomprehension at how quickly Malaya had been abandoned. Now, it was felt, the invaders would be given a good hiding. Hopeful rumours bounded around of reinforcements racing to the island's relief. Bizarre claims that American troops had landed at Penang and occupied Kuala Lumpur briefly cheered the surviving Malay Volunteers. About 1,000 mostly European Volunteers from the Malay States retreated to Singapore. Most were formed into a depot unit while roughly a hundred men were sent to regular units as replacement officers and liaisons. Singapore's two Volunteer battalions were moved from the south coast to defend Singapore City. Evans, disillusioned after spending weeks in a beach pill-box, was eager to see action.[54] His unit had been trained as anti-tank gunners on 18-pounders made in 1916; he was sure it would inflict savage punishment on the invaders. Its guns were based in the centre of the city, facing down a broad avenue to engage Japanese tanks. Instead it spent most of its time chasing looters and only fired a few shots at the very end of the battle.

War had not mended the disarray of the Volunteer forces. James Taylor Rea, a Singapore civil servant, was called up just five days before the city fell.[55] Nobody at the depot seemed to know what to do with him. He went from one officer to another for instructions only to encounter indifference or contradiction. Finally he was given a rusty rifle, but no ammunition nor a steel helmet.

Volunteer units guarding Singapore City saw little of the heavy fighting as Japanese troops forced their way on to the island. Some FMSVF and SSVF men were combined with decimated regular units in makeshift formations that vainly battled to stop the enemy forces. Orders to prepare for a final stand in the city as the Japanese closed in were welcomed by many of the Volunteers. Finally, they believed, there would be a chance to kill at least some of the attackers. Many European Volunteers had got their families out of the colony and were willing to die in the ruins of Singapore. J. K. Gale said his unit responded with enthusiasm when told they were expected to fight to the death.[56] They were shattered by the news a few hours later that British forces had surrendered. Major L. V. Taylor of the 4th SSVF Battalion wrote, 'I was stunned at the thought that we were going to surrender, particularly as I had mentally reconciled myself to the "last man last round" situation.'[57] Volunteers were suffused with a mix of

Malay and Singapore Volunteer Forces, December 1941

Straits Settlements Volunteer Force

1st Battalion   Singapore (SVC)
    HQ Wing – signals, intelligence, pioneer and medical sections   *Mixed race*
    3 rifle companies   *European*

2nd Battalion   Singapore (SVC)
    HQ Wing – signals, intelligence, pioneer and medical sections   *Mixed race*
    5 rifle companies   *1 Chinese, 2 Malay, 1 Eurasian, 1 Mixed race*

Singapore Royal Artillery   *European*

Singapore Royal Engineers   *Mixed race*

Singapore Fortress Engineers – converted to bomb disposal   *Mixed race*

Singapore Fortress Signals   *Mixed race*

Singapore Volunteer Intelligence Platoon   *Mixed race*

Singapore Volunteer Pay Section   *Mixed race*

Singapore Volunteer Armoured Car Company   *European*

Singapore Volunteer Field Ambulance   *Mixed race*

Singapore Army Service Corps   *Mixed race*

3rd Battalion   Penang & Province Wellesley
    HQ Wing – signals, intelligence, pioneer and medical sections   *Mixed race*
    4 rifle companies   *2 European, 1 Eurasian, 1 Malay*

4th Battalion   Malacca
    HQ Detachment
    2 Rifle Companies   *European, Chinese and Eurasian platoons*

SSVF estimated total strength 3,250 men

Federated Malay States Volunteer Force

1st Battalion   Perak   *865 men*
    3 rifle companies
    3 machine-gun platoons

2nd Battalion   Selangor   *778 men*
    3 rifle companies
    2 machine-gun platoons

3rd Battalion	Negri Sembilan	*775 men*

    3 rifle companies
    1 machine-gun company

4th Battalion	Pahang	*657 men*

Signal Battalion

Light Artillery Battery

Armoured Car Squadron (became regiment after start of war)

Field Survey Company

Artillery Survey Company

Motor Transport Company

Field Ambulance

Railway Maintenance Company

Independent Company

Plus some logistics detachments

Estimates of FMSVF strength range from approximately 5,000 to 7,400 men. Force included some 1,200 Europeans.

Unfederated Malay States Defence Forces

Johore Volunteer Engineers   *258 men*
    1 company   *European*

Kedah Volunteer Force   *571 men*
    Battalion HQ
    HQ support company
    3 rifle companies

Kelantan Volunteer Force   *136 men*
    1 rifle company

Johore Military Forces

    Regular forces of the sultan
    Infantry battalion and artillery

Source: Colonial Office Reports and SSVF, FMSVF and UMS returns.

relief, anger and humiliation. Guy Turner, of the 4th SSVF Battalion, recalled the utter relief of silence after days of violent noise and confusion.[58] Littledyke, the Volunteer who left home wondering if he would ever see it again, said his unit was ordered to put its rifles in a neat line on the ground, tear up their personal documents and then wash and shave before surrendering.[59] Evans's artillery unit was told to spike their guns only to have the order rescinded because the Japanese demanded the weapons be turned over in working order. A few Volunteers wanted to fight on and could only talk of killing Japs. Others sat in frozen silence trying to comprehend what had happened. Some nervously discussed what would happen next. Most men stood in groups, agonising over a single question – how could Britain have lost? It was a reversal of virtually everything they had been taught or believed in. Evans summed up the mood of most: 'The clouds had enveloped us and a feeling of anti-climax akin to shame mingled with expectant fear inside me.'[60]

*

Thousands of Volunteers were rounded up along with the regular troops following the fall of Singapore. A surprising number reacted to defeat with searing denunciations of their own officers. Older and inexperienced Volunteer officers often lacked the mental and physical strength to lead men in battle. Photos of pre-war regimental gatherings invariably depict numerous portly middle-aged officers. Seniority, social prominence and a taste for bureaucratic routine often were the main criteria in officer selection in the inter-war era.

Even men who had seen action in the First World War swiftly crumpled beneath the strain of modern battle. Taylor, of the 4th SSVF, said his commander, who had a good 1914–18 record, was overwhelmed from the start: 'Now manifestly unsuited and too old to command an infantry battalion in 1942, [he] had succumbed to battle fatigue.'[61] All but one of his battalion's officers were over 30. Hoops felt his battalion commander, a lawyer in his mid-50s, was totally unfit to lead troops in war.

Too many officers were concerned only with their own survival and comfort. Thornton was appalled when he went to Brigade HQ in Port Dickson to find out where his unit was after returning from an assignment:

> 'Some well-known Volunteer Officers were busy forgetting the war
> in liquor. They could not tell me where Sel. Bn. [Selangor Battalion]
> HQ might be! This from Brigade HQ. Despite the shortage of
> vehicles they had a truck loaded with beer and spirits.'[62]

Gale, the FMSVF Volunteer, said his armoured car could not be evacuated because a ship was loaded with officers' baggage. 'In many cases the respect had changed into contempt,' he said.[63] Relations between officers in some units were strained by rivalries dating back years. 'Underneath the surface petty jealousies grew an atmosphere of icy politeness[,] of cynical aloofness,' recalled one junior officer.[64] Volunteers also complained that a few long-time NCOs enjoyed bullying weak, young recruits.

Anger and resentment erupted as the Volunteers were swept into prison camps and military discipline crumbled. Many officers still expected to be treated with deference and demanded superior treatment in the prison camps. They were swiftly disabused. 'Our officers ... expected to maintain the usual discipline, saluting etc., but we soon disillusioned them on that score,' wrote Middleton.[65] Unlike in regular units, men in Volunteer formations were usually the social equals of their officers; some actually were their superiors in civilian life. Evans said a few officers and NCOs used the final days before the surrender to hoard unit supplies and cash. These men took the supplies into captivity, he said, refusing to share them with others.[66] A small minority gave the Volunteers a bad name in the years of captivity.

Captivity also brought out the social gulf between the Volunteers and the working-class soldiers of the regular British forces. Volunteers had joked during the campaign about being mistaken for officers by regular soldiers because of their upper-class accents. Others complained of sullen resentment from the regulars. Kinahan, the bomb disposal sapper, said he had never understood what life was like for most Britons until he was interned with ordinary soldiers in a prison camp.

> 'I had a pampered background and English public school education. The horrors of the great recession of the early 30s had largely passed me by, whereas most of my fellow prisoners came from humble homes which had suffered all the privations of that ghastly period in our history.'[67]

Chinese Volunteers were singled out for the harshest treatment after the British defeat. Japanese security forces saw the Chinese as a major threat to the new order.[68] SSVF and FMSVF Chinese Volunteers were at the top of their target list, followed by communists, 'anti-Japanese' political groups, financial donors to China and 'rascals or hooligans'. No order appears to have been issued to disband the Asian units after Singapore fell as had happened in Malaya. Some prescient British officers told their Asian troops to change into civilian clothes and slip away. Thousands of Chinese residents were rounded up by the Japanese for screening soon after the British surrender. Survivors said the huge throng was crammed into a few city blocks and ringed by Japanese troops. Chinese Volunteers in civilian clothes were among those rounded up.

Among them was Wong Sin Joon, a Singapore Volunteer, who gave a vivid post-war account of what happened. Members of the SSVF were told to identify themselves. Anyone who admitted being a Volunteer was told they would be released and given a job in the new police force. Several Volunteers who stepped forward were manhandled and marched away. Wong, who did not identify himself, was detained as he tried to leave with several civilians. There were reports after the war that some Chinese SSVF men pointed out other Volunteers in the crowd to the Japanese. Wong was taken to a nearby school with dozens of other Volunteers. Next morning about 70 Volunteers, hands tied behind their backs, were taken in trucks to a beach. What was going to happen became apparent as soon as they saw waiting Japanese troops.

> 'We could hardly move when we saw the firing squad. Some of us cried, some calling for their parents. As regards to myself I cried but could shed no tears, my limbs were as cold as ice when I looked around and saw the firing squad in their position.'

Wong and the others were forced to line up in front of several machine guns. Bullets ripped into the huddled men. Wong and a few others were only wounded. They lay among the dead bodies until the Japanese left. Wong and the other survivors crawled into the bush. Eventually they reached a Malay village where the people refused to help them. British soldiers later found Wong and took him to a field ambulance unit, where he was treated and hidden. Brigadier-General K. S. Torrance told an inquiry after the war that British and Australian soldiers were made to bury about 100 Chinese Volunteers who had been executed by the Japanese. Other accounts say some Malay and Eurasian Volunteers and regulars were also shot.

Official accounts suggest comparatively few Volunteers were killed or wounded in the campaign. Surviving records are sketchy and a great deal of documentation was lost during the war. A post-war report on FMSVF losses estimates 135 men were killed or missing. Of those, about 60 were non-Europeans. A 1946 Colonial Office report put Volunteer losses at 96 dead. Both estimates are clearly inadequate. Losses among Asian Volunteers appear to have been significantly undercounted: men executed by the Japanese or killed during the long occupation were not included. Details of casualties were probably lost when Volunteer units were disbanded or disintegrated in the retreat. Some 400, mostly European, Volunteers perished in the years of crippling privation, hard labour and cruelty in the Japanese prison camps. Volunteer forces had comparatively few battle losses because they served mainly in rear areas. That is no reflection on their courage and dedication. Many Volunteers were not only willing, but fully expected, to die. The overwhelming majority did everything they could to defeat the invading enemy. Their bravery and dedication, along with those of so many other British and imperial soldiers, were wasted by the folly of their own government and leaders.

Chapter 3

FORLORN HOPE

Dalforce

A FORCE OF CHINESE IRREGULARS was formed under a British police officer as part of the forlorn attempts to halt the Japanese forces that surged down the Malay Peninsula at the start of the war in the Far East. It was a sign of British desperation that the force contained communists, gangsters and other foes of the colonial regime. Some of the men were enlisted from prisons where they had been held on political charges. It was a predictably doomed venture. Virtually untrained men armed with old shotguns were slaughtered in one-sided fights with some of the Japanese Army's finest troops.

Lieutenant-Colonel John Dalley, a police special branch officer, was given the last-minute task of organising the Chinese. Dalley, shrewd and sometimes unorthodox, had been organising special forces for the military. Some in Singapore's Chinese community, which was split by political, social and regional differences, opposed the idea of using civilians for such a role. Communist leaders, however, demanded weapons to fight the Japanese. Dalley, with his experience of chasing subversives, was put in charge. It was probably thought that Dalley was best qualified to handle such men and clear up any complications, such as squashing the force if Britain emerged triumphant. British officials christened the new unit Dalforce. Its Chinese members adopted the more imposing 'Singapore Overseas Chinese Volunteer Army'.

Dalforce was formed in mid-December 1941. It was led by British officers with Chinese NCOs and men. Recruits comprised a remarkable range of the Chinese community: sons of leading merchants, gangsters, communists, nationalists, rickshaw pullers and coolies. Women also volunteered, although it is not clear what role they played. A desire to fight the Japanese united the disparate groups that made up the force. Some reports claim it was divided into Communist and Kuomintang units. It recruited some 2,000 men. Volunteers exceeded the number of recruits the force could take. Some units were still being formed when the British forces in Malaya surrendered. Reaction in the British community to the force was mixed. Tom Evans, who fought in the Singapore Volunteer Artillery, said younger settlers liked the idea while their elders were deeply mistrustful: 'We always thought there should be a Chinese army. Others thought they would be disloyal to the British.'[1]

Training was almost nonexistent. I. A. McDonald, a member of the Johore Volunteer Engineers who was posted to Dalforce as an officer, said the men received a week's preparation at most.[2] Training was little more than showing the men how to load a weapon, he said, and one or two other things. There was no time to train the recruits to shoot properly or show them how to fight. Most were armed with old shotguns confiscated from civilian police who had fled their post. McDonald said each man was given seven buckshot cartridges. It was not enough for a duck hunt let alone the unit's allocated role of patrolling the coastal mangrove swamps where the Japanese were expected to land. Machetes were also handed out to the recruits. McDonald said each man wanted a chance to scalp a Japanese invader. Uniforms consisted of clumsy blue outfits purchased in the cheapest sections of the bazaars. A khaki headband and a crude cloth badge completed the outfit.[3]

Dalforce detachments patrolled the coastline and held positions between some of the regular units.[4] Some of the first reports of Japanese landings came from Dalforce but its units that tried to block the Japanese advances suffered huge losses. McDonald said two-thirds of one company or about 100 men were lost on the first night of the Japanese landing.[5] Even so Dalforce provided intelligence and fought alongside regular units until the British defences collapsed. Survivors were ordered to change into civilian clothes, destroy their uniforms and slip away. Japanese security forces later hunted down Dalforce members and a number were executed along with other Chinese.

Chapter 4

A SULTAN'S TOY

The Malay States Guides

THE MALAY STATES GUIDES never quite lived up to their imposing and romantic name. Everyone agreed this was a very smart regiment. Its soldiers had to be at least 5 feet 9 inches tall. A third of the men of the regiment were over 6 feet. The men paraded in magnificent red tunics and green turbans with silver edging. Admirers compared the Guides' poise and superb marching to a British Guards regiment. Others had doubts about the force's military value. Critics claimed that the Guides were tin soldiers. They jeered that the regiment was just a toy wheeled out to please the vanity of Malay rulers at ceremonial parades. The Guides were indeed something of an orphan in the Empire's armed forces. The regiment was not a police force nor a fully-fledged infantry unit; it did not belong to the Indian Army or the British Army; the rank-and-file were organised on Indian Army lines but the European officers were closer to the outlook and methods of the British Army. It never quite seemed to know its true purpose. Officers and men became used to an idle, undemanding life with little to do besides ceremonial marching and occasional, sedate training exercises. Some of the Indian officers and men ran private businesses and treated their regimental duties almost as a sideline. The regiment was notorious for internal rivalries and bickering. It fell apart when it finally faced a real war.

There had been no rush to add Malaya to the growing list of colonies as the British Empire expanded. Britain's interest in the region was for a long time concerned mostly with safeguarding sea routes linking India and China. Singapore and a handful of British enclaves along the Malay peninsula, which had been acquired mostly in the early 19th century by the East India Company, were thought sufficient to guard the Malacca Straits and the vital trade link to China. London saw no need to occupy the patchwork of petty, warring native states covering the Malay peninsula. British detachment did not change until the 1870s when war and unrest in the native sultanates, vague fears that Germany had designs on the region, and the ambitions of local British officials forced a change. Britain still did not conquer and annex the Malay states, however. Instead it took charge quietly with treaties that gave *de facto* control to British officials who resided at the courts of the Malay sultans and ostensibly offered advice. These British residents, as they were known, soon held the real power. The rulers, whose authority over their fractious states and feuding nobility had been largely nominal, mostly accepted the changes. Malaya became one of the most peaceful British colonies apart from intermittent, mostly minor uprisings. Only a handful of British and native troops was needed to guard it.

The Malay States Guides traced their history to the years when British influence was starting to spread across the peninsula. Some sultans formed modern constabularies with British assistance to suppress lawlessness in their states. These forces were modelled on the Indian Army and employed British officers and Indian sepoys.

Captain Tristian Speedy was a police official in the British enclave at Penang when he was hired by a Malay ruler to end clan wars in Perak. Speedy was one of those robustly eccentric figures who did so much to expand the boundaries of the British Empire by flouting the instructions of government bureaucrats and following their own grandiose visions. A massive man, whose sprawling beard covered his chest, Speedy was born in India. He became an officer in the Indian Army, fought in the Indian Mutiny and then served in Abyssinia. Speedy went on to join the Indian Police, later taking a post in Penang, where he played the bagpipes in public. European residents were horrified by his exuberant behaviour.

Bored by Penang's stifling routine, Speedy happily accepted the offer to form a military police force for the Mantri of Larut. A high salary helped lure him from British service. He returned to the Punjab in 1873, where he had served in the army, and recruited a force of 110 Sikh sepoys to form the Perak Armed Police. Speedy's little unit fought alongside British forces in the Perak War of 1875–6 after the first British resident was murdered by a Malay chieftain. Speedy was delegated to assist the British officials sent to replace the slain resident. A strong-willed individualist like Speedy inevitably clashed with his new civilian masters. It did not help that Speedy was paid far more than his new superiors, who soon found many reasons to criticise him. Speedy resigned in 1877, tired of the growing restraints on his authority and the constant petty bickering.

Speedy's force was recognised as a valuable prototype, even if he was not regarded as a model commander. B. S. F. Walker, a regular army officer, was named Perak commissioner of police with instructions to strengthen the force. He recruited 250 Sikhs from the 14th, 15th and 45th Regiments of the Indian Army in 1883. The unit had some 650 men by 1884, mostly Indians with 100 Malays. Its European officers came from the British and

Indian Armies on temporary assignment. Small detachments were scattered around the state to back up the civilian authorities and police. It was renamed the 1st Battalion, Perak Sikh Military Police, in 1884. British officials in Malaya offered the unit to London for imperial service the same year. This was declined, but imperial officials valued the unit sufficiently to earmark it as the reserve force for Malaya and Singapore. Two other states, Selangor and Pahang, formed Sikh military police forces on similar lines.

Troops from the various forces helped suppress a rebellion in Pahang in 1891. Malay chiefs rebelled after the British persuaded the sultan to strip one of them of his title. The ensuing guerrilla war was one of the few serious attempts to resist encroaching British rule. Sikh police stormed and captured a rebel stronghold at Kuala Tembeline. Stability was soon established across the state and the civil Malay police had less and less need for the Indian military wings. Some British officials wanted to disband the various state police forces, saying they did not speak Malay and were 'about as suited to police work as the Household Brigade'. Other officials favoured retaining the Sikhs as a quasi-military force to help keep a check on the Malay majority.

A new role was found for the various Sikh forces when London decided to restructure the Malay states. Perak, Pahang, Selangor and Negri Sembilan were shuffled into a loose confederation as the Federated Malay States (FMS) in 1895. Its founding treaty required the member states to maintain a small military force. A regular infantry regiment was formed from the now redundant Sikh military police units. The new regiment was created in 1896 and based on the Perak Sikhs, as the senior force, with drafts from the Selangor and Pahang forces. (Negri Sembilan did not have a military police force.) It used the Perak Sikhs' headquarters at Taiping. Walker was the first commanding officer, with the rank of lieutenant-colonel.[1]

The new regiment was called the Malay States Guides in apparent imitation of the India Army's famous Corps of Guides. Six companies were formed with a depot company to train recruits. (A seventh company was raised temporarily during the Boer War to help garrison Penang after regular British troops were withdrawn.) Four companies were made up of Sikhs, one of Punjabi Muslims and one of Pathans. A 1903 report said five Hindu sepoys rounded out the force. Muslim sepoys needed permission from their officers to grow beards unlike the Sikhs. The regiment had 10 British officers, 8 native officers and 596 NCOs and men in 1896. Its strength rose to almost 900 men by the First World War. Many of the sepoys had served in the Indian Army. European officers came from the British and Indian Armies. Native Indian officers received commissions from the governor of the Straits Settlements. Efforts were made to strengthen the force. Infantry companies were issued Maxim machine guns. A battery was formed shortly after the regiment's formation with seven 7-pounder mountain guns and two 15-pounder field guns. It was a separate, slightly aloof unit with 150 gunners and 50 mule handlers to transport the guns. Gunners wore dark blue uniforms and turbans.

Everything seemed promising in the regiment's early years. Life was pleasant and undemanding, especially at the large regimental headquarters at Taiping. The soldiers were fairly well paid and many had families in the married quarters. Men were given money to buy their own food instead of being fed in communal kitchens. Officers were expected to make sure the men did not damage their health by skimping on meals to save money; men were banned from buying alcohol in local shops to try to curb excessive drinking. A daily rum ration could be purchased from the regimental canteen. Reports to the Imperial Defence Committee in London rated the unit as very efficient.

Annual inspections praised the force's smartness, efficiency and keenness in the early years – a contingent from the new regiment was sent to march in the celebrations of Queen Victoria's Diamond Jubilee in London in 1896. The regiment was given an important role in defence plans for Singapore. And yet the evaluations also hinted at problems. A 1903 report refers to a past 'tendency to join in conspiracies and create party and caste feelings in the Regiment'.[2] Discipline was marred by occasional drunkenness and insubordination. Army inspectors sometimes expressed doubts about the regiment's training standards. It was suggested that some exercises were staged or too easy. A 1901 report said the Guides only did well at target practice because targets were deliberately placed too close to the firing lines. The men, it added, should be made to shoot under more realistic conditions that resembled combat. Peace, ceremonial soldiering and the lack of any real purpose were believed to be sapping the regiment's morale. The regiment spent too much time drilling and very little time training for war: 'the great fault of the Malay States Guides is the want of system in the training', an inspector said in 1911.[3]

Soldiering in the Guides almost resembled a part-time job. Men and officers spent a few hours each day on parades and sports before rushing home to their outside interests. Some of the Indian officers and soldiers ran businesses. Others reputedly used the large amount of spare time to bicker and plot against rivals. It rarely had the kind of contact with other units that improved training and introduced new ideas. Proposals to send the Guides overseas on active service were rebuffed because the War Office saw the force as a local constabulary. Offers to serve in Somaliland, the Boxer Rebellion in China and the Boer War were all declined. Instead the regiment provided a fire brigade for the civilian areas of Taiping.

Some senior British officers sensed that the Guides were less impressive than they appeared on parade. And yet observers could not agree on what was wrong. A surprising number of outside observers pointed at the regiment's British officers. The officer's mess was frequently split by squabbling cliques. The regiment could not attract the kind of bright and energetic officers it needed to thrive. Too many of the officers were staid plodders embittered by real or imagined personal grievances. Some complained they had been given false information to persuade them to join the regiment. One disillusioned officer asserted he was told the Guides were like the Burma Frontier Force with junior officers overseeing large territories. Others complained they had no real authority and were always being overruled by the commanding officer. Officers from the British Army found it difficult to deal with native troops and performed poorly, a report noted.[4] The British officers generally had little contact with the men. Unit affairs were mostly left to the Indian officers and NCOs. Few of the European officers were even proficient in Urdu, the regiment's working language. Some of the officers insisted on giving orders in English even though few sepoys could understand it. All of the officers complained about poor pay. Even London, always eager to curb costs, agreed that the salaries were low and approved increases in 1912 to attract better candidates. Serving officers were enraged when they were told that only new arrivals would get the higher pay rates.

Things were not much better with the rank-and-file. Discipline was crumbling because of regular drunkenness. A 1907 inspection found a fairly high desertion rate of 5.4 per cent in the previous 12 months. Some regimental historians suggest the Sikhs were split by fierce regional loyalties. There were claims of discrimination whenever a member of a rival faction was promoted. Some men in A Company asked to leave the regiment after a quarrel over a woman in 1910 inflamed the rivalry. Two men were expelled after mediation by a Sikh priest failed to end the dispute and British commanders then tried to end the tension by grouping men from different regions in separate companies. Jealousy and cliques also divided the Indian officers. Sepoys supposedly were encouraged by Indian officers and NCOs from their home regions to undermine their counterparts and rivals from other areas.

The rot of years of suffocating routine and bickering was exposed when the regiment finally got a chance for active service with the outbreak of the First World War. It was picked for service in East Africa, and sent to Singapore late in 1914 to embark. Once there, the troops refused to go overseas. They argued that their contracts only obliged them to serve in Malaya. The reasons for the regiment's refusal are not clear. Some contemporary accounts suggested that the men were shaken by reports of heavy casualties in Africa. Other reports claimed some of the Indian officers and NCOs were reluctant to leave the lucrative businesses they had built up in their spare time. Outside influences were also blamed. Revolutionaries of the Ghadr movement and pro-German Islamic agitators had links with some of the men and attempted to foment anti-British sentiment in the ranks. Ghadrites, who aimed to create an independent Punjab state by overthrowing British rule, were active across Asia.

British commanders were horrified by the regiment's refusal to go overseas. Some officials said that the unit was disloyal and must be disbanded. Military authorities decided the time was not right for such drastic action and the regiment was sent back to Taiping. Breaking up the unit in wartime was seen as particularly damaging to British prestige and possibly dangerous. There were also too few troops left in Malaya and no obvious replacements for the Guides.

The Guides' battery stayed in Singapore to bolster its defences after the withdrawal of the regular British Army battalion. A few months later, on 15 February 1915, four companies of the Indian 5th Light Infantry mutinied in Singapore as the regiment was preparing to ship to Hong Kong. The 5th Light Infantry shared many of the same problems that had plagued the Guides. It was riddled with cliques and the British officers had little control over the men. Some of the mutineers went to the nearby barracks of the Guides' battery where they shot and killed the British captain in charge. Some of the Guides were persuaded, some accounts say forced, to join the mutineers, but most of the contingent refused. Battery members who stayed loyal fled to Johore, where they were disarmed and interned by the local sultan's forces. They were later allowed to rejoin the regiment.

Whatever the doubts about their loyalty, the Guides were used to help suppress a native revolt in the northern state of Kelantan later that year. Local Islamic leaders had called for the expulsion of all foreigners. Reports of the Singapore mutiny and British reverses in the war seemed to back up their claims that British rule was finished. A force of some 200 Guides was ferried up the eastern coast in a steamship and landed in small boats. Rebels armed with decrepit muskets attacked their camp a few nights later only to be easily beaten off. A rebel force was caught in open country the next day by the Guides, who killed and wounded several of the insurgents. However, it took five months of spasmodic clashes before the Guides and other British forces suppressed the uprising. The Guides' only casualty was a single soldier who was drowned.

The regiment had meanwhile reconsidered its refusal to serve in Africa. There were fears the unit would be disbanded and careers and livelihoods ruined. It now agreed to serve overseas with each man signing a new contract. It is not clear how much this turnabout reflected genuine repentance in the ranks or pressure from military commanders. Whatever the reasons, the regiment was sent to one of the war's most obscure backwaters. The Guides sailed in September 1915 to join the Aden Field Force. Some 900 officers and men were accompanied by 50 camp followers, including locally recruited Tamil labourers. They joined a British army which spent most of the war largely bottled up in Aden by a smaller Turkish force. The Guides' war diary records month after month of monotony in the baking wastes outside Aden. British detachments would go out to face the Turks, only to return after another inconclusive skirmish. One entry claims that the regiment formed an infantry square to beat off a Turkish attack in March 1916. Harsh conditions and disease depleted the regiment rather than the desultory bouts of fighting. By 1919, when it returned from Aden, its ranks were reduced to 500 men, mostly from sickness.[5]

The decision to use the Guides in a war zone suggests the authorities had regained some confidence in the regiment. That they were sent to a forgotten theatre, where British forces failed to distinguish themselves, was typical of the regiment's lacklustre fortunes. Doubts about the Guides' value had not vanished, moreover, and the Army quickly decided to disband the force once the war was over. Even its commanding officer recommended the regiment be broken up. Many of the men, worn out by harsh service in Aden, wanted to return to India. Without any fanfare, the regiment was disbanded in late 1919.

Chapter 5

LOYAL AND TRUE

The Malay Regiment

MALAYS WERE AMONG THE LAST RACES to be recruited as regular soldiers for Britain's vast colonial armies. They were maligned for decades by the British military establishment with a hotchpotch of racial stereotypes. 'The taste for military life has passed from amongst them,' one British officer wrote in the 1870s.[1] In fact the patchwork of Malay kingdoms had a long martial tradition when Europeans first established settlements on the coast. Small Malay armies fought well against far better armed Portuguese and Dutch expeditions. Fighting was a way of life for the native aristocracy.

Frank Swettenham, an early British administrator, described how a Malay gentleman went out in public: 'say, two daggers in his belt, two spears in his hand, a gun over his shoulders, and a long sword under his arm'.[2] British administrators suppressed the traditional Malay military system, based on the courts of the native rulers, as imperial control was imposed in the late 19th century. The relative ease of the British take-over led to a misguided contempt for the Malays as soldiers. 'No elements within reach of the Straits are trainable or capable of discipline,' wrote John Cameron in the 1860s.[3] Lurid Victorian stereotypes further coloured the disparaging British view of the Malays' fitness for military life. Critics scoffed that any Malay unit would be paralysed by laziness, homicidal outbursts and catatonic fear. It was a view based on two supposed traits of Malay character: running *amok*, a Malay term describing a reputed propensity to explode in murderous rages; and *latah*, the supposed trait of suddenly being frozen with fear for no ostensible reason. A plan in the 1890s to recruit Malays for companies of 'submarine miners' (to work with naval mines) to serve in Singapore, Hong Kong and Ceylon fell apart when Malays declined to sign up.[4] It all fitted neatly with the smug colonial view of the Malays as simple peasants content to loll around their villages under the benevolence of British rule.

The Malay Regiment was one of the most successful military units in British colonial history despite the disparaging view of the Malay character.

It fought heroically in the ruins of Singapore, achieving a reputation that outshone many British and imperial regiments. Calls to recruit Malays had come from a few influential British figures over the years and, as has been seen, General John French helped clear the way for Malays to join the Volunteer forces at the start of the 20th century by pointedly commenting on their proud military heritage.

Pressure to create a regular Malay military unit came first from the country's traditional rulers. Such a force would meet the Federated Malay States' obligation to provide a regiment for local defence, a role that had been filled by the Indian Army at the expense of Malay taxpayers. Supporters saw the formation of a Malay military unit as a step in advancing embryonic Malay national interests. Keen advocates spoke of recruiting 20,000 men for local defence. British officials tried to deflect and delay the calls for a Malay military force. It was claimed Malays were backward and incapable of forming an effective military unit. Opponents asserted that Malays could never be officers because they were incapable of mastering Western administrative skills. British bureaucrats used every paper-shuffling trick to delay and derail the calls for a Malay unit. The first formal proposal for a regular Malay regiment was presented to the Federated Malay States Legislative Council in 1913 only to be dropped because of the outbreak of the First World War. It was not until 1920 that the federal government acknowledged that the idea was being considered. Five years later it was referred to the War Office in London for further study. The exasperated sultans in 1931 demanded a decision. Britain did not want to alienate the native rulers who played a key role in the colonial edifice. 'There is the political consideration that the opportunity of fitting themselves for the defence of the country could not, without causing great disappointment to Their Highnesses the Rulers and their subjects, be any longer withheld from the Malay race,' a government statement conceded.[5]

There were other considerations. British civil servants and the traditional rulers were equally tired of helping pay for an Indian Army unit to garrison the colony. British officials complained their Indian counterparts would never set a fixed cost for the Indian unit and kept on sending unexpected additional bills. It was argued that Malays could do a better job at less cost. A small experimental unit was formed in 1932 to see if a Malay military unit could be successful. It was given six months to prove its value.

The experiment created huge interest. Admission was confined to Malays. More than a thousand young men applied for the 25 places in the unit. Well-educated and promising young men of the higher classes were encouraged to apply. Pride and the desire for a military life attracted candidates from many backgrounds. Poverty and unemployment inspired other would-be soldiers. British district officers were given the task of selecting recruits. Admission standards, physical and mental, were very high. About 25 per cent of the applicants were rejected for physical and health reasons. Intelligence, athletic and shooting tests winnowed out nearly all of the other hopefuls.

Colonial Office officials, sympathetic to the plan, carefully selected regular British officers and NCOs to run the experimental unit. It was recognised they would have to marry British Army standards with traditional Malay culture to produce a new military ethos. Pioneering native units, such as the Chinese Regiment, were studied to help pick suitable officers and NCOs. Captain G. Bruce of the Lincolnshire Regiment was given command. A second regular officer, Captain K. E. Exham, who was serving on secondment with the Malacca Volunteer Corps, was named regimental adjutant. Two regular NCOs, Regimental Sergeant-Major A. E. McCarthy and Company Sergeant-Major E. Oldfield, who were already in Malaya as instructors with the Volunteer forces, rounded out the training team. It was decided from the first that the unit would have British and Malay officers. All of the NCOs would be Malays once suitable men had been trained.

Bruce, an energetic and intelligent officer, was given six months to prove Malays could meet British military standards. His instructions from the War Office were '. . . to find out how the Malays would react to military discipline, and in fact if they could be made into really efficient regular soldiers'.[6] He spent a month learning basic Malay at the School of Oriental Languages before leaving London. The tiny band of recruits and their British trainers assembled at Port Dickson on 1 March 1933. They lived and trained in huts named after First World War battles and normally used by FMSVF units on weekend courses. British Army discipline was combined with 'appreciation of Malay sensibilities and customs' from the outset.[7] The trainers and recruits worked relentlessly for the next five months. Bruce recalled that he told the 25 recruits at the outset what he expected:

'. . . they were going to be drilled and trained until their hands, feet and hearts burned. They were not going to be just smart soldiers. They were going to be the smartest . . . soldiers anybody in the Peninsula had ever seen, heard of, dreamt of.'[8]

Intelligent, sympathetic treatment from the British staff and the eagerness and talents of the Malays produced swift and impressive results.

The British Army's penchant for swearing on the parade ground was also enthusiastically adopted.

Bruce, keen to win public support, invited the public to attend the contingent's Sunday morning parades to help dispel doubts about the unit. Sir Shenton Thomas, High Commissioner of the Federated Malay States, arrived on 18 July 1933 to determine if the experiment was a success. A flawless display of marching impressed the visiting delegation. Approval to expand the force to a company followed and more progress ensued. A mid-1934 government announcement said the experiment was a success and a full battalion would be formed. It officially became The Malay Regiment with the motto 'Loyal and True' on 1 January 1935. It also became the FMS garrison unit in 1937 when the Burma Rifles unit left and soon the regiment was running NCO courses for the local Volunteer forces.

The force reached its authorised strength of some 800 officers and men by October 1938. A shortage of Malay officers, the only serious deficiency, stemmed from training delays. Standards for all ranks were kept high. Hundreds of men continued to apply for the few spots in the regiment. District officers and village headmen made the initial selection of candidates. A visiting regimental board then made the final choice. Recruiting was extended beyond the federated states to the other Malay states and the Straits Settlements.

Whether or not it was due to the success of the Malay Regiment, the British Army began recruiting Malays in the late 1930s as local auxiliaries. The Malay Sappers were formed with 1,000 men in 1938 as part of the Royal Engineers. The unit manned searchlights and was moved in 1941 to the Royal Artillery. There were also eight Malay truck companies attached to the Royal Army Service Corps.

Confounding sceptics and ingrained prejudices, the new regiment was a model unit. 'The record of good conduct in the Regiment is probably without parallel in any other Regular Unit,' enthused an early history. Certainly few units developed so quickly and effectively. Its men were natural soldiers, enthusiastic, devoted and disciplined. A strong paternal spirit did not blunt the men's development. The first four Malay officers were appointed in late 1936. All four had joined as privates in the first batch of 25 recruits. Indeed many of the 25 founders were exceptional men: several went on to high command in the British and post-independence Malayan armies. Not untypical was Raja Lope Rashid, an aristocrat educated at Oxford, who was described as 'perfectly at ease' with even the 'humblest of his countrymen'.

Malay officers held commissions from the FMS high commissioner rather than the British crown. British officers held all the senior commands and far outnumbered Malay officers up to the start of the war. British members of the regiment were also far better paid. A European sergeant-major received $375 a month while a Malay with the same rank was paid $55. The men were encouraged to marry, wives and families coming within the regiment's embrace. Married quarters were constructed and families exposed to British notions of housekeeping:

> 'Under the strict but sympathetic eye of a European Lady Medical Officer, many soldiers' wives and families learnt valuable lessons in domestic service which were later carried to distant villages over the country.'[9]

While it was famous for displays of faultless marching, the new regiment soon saw more active soldiering. It was commended for helping suppress violent coal strikes in 1937 and detachments later helped quell civil disturbances in two of the Malay States. Its acceptance as a fully-fledged unit came in 1938 when it was merged into the new 1st Malayan Infantry Brigade with the British 2nd Battalion, Loyal Regiment, and the Indian Army's 1st Battalion, 17th Dogra Regiment. Intense training followed the outbreak of war in Europe in 1939. Jungle exercises became a regimental speciality. A local endurance record was set when a platoon under Lieutenant Mohamed Ali marched 104 miles in 4 days, 4 hours and 15 minutes over rough terrain. The men each carried a rifle and 80 pounds of equipment; none dropped out. However, six soldiers drowned during a 1941 exercise on the east coast.[10]

With the outbreak of war in 1939 there were calls to form a second battalion to boost regional defence but the decision to create another battalion did not come until March 1941. A regimental depot was then established to train recruits for both battalions and experienced officers and men were transferred from the 1st Battalion to help organise and lead the new unit. Heavier weapons, including mortars and Bren gun carriers, helped strengthen the two battalions in the final days of peace.

The 2nd Battalion became operational one week before the Japanese invaded Malaya. Combined, the two battalions had some 1,400 men at the start of the Japanese war, including 180 recruits with six weeks or less of training. The 2nd Battalion reached a peak strength of some 580 men in the final days of the campaign. The two units had 59 British officers and 19 Malay officers. Fifteen of the British officers were last-minute additions from the Volunteer forces.[11]

Both battalions were deployed on anti-invasion duties at the start of the campaign. 1st Battalion guarded the southern coast of Singapore island. Two companies of 2nd Battalion, which was still forming, were deployed in Malaya: one at Kelantan and the other in Province Wellesley. The 2nd Battalion's A Company was bombed at Kelantan a day after the Japanese landing on the east coast. It fought in several rearguard actions as British forces were pushed back down the peninsula by the advancing Japanese. D Company in Province Wellesley on the west coast was heavily bombed and machine-gunned by Japanese planes. It helped to repulse a Japanese attack on the mouth of the Nibong Tebal River. Royal Navy ships evacuated the company and other British units after they were trapped on the coast at Ponggor. Both companies reached Singapore where the 2nd Battalion assembled as a complete formation for the first time.

A. E. Percival, the hapless general who commanded the disastrous British defence of Malaya, later said the young Malay soldiers were the equal of any of the troops under his command. 'They set an example of steadfastness and endurance under the most difficult conditions,' he wrote.[12] Percival's praise was, if anything, less than the regiment deserved. Its bravery and endurance in the final, catastrophic days of the siege surpassed that of many older, more experienced regiments.

The two units held defensive positions on the south coast when the Japanese invaded Singapore island from the north. Units of 1st Battalion had constructed concrete machine-gun posts and other coast defences that were never used. Positions of 2nd Battalion slightly inland along the Jurong River were attacked at dawn on 10 February and the unit driven back. Further heavy Japanese infantry and artillery attacks came two days later. Dozens of Malay soldiers were killed and wounded. The battalion repeatedly checked the Japanese advance, only pulling back under extreme pressure to new positions. Both battalions were holding a line stretching inland from the coast by 13 February when a major thrust of the Japanese 18th Division hit the 2nd Battalion. Burning oil from a refinery flowed down a nearby stream and provided an apocalyptic backdrop as the Malays fought off several attacks. Eventually the defenders were forced back to new positions. Units of the 1st Battalion were hit by Japanese tanks on 14 February and fought hand-to-hand to throw back the accompanying infantry. Mass fire from 16 Lewis machine guns halted one Japanese attack.

C Company staged a last stand on Opium Hill after being cut off by Japanese troops and many of the men died in horrific close-quarter fighting. One of its decimated platoons made a final bayonet charge. Lieutenant Adnan bin Saidi was wounded as he ordered his men to fight to the death.

Japanese soldiers bayoneted the young officer and hung his body upside down from a tree. At least six captured Malay soldiers were tied up and then bayoneted by Japanese troops. A few survivors were badly burned as they escaped across the creek filled with burning oil.

Malay soldiers fought on as men from some British and Australian units abandoned their positions, as J. K. Gale of the Singapore Volunteer Artillery recalled:

> 'They were being attacked by vastly superior forces but managed to hold the enemy almost entirely ... On many occasions our troops withdrew when this barrage came over. Not so the Malay Regiment. Many of them went forward when the mortar fire started. Everyone had the highest praise for the way that the Malay Regiment fought. They were surpassed by none.'[13]

Lieutenant Alastair MacKenzie, a Volunteer officer assigned to the regiment a few weeks earlier, was appalled at seeing terrified white troops flee past the Malay positions. 'The Malays behaved well, though what their inner thoughts were at the sight of such rabble, one can only guess,' he said.[14] MacKenzie was enraged when his Malay sergeant was killed by fire from a British infantry unit. Some British troops stayed with the Malays and fought. McKenzie never forgot seeing Malay infantrymen and British gunners huddling together in a slit trench under withering Japanese mortar fire. Most were dazed except for 'one middle-aged Malay contentedly smoking his pipe'.[15] Old colonial attitudes did not always die even as the British Army perished in the ruins of Singapore. MacKenzie had a 'slight tiff' with a British officer who '... was concerned at the lack of British troops and preponderance of Malays'.[16] Having watched other British units flee, MacKenzie's response was 'brief and terse'.

Seven Malay officers, six British officers and 146 men of the regiment were killed in the campaign, including several later executed by the Japanese. A larger, if never specified, number were wounded. Survivors from the two battalions were gathered at the Keppel Harbour golf course following the British surrender. Some of the Malays were given permission by the two battalion commanders to put on civilian clothes and slip away before the Japanese arrived. British officers were separated from the Malays by the Japanese and sent to a prison camp for Europeans. Some of the Malay officers and men were taken to a facility where other Asian troops of the British forces were being held. Several Malay Regiment officers, and some Malay officers of the Volunteer forces, were separated from their men. Five of the Malay Regiment officers were executed with a large group of

Chinese Volunteers. The officers refused demands to serve the Japanese or at least put on civilian clothes and accept release as a sign they no longer served Britain. A later British Army report said they even refused to remove their rank badges.[17] There were also vague reports that some Malay Regiment soldiers were shot in a separate incident, possibly with the large group of Chinese Volunteers who were executed after the battle (*see* page 46). Some of the interned men were released eventually while others were sent to labour camps. Most of the battalions' families had been moved to Singapore for safety a few weeks earlier. They and some of the surviving soldiers walked to their homes in Malaya. Japanese forces frequently detained and harassed them along the way.

Many survivors of the regiment volunteered for duty as soon as Japan surrendered. A skeleton headquarters was set up at Port Dickson and by March 1946 some 600 veterans were helping re-form the regiment. Rapid expansion followed. Seven battalions were formed by the time of Malayan independence in 1957. The regiment played a major role in the 12-year campaign against communist insurgents and was a foundation of the modern Malaysian Army.

Chapter 6

WHITE RAJAS

The Sarawak Rangers

THE WHITE RAJAHS WHO RULED over the little kingdom of Sarawak resembled something from one of the more eccentric works of Gilbert and Sullivan. James Brooke and his descendants ruled their steamy realm on the Borneo coast for more than a century. It was a bizarre melange of Victorian propriety, head-hunters, tamed pirates and claims of untold wealth and luxury. Brooke's dynasty epitomised the eccentricity the British rather liked to see in themselves and their Empire. Brooke, who soldiered in India as a young man, used an inheritance to outfit a ship in the 1830s to seek wealth and power in Borneo. He was a daring, determined man even by the swashbuckling standards of the early empire-builders. Brooke was soon fighting pirates and warlords. He made himself invaluable to the local ruler by subduing the rebellious province of Sarawak. Brooke's reward was to be made rajah of the state. The new monarch set out to fulfil his vision of a model kingdom. London provided tacit support to what was seen as a useful and cost-free pro-British bulwark.[1]

Brooke's dreams of peaceful government and trade first had to overcome Sarawak's chronic lawlessness. Pirates infested the coast and Dayak head-hunters dominated the interior. Both groups were addicted to fighting, raiding and plunder. Brooke recruited a ragtag band of followers and mercenaries that evolved into a private army. Work on a regular army began in the 1840s with 24 men under a native officer who had served in the Ceylon Rifles.[2] It expanded over the years as men were recruited to garrison coastal and river strong-points and pacify the interior. A central military force called the 'Sarawak Fortmen' was formed by 1862. It became the Sarawak Rangers in 1872.

Most of the Sarawak Rangers were coastal Malays and Dayaks from the jungle. One or two British officers ran the force with the help of Indian and Javanese NCOs. Indians were recruited as ordinary soldiers starting in 1902. It was not clear if this was because Dayaks were not signing up in sufficient numbers or if the rajah of the time wanted a force resembling the usual British model. Whatever the reason it seems to have triggered a recruiting spree that was soon bringing in men from across Asia. By 1907 the Rangers had 458 other ranks, including some 290 Dayaks, 52 Malays, 40 Javanese and 66 Indians. A band with 17 Filipinos rounded out the little legion. The regiment was run loosely along British lines and was accompanied by Dayak auxiliaries during the local wars.

Suppressing intermittent rebellions and riots were the Rangers' main tasks. Punitive expeditions of Rangers, police and loyal Dayaks, led by the current rajah or one of his district officers, would plunge through the jungle in pursuit of rebels. Tribes that did not want to abandon the traditional joys of head-hunting were a frequent target. Some of these improvised forces were quite large, and might spend months chasing hostile bands in the deep jungle. A 1902 expedition had some 12,000 men, mostly Dayaks, and only turned back when it was decimated by cholera. Rangers also backed up the police in handling unrest in the towns. A dispute between a Javanese labourer and a Chinese resident led to serious rioting in 1923. Order was restored after the Rangers and police shot and killed 13 protesters. Personality clashes between the rajahs and the Rangers' British officers could be as explosive as the intermittent campaigns. Several officers were dismissed over the years for transgressions ranging from drunkenness to filching government funds. The regiment was also at the centre of a bitter quarrel around 1900 between the then rajah and the Anglican archdeacon, who had tried to make the Rangers attend church services.

The Sarawak Rangers reached their apogee with a strength of some 540 men by the end of 1930. But it seemed the little force had been too successful: Sarawak enjoyed the peace that James Brooke had envisaged almost a century before. A global slump in rubber prices during the Great Depression also meant the state had to make stringent savings. The Sarawak Rangers were disbanded in February 1932. Some of the men were transferred to the Sarawak Police to form a military wing designated as Section B. Others, reputedly offended by their loss of military prestige, ended up supporting a rebel chief. Section B took part in the brief defence when Japanese forces invaded, although there are vague reports that the Rangers were revived in some form in 1941 because of the worsening regional situation. Sarawak, liberated by British forces at the end of the war, became part of independent Malaysia in 1963.

Chapter 7

SECOND TO NONE

The Volunteers of Hong Kong

H ONG KONG'S FIRST VOLUNTEER DEFENCE FORCE was formed after news arrived in the spring of 1854 that Britain was at war with Russia. It was not entirely unwelcome news for the little outpost. Russia's growing strength in the Pacific was regarded as a menace to Britain's Far Eastern interests. Whatever its causes, the Crimean War was seen as a splendid chance to squash St. Petersburg's impudent pretensions in Asia. Hong Kong's Royal Navy squadron promptly sailed out to seek the Russian Pacific Fleet. With it went the colony's governor. It was not clear if he was seeking glory or just escaping the thankless tedium of governing the sleepy port and its prickly inhabitants. The warships had barely disappeared over the horizon when the colony seems to have realised it was now virtually defenceless.[1]

The Ninety-Nine: The Early Years

William Caine, the deputy governor, was left in charge. Caine was a humourless man, driven by a sense of duty that was pedantic even by Victorian standards. He was detested for rigidly enforcing the smallest regulations. Still, he showed more concern for the island's defences than his absent chief. Caine decided to form a local European volunteer force to boost the small, disease-ridden garrison. Hong Kong's warehouses and the homes of the Western residents were a rich prize in a lawless, violent region. Pirates infested the coast; China barely tolerated the British presence; and the island's tiny European community was vastly outnumbered by the local population. Nightmares of being slaughtered in a local uprising dangled at the back of most Europeans' minds. A volunteer corps, Caine informed London, would help forestall any wickedness.

Caine was swiftly and venomously denounced by some of the people he was trying to protect. One public meeting ended in bedlam. Insults ricocheted across the room as rival groups denounced the plan and each other. Some residents said a volunteer force would allow cowards, weaklings and slackers to shirk their duty to defend the colony. They called for a militia, in which all European males between the ages of 16 and 60 would have to serve. Others, imbued with contemporary notions of individual liberty, said compulsory service was another name for tyranny. Yet another faction insisted that Caine's plan was a ruse to ship the colonists off to the Crimea and the horrors of life in the ranks of the British Army. Cynics said the settlers were fortune hunters who would never do something for nothing – including defending their own skins. Local newspapers commented that, while Caine might be an expert on the Chinese, he clearly knew nothing about Europeans. It took several days to calm the colonists and persuade them there were no plans to impose compulsory military service. A second appeal, coupled with a warning of the outpost's precarious defences, was answered by 99 men. Years later 'The Ninety-Nine' became a toast at regimental gatherings. Hong Kong's first Volunteer force, however, was to be so fleeting that all trace of it was lost for decades. Government and regimental records for years dated the founding of Hong Kong's Volunteer forces to 1862.

It was very different when the proud little force assembled in 1854. Enthusiasm and predictions of a long and glorious future enlivened its early days. Enrolment rose to 127 as more men signed up. Local officials were happy with the turn-out in a colony that had just some 300 eligible European male residents. British nationality was not a requirement; all European and American male residents were welcome – Westerners working and living in China often formed a united front for mutual protection. The corps' make up mirrored the population of the tiny outpost. Most Volunteers were British – Portuguese were said to make up the second largest group. At the time 'Portuguese' often meant Eurasians of Portuguese and Chinese ancestry.[2] The Portuguese were to play a long and important role in the Volunteers despite frequent shabby treatment by the British establishment. As late as 1910 a British Army report said that, in the view of the colony, the Portuguese 'possess no value as soldiers'.[3] At least they were admitted to the force. Eurasians of British parentage faced bigger barriers, and did not join in significant numbers until the years just before the Second World War.

Shopkeepers, civil servants, traders and lawyers filled the ranks of the first Volunteer force. Tavern keepers and journalists – equally disreputable trades at the time – were among the best represented professions. Recruits ranged in age from teenagers to men in their fifties. Volunteers were armed with old muskets and rusty bayonets from the Hong Kong arsenal. Recruits augmented the government equipment with whatever guns, swords, knives and clubs they owned or could borrow. Records make no mention of uniforms, and it is likely the men drilled in everyday work clothes. Recruits trained almost every day at first, learning to form ranks and march. When critics hooted that the would-be warriors would not frighten a nervous spinster, Caine insisted they were starting to look like soldiers. Local cynics were to have the last word sooner than even they might have imagined. Turn-out at drills plummeted as the supposed Russian threat dwindled and searing summer heat gripped the island. Marching up and down in heavy European attire exhausted mostly middle-aged men used to spending the day in offices, counting houses and shops. Just a third of the force turned out for a parade in August. Drills were quietly cut from daily to once a week. Caine tried to insist all was well, and that it would take time to build the unit. But the corps was melting away as rapidly as the sweat streamed down the marching recruits' faces. By 1855 the unit had vanished.

Officials and some residents believed a volunteer defence force was needed despite the discouraging demise of the first unit. Britain's presence in the region was tenuous. Outwardly dismissive of the Chinese, the tiny British community fretted over its isolation. Tales of the Indian Mutiny, particularly harrowing reports of massacres, added to the unease. Hong Kong's European residents glumly compared events in India to their own situation: a tiny handful living amid thousands of Chinese on Hong Kong island with millions more on the nearby mainland. A newspaper, the deceptively titled *Friend of China*, advocated expelling what it termed undesirable Chinese elements. Those allowed to stay on the island would be forced to carry passes. If the ungrateful Chinese still refused to recognise their good fortune at living under European rule, the newspaper suggested a stark public lesson: 'A few hangings in the cross roads would soon give encouragement to the well disposed, and strike terror into the hearts of those who designate us barbarians.'[4]

A second attempt at forming a volunteer force was made in 1862. Hong Kong had grown and become more confident in just a few years. Local leaders believed the community had a duty and enough stout residents to contribute to its own defence. A petition was submitted to the governor for permission to form a unit. It would be self-governing and largely pay for itself. The new corps was led and moulded by Captain Frederick Brine, an inspiring and energetic Army officer, who also had a major role in European volunteer units in Shanghai, Hankow and Yokohama. Brine's enthusiasm for volunteer troops was not shared by the general in charge of regular British forces in Hong Kong. Regular officers often loathed what they regarded as ungainly civilians playing soldiers. Attempts were made to deny the volunteers the use of Army weapons. Civil officials backed the new unit, and the general's opposition was overridden.

It was decided the new force would be an artillery unit called the HongKong (*sic*) Volunteers. Members of the force would pay annual subscriptions to help cover the cost of weapons and other equipment. Polished men with social and educational attainments were starting to replace some of the rough characters who had dominated the colony's early years and the new unit wanted men of suitable breeding and class to set a proper tone. Life in the Volunteers resembled an officers' mess of the British Army or a gentleman's club. Members of the force, whatever their ranks, largely treated each other as equals, trampling military protocol. Like all good clubs, prospective recruits had to be proposed by a member of the corps and approved by the commanding officer. A special category existed for 'honorary members', who could use the rifle range and attend social events for an annual fee while avoiding drills. The force had 123 officers and men by June 1862. A band and a rifle unit were added in 1863 and a field battery was acquired the following year.

It was intended from the start that the force would be a serious military unit. Brine set training and proficiency standards for the first time. Volunteers had to attend at least 24 musters a year and pass a drill examination. A long list of misdeeds was punished by fines, including $1 for accidentally firing a musket or improper use of bayonets. Talking in the ranks merited a 50-cent fine for each offence.

Hong Kong's Volunteers were mobilised for the first time when they were called out to aid the authorities in December 1864. Ironically, they were fielded against Europeans rather than the dreaded Chinese. An economic slump was buffeting the colony. Hong Kong was full of angry European sailors left jobless after local shipping firms had replaced them with cheaper Malay seaman. A riot in September left several dead and injured. Tension increased when soldiers of the regular garrison and local police fraternised with the protesters. Volunteer riflemen kept watch on the regulars after they were moved out of the town to prevent more trouble. Volunteers also patrolled the streets of the settlement until calm was restored. Continuing hard times and waning enthusiasm because of the lack of any major threat to the colony seem to have caused Hong Kong's second volunteer force to collapse. Several local businesses went under because of the slump. Volunteer numbers plunged as men left the colony or focused on work. Fewer and fewer showed up for drill sessions. A May 1866 government notice curtly announced the disbanding of the unit.

Hong Kong was, however, becoming an important link in a chain of British bases girdling the globe. Batteries were erected in the 1870s to defend against sea and land attack as London built up the colony's defences.

A third attempt was made in 1878 to raise a local force to bolster the regular forces. Fear of Russia's imperial ambitions and its growing presence in China was again worrying the British outposts in Asia. The authorities, keen to ensure the Volunteers survived this time, played a greater role from the start, issuing a call for men, providing equipment and some funding. Recruits were required to attend regular training and maintain minimum standards at drill and shooting or face dismissal. Hong Kong's European community generally supported the plan, even if local wits repeated the tired old joke that the recruits would wilt when they drilled in the sun. Some business leaders also worried that service with the force would interfere with employees' work. In the event training was conducted in the early morning and the evening to soothe concerns about disrupting working hours and marching in the heat.

The imposingly entitled Hong Kong Volunteer Artillery and Rifle Volunteer Corps began life with 107 recruits. Plans called for artillery and infantry units. Artillerymen wore a dark blue serge smock with scarlet collar and cuffs, white shoulder straps and white metal buttons. White trousers were worn in summer, blue serge trousers with a narrow red stripe in winter. Infantry Volunteers wore scarlet serge smocks with blue facings and shoulder straps emblazoned with HKR for Hong Kong Rifles. White solar helmets were worn in the summer and blue forage caps in winter.

Hong Kong's third volunteer force fared no better than its predecessors despite all the official encouragement and able organisation. Enthusiasm was flagging by 1880 with as few as 12 men showing up for evening drill. A lack of any evident threat to Hong Kong, mixed views in the colony over the need for such a force, and personal disputes between some of the officers damaged morale and bled the unit of men. Weapons and equipment borrowed from the garrison were returned for reasons that are not clear. It all proved too much. The unit lapsed into virtual somnolence and was disbanded in November 1882.

A Most Superior Corps

A new artillery unit was formed a few weeks later as the Hong Kong Volunteer Corps. Hong Kong officials had decided to disband the old unit to create a new force and weed out both the unsuitable and the undesirable. This time the unit would continue, in one guise and another, until the end of British rule. Tougher standards were imposed to avoid the problems that wrecked earlier units. Recruits were required to pass a medical exam for the first time. Volunteers who missed drills without a valid excuse faced fines and expulsion. Other lessons adopted from the past included more state funding and confining drills to the cooler months from October to March.

Again the plan received an enthusiastic response from the European community. By the end of 1886 the corps had 191 members, the usual mix of government officials and employees of the colony's leading trading companies. Volunteers trained on the coastal artillery and manned a battery of 7-pounder RML guns. The corps was disbanded and immediately re-formed in 1893 purely to put it under a new ordinance. Its provisions put the Volunteers under the control of the military authorities and brought its legal and administrative structure into line with the regular army.

The new Volunteers were organised as a field battery and a machine-gun company. Infantry and engineer units and more machine-gun companies were added over the next few years. A drum and fife corps was formed around 1897 from 23 musically-inclined members. Uniforms similar to those issued to the previous Volunteer unit were worn. Officers wore Royal Artillery Militia uniforms on ceremonial occasions. Khaki for all ranks was adopted in the mid-1890s. It was still very much a socially superior unit, with the manners and camaraderie of a gentlemen's club. Prospective members now had to be proposed by two members and gain the approval of a company commander and the commanding officer.

Hong Kong's regular military authorities were not entirely pleased with some aspects of the new unit. Familiarity between the ranks was said to be rampant. One report said proper discipline would not be possible until the unit had separate officers' and NCOs' messes. Such cordial, if unmilitary, conditions were hardly surprising when many of the Volunteers moved in the same professional and social circles. Senior civil servants and local tycoons were not going to emulate the humble privates of the British Army or the Territorial forces. Regular commanders nonetheless were adamant that such unmilitary familiarity must be staunched and a new headquarters building was opened on 15 December 1906 with separate facilities for different ranks – construction costs meant the men had to go without new winter uniforms.

It was the high noon of Empire and Hong Kong was outwardly proud of its little Volunteer force. Civil and military officials talked of expanding the corps to play a greater role in local defence. Recruiting figures told a different story. Authorities once again struggled to keep up the unit's numbers. Growing numbers of Hong Kong's privileged young men happily ducked serving in the ranks as sport and other types of amusement proliferated in the expanding colony. Recruiting jumped whenever it seemed the colony was threatened, plummeting when conditions returned to normal. Officials in charge of colonial defences complained about the poor physiques

Hong Kong Volunteer Corps, 1902

	Strength	Establishment
Staff	6	7
Field Battery	77	110
A Machine Gun Company	56	41
B Machine Gun Company	51	41
C Machine Gun Company	43	41
D Infantry Company	54	57
E Engineer Company	25	30
Band	6	24

Source: PRO CAB 9/5/15.

and equally flabby enthusiasm of local young gentlemen, and bureaucrats in London and Hong Kong came up with various schemes to boost recruiting. Discreet pressure was exerted on trading firms in London that sent young men out to the settlement. Young government officials arriving in Hong Kong were pressured by department heads to join the Volunteers.

It all made little difference and recruiting was often lamentable. A hard core of keen Volunteers formed the corps' backbone. Bombardier F. O. Day was commended in 1906 for attending 177 drills in the past year. But the tedium of peacetime drilling in the ranks had little appeal for officials and businessmen used to making major decisions and commanding others. And there were far more pleasant ways to fill the hours after work. Hong Kong Governor F. H. May complained in 1913 that some 800 eligible young Britons in the colony refused to join the corps, including 375 men with regular or voluntary military experience.

A few daring individuals suggested accepting Chinese to solve the recruiting problem. Hong Kong had a growing number of Westernised and prosperous Chinese residents with strong ties to the colony. Governor Sir William Des Voeux championed the idea in 1903, rejecting scathing contemporary British views of the Chinese:

> 'Hitherto, Chinese soldiers have gained a reputation for cowardice, because they have usually run away when faced by European troops. But knowing the remarkable courage with which individual Chinese commonly face death, I have always been of the opinion that this reputation was undeserved, and that if led by English officers they would make exceptionally good soldiers, as being able to withstand hardships, unsanitary conditions and insufficiency of food which would cause most European troops to succumb.'[5]

Most of the British community was implacably opposed to what they saw as the governor's heresy. It was a deeply held belief that the Chinese were cowardly and treacherous. 'All local opinion, however, condemns their enrolment as soldiers of any kind as they are considered to be quite unreliable and to be easily influenced by the Chinese authorities at Canton,' a 1909 British Army report stated.[6] Disdain of the Chinese was so strong that the Volunteers insisted on pulling their mountain guns in exercises rather than use local coolies – a remarkable lapse in a society where it was deemed that Europeans did not do menial labour. Puzzled military authorities in London suggested coolies be employed to improve efficiency in future.

Enthusiasm soared when the Volunteers were called out for a modest campaign in 1899. Britain had leased a swathe of the adjoining mainland from China that year to allow the colony to expand. Foreign rule was bitterly opposed by the inhabitants of what would become the New Territories. Armed Chinese villagers clashed with regular British troops. Worried officials ordered the Volunteers to help the regulars occupy the territory. A call to arms was issued late on a Sunday evening when most of the Volunteers were at dinners and other social events. Men in evening dress and other civilian attire hurried to the harbour with military sun helmets, bandoliers and whatever they could grab. About a hundred Volunteers with artillery and machine guns crossed to the mainland only to find that the Chinese had melted away. A Volunteer detachment later helped occupy Kowloon City. It confiscated weapons from the locals as the British flag was raised. It all resembled a holiday outing rather than a military expedition. Happy and excited Volunteers went home to tell families and friends that they had thoroughly enjoyed the day. Flushed with success, the Volunteers offered a machine-gun detachment for the South African war. London declined the offer.

Recruiting soared with the outbreak of the Boxer Rebellion in China, almost doubling the force's numbers to 311 men in 1900. Eager recruits marched and practised shooting, but the Boxers never appeared on the colony's borders. With numbers again falling, the local military authorities reorganised the corps in 1902 to give it a new role supplementing the regular coastal artillery.[7] It was formed into artillery and engineer units while the machine-gun and infantry companies were disbanded. The band survived the change. Volunteers were trained to man 10-inch and 6-inch coastal defence guns while the engineers operated searchlights.

New efforts were made to tackle the chronic problems of poor recruiting and retention. A plan was put forward to pay a £5 Christmas bonus for men who passed an annual fitness test. Ending the corps' amateur status,

Hong Kong Volunteer Corps, 1912

Staff	
Howitzer Section	
10-pounder Section	
Engineer Company	
Machine Gun Company	3 sections
Civil Service Company	
Scouts Company	mounted, foot and Maxim sections
Cadet Company	
Total establishment:	**328**

Source: HKVC 1912–13 Report, PRO CAB 9/5/15.

it was suggested, would attract more men and force them to serve their full terms. Volunteers were until then more or less able to leave whenever they wished. But the Colonial Defence Committee in London was watching events in Hong Kong with growing unease. A rebuke from the imperial capital said gentlemen could hardly be expected to do the stultifying, heavy labour of garrison artillery. Plans to pay the Volunteers were also censured because they would attract the wrong sort of recruit, and cause gentlemen to resign in understandable horror.

Numbers steadily dropped after the reorganisation. Volunteers disliked serving in the coastal forts and missed exercises in the open country. Embattled local military officials tried to defend the changes while conceding strenuous work on the guns was not popular. Machine-gun training was resumed to try to keep the men happy. In the end garrison chiefs admitted in 1905 that their plan was a failure and began phasing it out. The Colonial Defence Committee primly commented that businessmen in an Asiatic colony did not have the right physique for heavy manual labour. Hong Kong's Volunteers were re-formed into field artillery, machine-gun and infantry units. Morale improved and resignations dropped as the men went back to the more pleasant routine of field exercises and drill-hall meetings.

The first of many attempts was made to improve recruiting by forming a unit based on particular loyalties or interests. A plan was mooted around 1900 to raise a Scottish company. Such units were sprouting in Volunteer units around the British Empire because of the feats of Scots units in the regular army. Too few Scots were available, or willing, to form a company, so interested English, Welsh and Irish residents were accepted. It soon became one of the most popular units in the corps.

A mounted infantry troop formed in 1905 to patrol the rugged border areas of the New Territories was also popular. Its success was largely the work of its zealous commander, C. H. Ross, who had headed a mounted unit in the Shanghai Volunteer Corps. Ross seems to have personally provided most of the Hong Kong unit's mounts. Recruits clamoured to join and its official strength was increased in 1907 to an officer, two NCOs and 40 troopers. An annual field camp was held over the Christmas holidays, which Ross said all of the company attended except for four married men, 'who apparently cannot leave their families at Christmas time'.[8] Ying Kee, a Chinese cook hired to feed the men in camp, was officially praised for his work.

Engineer, scout and cadet companies were also formed. A Hong Kong Volunteer Reserve Association, for men over the age of 35, was established as a back-up force. Members were not required to do much training and only had to serve in an emergency. It was soon as large as the Volunteer force, a fact that did not please officials trying to keep up the latter's strength.

The force continued to struggle with a manpower shortage as members drifted away and few new arrivals showed any interest in military service. A visiting general said it was a pity Hong Kong did not have a planter class like India to give the corps backbone.[9] Unable to keep up numbers, the force's official establishment was cut from 433 men to 328 men in 1912. The infantry company, with 20 men against an establishment of 90 men, was disbanded. It was replaced with a Civil Service Company open only to local government officials. It attracted 18 men and did not last long. Corps commander Captain C. V. S. Skrimshire complained in 1912 that many of his men thought playing cricket or tennis was more important than attending drills.[10]

World War I

Peacetime volunteering, with its pleasant round of drills, camps and regimental dinners, came to an abrupt end in August 1914. Hong Kong's regular battalion was recalled for service elsewhere. The Volunteers were mobilised to bolster the colony's defences. Members helped man the coastal forts and guarded key government locations. Marauding German warships were among the envisaged threats to the colony. Responsibility for internal security was shared with the police. Volunteers went to work or attended social events in full uniform, propping rifles against walls or desks. Men frequently had to leave in the middle of meetings or dinners for sentry duty and irate employers complained that Hong Kong's important economic contribution to the war effort was being impaired by constant disruption to office routine. Military duty was accordingly confined to the Volunteers' free time after talks between the military authorities and local business leaders. Guarding government offices soon became tedious for men who did not want to miss the war. Dozens of younger men left to join regular units. The Volunteers' ranks were a rich source of officer material for the British armies in Europe and the Middle East and the exodus of younger men inevitably depleted the force. Conscription of all white British males was introduced in 1917 to make up the shortfall. Men between 18 and 55 were enrolled in a new formation, the Hong Kong Defence Corps, which merged the Volunteers and other reserve units into a single force.

A prison camp was erected at the start of the war to hold German and other enemy aliens. Men from the Volunteers guarded the camp. Most of the internees were old Hong Kong residents. Zealous sentries were met with jeers from imprisoned friends and colleagues asking if they had remembered to load their rifles. Tension eased after a few months and life in the camp settled into a routine. Permission was granted for the prisoners to form a drama group and tools were provided to construct a camp theatre. The prisoners immediately began work on a mass escape, and the tools were used to dig a tunnel under the camp fence. On the night of the break-out, the first three would-be escapees emerged from the tunnel on the other side of the fence and darted into the gloom. A fourth man was spotted by a sentry, who fired and hit the prisoner's bag, forcing him to dive back into the tunnel, and abruptly ending the escape. An Indian constable arrested the three escapees the next morning.

A post-war 1919 report on the Hong Kong Defence Corps said that the unit had 826 men. It was rated a useful force with an infantry battalion of three rifle companies and a machine-gun company; artillery and engineer companies; mounted, signals and stretcher-bearer sections. A cadet company boasted 88 members. Congratulating Hong Kong on its wartime efforts, the Colonial Defence Committee also warned that the colonies would have to take greater responsibility for their defence in the coming years.[11]

The Inter-War Years

Peace did not see a return to the amiable Volunteer soldiering of the golden days of the Empire. British power was starting to buckle. Asia was undergoing vast changes. Unrest and civil war were sweeping China and Japan was aiming at domination of the continent. Tokyo had been a key British ally, allowing London to strip its Far Eastern forces over the years before World War I. Ties with Japan unravelled swiftly after 1918, but Britain did little to build up its regional defences. London, drained of blood and wealth by the war, decreed the colonies must help lower the cost of imperial defence. Volunteer forces were expected to form a major part of local garrisons and meet the same standards as the regular army. Few in Hong Kong realised or were willing to admit it was once again a vulnerable outpost. A few prophetic observers who warned of the risks of another war were drowned out as killjoys and bores.

Volunteer soldiering was revived with a 1920 ordinance forming the Hong Kong Volunteer Defence Corps (HKVDC).[12] Standards were stiffened as part of the plans to put more reliance on local forces. Volunteers on active service were now under the same regulations as the army and could be deemed deserters for not answering call-outs. Fines were introduced to make men complete their enlistments, and end the old habit of Volunteers drifting away if they lost interest. In the most telling sign of change, applicants were no longer proposed and seconded.

Tougher standards, however necessary, hardly helped cure lacklustre recruitment. Military service was the last thing most people wanted to think about. The idea of another war seemed inconceivable. All of the Western world wanted a good time after the horrors of the recent conflict. Young British men in Hong Kong were no different, and most had the money and the freedom to indulge themselves. Weekends of drill and kit inspections stood little chance against the pleasures of the roaring 1920s. Military and civilian authorities were soon complaining about Hong Kong's general indifference to its own defence.

The inter-war period presents two conflicting portraits of the HKVDC. One is of a small, but increasingly capable military force with a hard core of dedicated and capable soldiers. The other view is of a dire lack of recruits and widespread public apathy.

Annual force assessments are peppered with complaints about poor recruiting. Officials were particularly distraught over the dearth of white Volunteers, who were expected to form the HKVDC's backbone. In 1927, a typical year, 253 men left the HKVDC and just 133 enrolled. A note from the Imperial Defence Committee in the mid-1930s said its members could not 'conceal their regret at the very great falling off in the strength of the Corps'.[13] Official attempts to explain this quandary ranged from the lack of any threat to the colony to dwindling athleticism among the idle young. Bureaucratic frustration exploded over the disinclination of young civil servants to enlist despite browbeating by superiors. A 1934–5 HKVDC report said low recruiting was hardly surprising if civil servants

Hong Kong Volunteer Defence Corps, Strength 1927/28

Unit	Strength	Unit	Strength
HQ and Band	28	Battery	39
Engineer Company	29*	Signals	29
Mounted Infantry Company	19	Armoured Car Company	63
1 Platoon (Machine Gun)	32	2 Platoon (Machine Gun)	44
5 Platoon (Scottish)	22	6 Platoon (Scottish)	25
7 Platoon (Scottish)	40	9 Platoon (Portuguese)	39
10 Platoon (Portuguese)	54	Medical Section	8
Reserve Company	16	Auxiliary Company	16

* *'Electric light duty only; too few for field work.'*

Source: *HKVDC Report April 1927 – August 1928, PRO CAB 9/19/54.*

did not set a good example for the colony.[14] Of 150 new civil servants eligible for the corps in the mid-1930s, seven joined the new Hong Kong Naval Reserve and 24 enlisted in the HKVDC. A 1935–6 report branded the colony's young British men as feckless and ungrateful.[15] Just six of the 174 men recruited that year were white. Recruiting was hit further by the Great Depression as struggling companies sent fewer young men out to the colony. In yet another report detailing poor recruiting of government workers, the colony's civil service chief tried to deflect criticism from himself by earnestly informing the Imperial Defence Committee that he was a private in the corps.

Novelty units were created in an effort to boost recruiting. A Canadian section appears to have existed briefly in the mid-1920s and an ANZAC unit was formed in 1932 with 30 Australians and New Zealanders. Its uniform included Australian-style slouch hats. The new company was launched at an ANZAC Day dinner with talk of infusing the HKVDC with the Gallipoli spirit. Lack of spirit of any kind saw the unit swiftly fall apart. A 1935 inspection report blasted the unit for what it termed 'deplorable lack of *esprit de corps*' despite 'remarkable enthusiasm by a few members'.[16] The unit was disbanded with the 19 surviving members absorbed into other units.

The regional commander of British forces blamed the recruiting woes on the future rulers of the Empire. In a remarkable letter to the War Office, Major-General J. W. Sandilands also maligned the handful of men who did enlist. In a tirade that trampled some fondly held patriotic beliefs, Sandilands said Territorial soldiers in Britain were mostly labourers who served for pay. It was absurd to imagine such men were motivated by patriotism. Hong Kong's affluent young civil servants and businessmen would never serve for the tiny sums paid to working-class Territorial soldiers. Spoilt young colonists refused to accept that Britain's Far East possessions would ever be threatened or that they had any duty to defend them. Their only interest was making enough money to retire. Until then they lived for long leaves, every four or five years, when they went back to Britain for six months or more. 'It is not the slightest use preaching to them about the glories of the British Empire, the need of patriotism, the obligation of service,' he wrote. Sandilands bizarrely remarked that men who joined the Volunteers did so 'for certain odd reasons which are best known to themselves'. Conscription was the only solution, he concluded. Sandilands' outburst, beyond enhancing his reputation for eccentric irascibility, was filed and forgotten.[17]

Poor recruiting, British military weakness and regional instability helped bring down the barriers to Asian enlistment. Some Chinese and Eurasians were eager to enlist even if most of the British were not.

Singapore and other Far Eastern colonies had been recruiting Asians for years for their Volunteer units but it is not clear when the first Chinese joined the HKVDC. The first reference to a Chinese on the official strength was a 1905–6 report listing a Chinese orderly room clerk[18] and Chinese medical students had formed a small makeshift first-aid detachment at corps' exercises in the 1890s. A handful of Chinese appear to have been serving in various Volunteer companies by the 1920s. An HKVDC report in the early 1930s refers to Chinese in the medical section.[19] Some of the early Chinese recruits had Western educations and local ties going back several generations. These polished, accomplished individuals could blend into colonial society. Like the British, they had much to protect. Most British officials and residents accepted the change only grudgingly and sizable numbers remained implacably opposed. Vitriolic opponents of integration insisted the Chinese were only in Hong Kong to make money and had no loyalty to Britain. Others claimed the Chinese were far too weak, physically and morally, to make reliable soldiers.

Opening the ranks to Asians did bring a modest improvement in recruiting. HKVDC enlistment figures for 1934 show that 75 Portuguese, 49 other Eurasians, 25 Indians and what was described as 31 'Chinese and others' were admitted that year. Just six whites joined.[20] It was not much of an improvement in a colony with some 2 million people.

Chinese recruiting jumped with the formation in 1937 of an all-Chinese machine-gun unit, No. 4 Company, followed by a second unit, No. 7 Company. Both companies were commanded by British officers. Chinese

Volunteers began to appear in the artillery units, initially joining Nos. 3 and 4 Batteries. Unit records for 1941 show Chinese gunners in all HKVDC batteries. A few Indians and one Vietnamese are listed too. Chinese also served in the searchlight sections. There appears to have been no talk of Chinese officers even though some HKVDC commanders now conceded that Asians made excellent soldiers.

Opposition within the HKVDC to Chinese Volunteers persisted up to the outbreak of war. Even the European commander of one of the Chinese companies said he understood why some colonists insisted that Chinese should not be recruited if Hong Kong was attacked. Attempts were made to assure the white population that Chinese troops were not a danger. Major-General A. W. Bartholomew, the garrison commander, had told the colony in 1936 that very high standards were used to select non-Europeans for military service.

> 'Great discrimination has been exercised in the selection of the non-British recruits. Moreover they are being trained for specific duties to which they are particularly adaptable, and I have no reason to lack confidence in their staunchness and loyalty in the event of war.'[21]

Possibly even more despised were the Eurasians. Portuguese Eurasians were accepted begrudgingly from the first days, but other Eurasians (mostly descendants of unions between British men and Chinese women) seem to have been less welcome. An early governor of Hong Kong voiced the traditional British disdain of mixing races when he wrote in the 1850s, 'A large population of children of native mothers by foreigners [Westerners] of all classes is beginning to ripen into a dangerous element of the dunghill of neglect.'[22] British Eurasians were caught between two cultures. Many yearned to serve an empire they venerated even if it generally treated them with disdain. Some hoped volunteering might win them some kind of acceptance by the British.

It was decided in the 1930s to turn No. 3 Company into a separate unit for non-Portuguese Eurasians. Most of these Eurasians had been in No. 1 Company. HKVDC leaders said segregated units were more effective for cultural and linguistic reasons. It was claimed the different races were happier serving with men of their own kind. A note in the 1935–6 HKVDC report welcomed the change because it made No. 1 Company an exclusively British unit. 'I consider that this was a sound move, putting as it did, all the Eurasian element in one separate unit,' wrote one officer.[23]

A separate Portuguese company had been formed after the 1914–18 war. It is not clear why the corps had accepted these Eurasians a little more willingly than other mixed-race men. Perhaps miscegenation was less disturbing if it did not involve British blood. And the Portuguese were insistent they were Europeans.

Certainly the HKVDC needed them. The British monopoly on command was shattered when several members of the Portuguese company were given commissions. Officials justified the move as the only way to boost Portuguese enlistment and counter the lack of British recruits. A senior British officer said he wished British Volunteers were as eager as the Portuguese.

Portuguese Volunteers went on serving loyally even though they were never accepted as equals. Jose Gasano, a Portuguese Volunteer, enlisted with his four brothers just before the war. 'We didn't have to, but we simply couldn't let the English boys be called up and do nothing. We wanted to fight for our homes and families,' he recalled.[24]

Volunteer publications of the inter-war era project an image of different races cheerfully serving the British Empire.[25] But there is no suggestion of equality and an undertone that different races prefer serving in separate units permeates the texts. While British Volunteers drilled and practised with men of other races, even shared tea or jokes for a few moments, that usually was the limit of familiarity. Most whites could only see non-whites in the ranks, or anywhere else, as social and racial inferiors.

However, resentment erupted in 1939 over rumours that Asian Volunteers would be paid less than whites if the HKVDC was mobilised for war. In fact a confidential War Office proposal to pay non-whites less had already been overruled quietly by the colony's governor but the issue was still raised at a meeting of the colony's Legislative Council after rumours spread about segregated pay rates. Council member Lo Man Kam passionately insisted all Volunteers must be treated equally. It was not a matter of money, he said, but a fundamental principle that men fighting for a common cause had the same rights.

> 'Sir, the Colony is justly proud of its Hong Kong Volunteer Defence Corps. But in order that its splendid *esprit de corps*, its efficiency, may not be impaired, it is essential that all its members should be able to feel that, as fellow members working in union for a common cause, they do in fact receive equal treatment in every respect, and in all matters, without any discrimination between race or creed.'[26]

Applause erupted as he thundered that any hint of racial discrimination was intolerable. Agitated colonial officials insisted there were no plans to discriminate against any Volunteers.

Hong Kong Volunteer Defence Corps, Strength 1936

Unit	Strength	Unit	Strength
Headquarters	8	Machine Gun Signals	21
Reserves	25	Infantry HQ	1
Battery	71	A Rifle Company	128
Engineers	33	B (Anti-Aircraft) Company	79
Signals	49	Reserve	1
Mounted Machine Gun Troop	33	Medical Detachment	17
Armoured Car Company	23	Reserve Officers	13
Motor Machine Gun Company	38	Army Service Corps Reserve	92
1 Machine Gun Company	50	Railway Detachment	51
2 Scottish Company	49	Nursing Detachment	99
3 Machine Gun Company	61		

Source: HKVDC Report 1935–36, PRO CAB 9/19/54.

Foreigners, mostly Europeans and Americans, had served in Hong Kong's Volunteer defence force over the years. Plans in the 1920s to ease the chronic shortfall of British recruits by stepping up recruiting of foreigners were sidelined by a farcical dispute over constitutional precedent.[27] Colonial Office officials received a letter from the Hong Kong administration in 1927 about plans for an Army Service Corps unit for the local defence force. It would provide much needed logistical support for the Volunteers by enlisting local civilian professionals and foreign recruitment was a key part of the scheme. A highly qualified Chinese man with U.S. citizenship had been touted as an officer in the envisaged unit but Hong Kong's governor had last-minute qualms that the 1700 Act of Settlement banned foreigners from the British armed forces. Plans for the unit were shelved while advice was sought from London. The governor's interjection created a small uproar. It was pointed out that the Portuguese company had four officers and 117 men. Excluding them would decimate the HKVDC and offend the entire Portuguese community and other foreign residents.

Whitehall officials solemnly debated the issue before duly informing Hong Kong that foreigners might serve as ordinary soldiers. London was not too enthusiastic, however, adding that the number of foreigners in any unit should not exceed half its strength while also reluctantly agreeing that the governor was right that foreigners could not be officers. Dismissing the Portuguese officers would cause offence, so London said they should quietly be offered British citizenship. An embarrassed reply from Hong Kong said further inquiries had revealed the officers were British subjects. It said much about the social divisions in the colony and how men could serve together for years and yet know so little about each other.

Concerns about foreign enrolment led to another protracted exchange with Whitehall in 1936 when about 30 German residents asked to join the HKVDC.[28] War Office officials were sympathetic, saying it might be a good way to improve poor relations with Nazi Germany. The Foreign Office, after ruffling the Army by asking if the HKVDC was a police force, opposed the plan. It said Germans living overseas were being organised into Nazi groups loyal to Adolf Hitler. Such men would not be reliable in a crisis. The Army Council swiftly reversed its position and the men were rebuffed. HKVDC records indicate, however, that there were some Germans in its ranks. Perhaps the 1936 approach from the 30 German residents was a request to form a separate unit. German and Dutch Volunteers appear to have resigned in 1937, after their governments warned they could lose their citizenship by serving a foreign power.

The Path to War

HKVDC commanders tried to boost the force's professionalism and firepower as the Asian political situation deteriorated in the inter-war years. Government parsimony, public apathy and the indifference or hostility of some colonial officials frequently blunted their efforts. Returned veterans of the recent world war had injected realism into training and planning. Political reality was tacitly acknowledged when Volunteer units joined regular forces in periodic war games simulating invasion of the settlement by an unnamed power that clearly resembled Japan. The medical section attended lectures on treating poison gas casualties. Specialist units were formed or expanded to provide technical and logistical support. Regular army commanders encouraged the creation of these new units because their own support wings were being pared by government spending cuts. Artillery, machine-gun and infantry units remained the HKVDC's backbone. A 1927–8 report spoke of building the force into a machine-gun battalion with 40 Vickers guns for beach defence; it had just eight at the time.[29]

Despite such grandiose plans, even minor weapons and items of equipment often had to be begged or pilfered. A scheme was set up to solve a shortage of pistols by using weapons the police had confiscated from criminals. It only produced a few weapons, and the corps was short of 257 revolvers in 1939. Training camps had to be cut in the mid-1930s to find money to buy uniforms for non-European recruits coming into the force.

Two armoured cars were built by bolting naval armour on to truck chassis. Frequent break-downs meant the vehicles were often out of service.

Unit commanders complained the vehicles were left outside in all types of weather because of a lack of shelter and a request was submitted for canvas covers. Demands for more armoured cars to create an effective fighting unit were ignored for years. Significant expansion did not come until 1940 when four more armoured cars were built in the colony. Members of a motorcycle machine-gun unit had to use their own bikes. A 1932 report complained that expansion plans were threatened because young men were buying cars rather than motorbikes that could be lent to the unit.[30]

The mounted unit tried to ignore mechanisation as it trotted around the colony's border with machine guns strapped to pack animals. A 'severe blow' hit the unit in 1930 when 14 ponies died of glanders. Sympathetic local gentlemen donated replacement animals. The unit was still a social cut above the rest of the corps and appears to have been the only part of the force with a waiting list. New recruits had to be content with holding the horses' bridles on exercises. Changing tastes saw the troop complaining in 1935 about 'a regrettable lack of keen riding people in the colony'.[31] Recruits were gravitating to the new motorised units as young men shifted their allegiance from the horse to the internal combustion engine. The mounted troop bowed to modernity by purchasing a Chevrolet car to carry six men and two machine guns.

An anti-aircraft unit formed in 1931 was armed with old Lewis guns because there were no funds to buy modern weapons. Contemporary photographs of field exercises show the men of the unit precariously balancing the guns as they beat off imaginary air raids. Plans called for anti-aircraft crews to keep their weapons at workplaces so that they could defend them against surprise air attacks. A brochure was produced to attract recruits with a progressive outlook. A radio set was eventually issued to the signal section in the 1930s but workmen restoring government buildings repeatedly severed the aerial. A Sikh section was added to augment the signal section's existing Muslim arm. Both wings were made up of local Indian post office technicians.

Chinese businessmen donated four motorcycles in 1935 to form a dispatch rider section for the signals company. A separate railway unit was created to run troop trains and repair or demolish track. Most support units were too small and ill equipped for major operations. Ambitious plans were rarely achieved, such as a scheme for a wartime Army Service Corps cadre with an envisaged strength of 229 Europeans and 414 Chinese.

Fighting skills were not always the corps' top priority in the inter-war period. Trivial pet projects sometimes consumed considerable time and energy. Efforts to develop a band formed with Portuguese Volunteers in

1927 overshadowed more practical needs. It was expanded to 37 men in 1931 and more instruments were bought despite a decision to delay purchases of machine guns for budgetary reasons. Attempts were made to find ex-regular army bandsmen to improve its performances.

Time and effort was lost in other ways. A request to ally the tiny 15-man pay section with the Royal Army Pay Corps led to a lengthy exchange in the late 1930s with London. It was approved by the King after months of correspondence between the HKVDC, the Hong Kong government, the RAPC and the War Office.

Bureaucratic inflexibility in London also hurt efforts to strengthen the HKVDC in the final years of peace. Regular army commanders in Hong Kong asked London to shorten the 12-month process of ordering ammunition for the Volunteers. The long lag disrupted training and made it difficult to build reserve stocks. A terse reply suggested Hong Kong order bullets two years in advance if it wanted to avoid delays.

Political tension steadily increased in Hong Kong during the 1930s. Chinese protests and strikes against both British rule and Japanese aggression in China shook the colony. HKVDC troops were called out to help the regular army and police, guarding government installations and patrolling the streets. Columns of Volunteer and regular troops with bayonet-tipped rifles marched through the poorer areas in shows of force to awe the Chinese population. Refugees from the war in China poured into the enclave, adding to the overcrowding and tension.

Japanese forces appeared on the mainland border in late 1938. British hopes of peaceful relations did not last long. Japanese troops challenged British control with frequent border incursions, shelling and air attacks. Hong Kong's rulers still wanted to believe it could escape the conflict enveloping China. Hopeful rumours abounded of Japan's offensive in China bogging down or of secret agreements to avoid British territory. Europeans comforted themselves by ridiculing the Japanese as subhuman freaks. Jokes about the supposed Japanese inability to fly aircraft or see at night became a staple of European dinner parties.

An increasingly important role was given to the HKVDC in the colony's defence plans in the last years of peace. Enlistment in the corps finally began to rise as the threat of war became undeniable, reaching 1,000 officers and men by the late 1930s. Most of the corps was organised into machine-gun units for coastal defence on Hong Kong island. It was wryly commented that each man would be assigned his own beach to defend if the Japanese invaded. The mounted troop was forced to give up its horses for active duty, although its routine of gymkhanas and dinners continued.

A machine-gun crew of the Hong Kong Volunteer Defence Corps on a training exercise on the eve of the Second World War.

Above left: Relaxed men of the Singapore Royal Artillery (Volunteers) on parade in the 1930s. European Volunteer units maintained high social standards and a club-like degree of informality reminiscent of the 19th century.

Left: Riflemen of the Malay Regiment in a mock attack during exercises after the Japanese landed in Malaya. The regiment's two battalions earned a distinguished combat record in the doomed defence of Singapore a few weeks later.

A Karen rifleman of the Burma Rifles during the inter-war period. Members of the minority hill tribes in Burma were recruited rather than the Burman majority.

Hong Kong Volunteer Defence Corps, Strength 1941

Unit	Strength	Unit	Strength
Headquarters	54	1 Company	104
Artillery HQ	5	2 Company	98
1 Battery	68	3 Company	114
2 Battery	86	4 Company	78
3 Battery	78	5 Company	99
4 Battery	97	6 Company	96
5 Battery	67	7 Company	41
Engineers	123	Army Service Corps	72
Signals	40	Stanley Platoon	29
Fortress Signals	17	Pay Unit	17
Armoured Car	29	Reserve Force*	72
		Medical Section	169

Source: PRO CAB 5/56/1999.   * *Men over 55.*

Years of negligible funding and improvising with cast-offs gave way to frantic efforts in 1939 to expand and re-equip the corps. Ambitious plans called for expansion to 90 officers and 2,000 men but Hong Kong, like other colonies far from the battlefields in Europe and the Middle East, came last in the scramble for equipment. A list of urgently needed items for the HKVDC included 552 helmets, 482 rifles and bayonets, quantities of mosquito netting and two 'urine tubs' at 13 shillings and 6 pence.

Conscription was introduced in Hong Kong for white male British residents, aged 18–55, when Britain declared war on Germany in 1939. Even the most blinkered colonists realised the conflict in Europe raised the chance of war with Japan. Japanese border violations steadily increased. HKVDC enlistment jumped dramatically as hundreds of residents signed up. Men aged up to 41 were taken by the HKVDC or the much smaller Hong Kong Naval Reserve. Hundreds of Chinese volunteered for military duty. A register was compiled of British women and children 'of all races'[32] to be evacuated if Hong Kong was attacked. Eurasians and Indians were listed, but not Chinese, including dependents of Chinese Volunteers. White British women and children were ordered to leave for Australia in 1941 as the political situation worsened but dependents of Asian and Eurasian HKVDC men were not evacuated even though they were likely to be singled out for harsh retribution if Japan captured the colony. Hong Kong officials insisted they had no choice because of Australia's ban on non-white migrants. Survivors said later that a few Eurasian women and children slipped in among the European evacuees amid chaotic scenes at the docks.

All evacuees were sent to the Philippines before going on to Australia. Inspectors in Manila singled out the Eurasians and sent them back. Efforts to find havens for non-European dependents in Fiji or Mauritius were overtaken by the Japanese invasion.

A July 1941 report gives a final snapshot of the HKVDC on the eve of war.[33] Its strength was reported to be 101 officers and 2,139 men. Colonel H. B. Rose, corps commander and author of the report, said every eligible European had been recruited. European civilians were no longer being sent to the colony, and some firms were moving staff to offices in other parts of Asia. Chinese of the 'right type' could be recruited, but Rose claimed they found it hard to take time from work to train and most preferred to serve in the less-demanding civil defence.

Rose gave an upbeat report on his command's readiness for war. Training had been increased substantially since 1939. Volunteers were doing two weeks in camp annually; an eight-hour weekly stint of field training; evening parades once or twice a week; plus weekend exercises. Regular instructors were overseeing the training. HKVDC officers and NCOs attended frequent special courses under regular instructors. Cooperation with the regulars was very good and standards were generally high. Overall, Rose concluded, corps spirit was excellent and the men were keen and cheerful.

Some regular officers were impressed by the part-time soldiers' resolve and their contempt for the enemy. 'A manifest sense of bravado was apparent among the Volunteers,' one officer recalled after the war. 'The Volunteers were ready for a fight ... their way of life [was] threatened. Its men were determined and angry.'[34] Major-General C. M. Maltby, the garrison commander, had some concerns about the Volunteers' readiness in an August 1941 evaluation.[35] Its men, he said, were weak on tactics and other basics. Time was running out, however, and not much more could be done to boost the force's readiness. Hong Kong had just six regular and colonial infantry battalions. The HKVDC was going to have to play a major role in the coming battle.

Doomed Outpost

Japanese forces swept across the Hong Kong frontier on 8 December. Pearl Harbor was attacked at the same time on the other side of the international date line. London had all but written Hong Kong off. Britain's imperial defences had been crippled by appeasement and parsimony. Paltry, last-minute reinforcements could not begin to erase decades of neglect. Hong Kong's 12,000-strong garrison was an ill-matched mix of regular and

Volunteer British, Indian and Canadian troops. Many of the troops were poorly trained, inexperienced and bereft of modern equipment. The defenders had no chance against the far larger battle-hardened Japanese army that invaded the settlement. Moreover, Hong Kong was virtually indefensible. A huge civilian population and the small garrison were trapped in a tiny enclave, exposed to air, land and sea attack. There was no room to manoeuvre, retreat or escape. Hong Kong was ordered to fight to the end even though the British government must have known there was virtually no chance of any help arriving.

No attempt was made to defend the frontier when the Japanese attacked. British plans rested on three regular army battalions holding the aptly christened 'Gin Drinkers' Line', a series of incomplete fortifications close to Kowloon. Virtually all of the other British forces were deployed on Hong Kong island. The HKVDC comprised a significant part of the garrison: five batteries; seven infantry and machine-gun companies; armoured car and reconnaissance units; a reserve company of older men; and engineer, signals, logistics, pay, railway, ambulance and nursing detachments.

Only fragmentary accounts survive of the HKVDC's role in the three-week defence of the territory.[36] It is not even clear how many Volunteers took part. The official report on the campaign puts HKVDC strength at 1,385 men. Various HKVDC accounts give figures ranging from 1,660 to 2,200 men. Post-war records suggest just 66 officers and men failed to report for duty when the force was mobilised on the eve of the invasion; many of them were Chinese and Portuguese. Hong Kong's Volunteer troops were scattered around the defences and did not fight as a single formation. Most of its combat and support units were positioned on Hong Kong island. Just 1st Company, the Engineer Company and the armoured cars were deployed on the mainland with 3rd Company on Stonecutters' Island.

Months of training and planning supposedly had ensured that mobilisation would be swift and efficient. Volunteers instead encountered confusion and incompetence at the regimental depot as they tried to draw stores and weapons on the eve of the invasion. Angry officers argued with supply orderlies as confused soldiers milled around. Harassed clerks could not find vital war stores. Some equipment was defective and there was no time for repairs.

Men of 1st Company only received part of their war equipment and ammunition though it did get 30 last-minute reinforcements, boosting its strength to 3 officers and 90 men. A mismatched collection of military and civilian vehicles took the Volunteers to their war positions – an old

HKVDC truck, a civilian truck, two vans, two cars and five motorbikes on loan from Volunteers or friends. Three new Bren gun carriers added significantly to the company's firepower and manoeuvrability. Orders sent the company to defend the military–civilian airfield at Kai Tak on the mainland. It found more confusion and little preparation at the Royal Air Force base. A search of RAF stores only yielded defective anti-aircraft sights for the HKVDC's antiquated machine guns. There were no stands to mount the guns. Volunteers dug positions and kept watch for Japanese paratroopers or what the orders called 'civil commotion'.

Engineers of the HKVDC and some Indian regulars were the only British troops on the undefended Chinese border. Many of the HKVDC sappers were highly skilled civil engineers who had been planning and practising demolitions in the region for months. The railway bridge was blown up after British signallers picked up a Japanese radio message warning that war was imminent. Bridges, roads and supply dumps were destroyed during the day as the tiny British rearguard steadily retreated. HKVDC armoured cars backed up the retiring detachment later in the day.

War burst on the colony when Japanese planes attacked Kai Tak and other targets. Hong Kong's entire air force, three antiquated torpedo bombers and two amphibious planes, was destroyed on the ground. Civilian aircraft parked on the field were also destroyed or damaged. Nervous, unpractised HKVDC men did not score a single hit with their elderly machine guns on the diving attackers. A second raid that afternoon flew far above the range of the airfield's defences. Bombs left a dozen small craters around the runway. A few civilian aircraft that were still airworthy flew out after dark. Among the passengers were officers with orders to set up links with the Chinese government and forces.

Kai Tak's RAF detachment withdrew after wrecking some of the airfield's installations, leaving the Volunteers and a few regulars. A civilian mob stormed and looted the abandoned Air Force officers' mess a few hours later. Artillery fire could be heard from the nearby hills.

Parts of the Gin Drinkers' Line were over-run on 10 December after just a few hours of fighting. Bren gun carriers and troops from 1st Company were sent with the armoured cars to support the retiring regular units. Excited Volunteers claimed they had scythed down howling waves of Japanese infantry. The men also reported being shot at by Chinese snipers who were aiding the Japanese. It was the first of many reports of a sizable Chinese fifth column operating behind British lines.

Orders arrived on 11 December for the rest of the company at Kai Tak to abandon the airfield and return to Hong Kong island. The next few hours were spent trying to wreck infrastructure and equipment. Amateurish attempts to blow up a water tower backfired when the charges failed to detonate simultaneously and most were blown clear without exploding. Efforts to hole the tank with machine-gun fire failed to rupture the base. The HKVDC engineers were more successful with demolitions at a nearby power station and a cement plant. Volunteer armoured cars and Bren gun carriers covered the retreat to the waterfront. HKVDC men also guided parties of regular troops to the piers as looters rampaged through the burning streets. All of the regular and Volunteer troops were evacuated to Hong Kong island by 12 December. Volunteers of 3rd Company and regular troops holding Stonecutters' Island also pulled back to the main island.

Hong Kong's settlers were bewildered and angry that the New Territories seemed to have been abandoned without a serious fight. Few could understand how British forces were being swept away by the Asians who had been lampooned up until a day or two before as comic freaks. Many of the Volunteers were confident Hong Kong island would never be taken. Few wanted to admit that Britain would abandon the colony. There was talk of reinforcements and rumours swirled of Chinese armies racing to attack the Japanese in the rear.

Hong Kong's forces were divided into two brigades to defend the western and eastern halves of the island. HKVDC units were scattered around the island. Three infantry companies, 1st, 2nd and 3rd, held positions in the rugged hills in the east of the island, while the other four initially were based in the centre and west with 5th Company holding the far western corner. 1st, 2nd and 3rd Batteries manned coastal positions on the south coast; 4th and 5th Batteries held the north-east corner of the island; and the armoured cars and support formations were attached to various headquarters and regular units.

The next few days were a blur of frantic activity, disarray and contradictory orders. Existing defence positions were strengthened, and new entrenchments and gun pits dug. More than 20 Volunteers were sent to replace dead and wounded officers of the regular army battalions. Japanese artillery firing across the narrow strait peppered the island. British guns, rationed to a few dozen shells each day, struggled to spot enemy positions on the Kowloon waterfront. A war diary compiled by 1st Company survivors says detailed defence plans, which had taken years to prepare, were abandoned without explanation.[37] New plans, sketchy and confusing, were issued and quickly countermanded. The company's three weak platoons were assigned to cover a stretch of territory it would have taken a battalion or more to defend adequately. Requests for information were brusquely batted aside by senior officers. Weapons and equipment lost or abandoned on the mainland were not replaced. Military communications were patchy, and officers sometimes had to walk miles to find working civilian telephones.

Japanese artillery fire inflicted mounting damage on the handful of British batteries as raiding detachments tested the island's defences. The antiquated guns of 4th HKVDC Battery helped smash a 15 December Japanese night attack. Any ideas that the defence could stop the Japanese reaching the island were soon proved illusory, however. Three Japanese brigades made separate landings on the island's north-east coast on the night of 18–19 December. Japanese troops surged ashore effortlessly and immediately began pushing into the hills behind the coast.

Stunned Volunteers were among the first troops to be over-run. A position of 4th Battery was captured without the rest of the unit realising it. All of 5th Battery was over-run before the crews knew the Japanese had landed. Twenty men taken prisoner were tied up and later bayoneted, their bodies tossed down the adjoining hillside. It was the first of several massacres of prisoners, hospital staff and patients.

1st Company and the other slender forces in the hills tried to hold off attacks by at least four Japanese battalions. Machine guns were positioned to cover narrow paths leading to the summits. Retreating Indian soldiers and police said the Japanese were close behind them. A few of the retreating men agreed to stay and help, but the Volunteer officers felt they had to be watched in case they fled, making them a liability. 1st Company's men fired machine guns into the night when noises were heard. 'Cease fire' was ordered and Japanese voices suddenly filled the lull. Every Volunteer opened fire blindly as the Japanese scattered. Next, bands of Japanese soldiers began to attack from different positions, confusing the defenders. A machine-gun post was over-run, one crewman shot at close range and the other bayoneted. Some defenders pulled back over the ridgeline and fled. A Japanese soldier, seeing the running Volunteers, fired a rocket to signal that the position was taken. Its light revealed a knot of Japanese soldiers who were quickly gunned down by the surviving defenders. An HKVDC officer and four men slipped away believing they were the only survivors. Finally a wave of Japanese troops surged over the last defenders, shooting and bayoneting many of them. Survivors said the Japanese turned the position's machine guns on them.

Not many Japanese were killed in the confused fighting. There were too many attackers and they moved too quickly and surely in the dark for the disoriented and weary defenders. Ten of the 31 HKVDC men holding the post were killed, five wounded and four captured.

Some 230 men of 3rd Company and Canadian troops, meanwhile, battled three Japanese battalions that enveloped the sides of a key hill called Jardine's Lookout. Volunteers in pill-boxes held off the Japanese for most of the first day after the landings. 3rd Company endured 85 casualties out of a strength of 115 men in desperate fighting. Japanese troops bayoneted wounded Volunteers and beat others to death with rifle butts.

Several Eurasian NCOs were praised for holding up large groups of Japanese troops and sacrificing their own lives to allow other Volunteers to pull back. One of their officers, noting most had British fathers and Chinese or Eurasian mothers, said such bravery and resolution was a surprise from a group Hong Kong had looked down on as weak and craven.[38]

Forced back to new positions, 1st Company received orders to hold its post to the last man. Its diary exudes bewilderment at frequent and harsh criticism from brigade headquarters that seemed to question the men's courage despite mounting casualties. Senior officers appeared to have had little idea of what troops faced in increasingly hopeless attempts to halt the invaders. Other units also felt their courage and dedication were being questioned.

Nobody could doubt the courage of one of the garrison's most unlikely units. The HKVDC reserve force was composed of men aged 55 and older. Some of the businessmen and socialites in the company were close to 70. At least one was a veteran of the Boer War. Life in the company was suitably sedate with the men doing occasional guard duty at government installations. Posted to guard the North Point power station, in the belief that it would be out of the way, the aged unit was in the middle of the Japanese landing forces on the first night. North Point's geriatric garrison and regulars from the Middlesex Regiment held off wave after wave of howling Japanese soldiers. Elderly Volunteers kept up a steady fire as Japanese shells slammed into the power station and flames engulfed the facility. A knot of defenders fought from the wreck of an overturned bus. Private T. E. Pearce, 67, mused that it didn't make much difference if he died under the bus or burned to death in the blazing station. He and another Volunteer died when the bus was over-run. Private Sir Edward Des Voeux, politely turned down a suggestion to leave a nearby building, saying he was far too old to rush about. He died at his post still firing at the advancing Japanese troops. Some of the dead and wounded Volunteers suffered sword slashes in hand-to-hand fighting before the station fell on the morning of 19 December.

Japanese forces over-ran many of the British positions in the north-east of the island within 12 hours after the first landings. British attempts to halt the Japanese pouring on to the island were smashed with terrible losses. Single companies and then mere platoons were decimated in hopeless counter-attacks on Japanese regiments. Losses among the defenders swiftly mounted and there were no replacements for the dead and wounded. Rose, the HKVDC commandant, took command of the West Brigade after its regular commander, Brigadier-General J. K. Lawson, was killed. Japanese troops captured Wong Nei Chong Gap with its north–south road bisecting the island. Improvised infantry units cobbled together from regular and Volunteer engineers, gunners and support troops failed to retake the gap in repeated attacks.

Japanese forces had thus effectively cut the island in half by 21 December. British troops in the south-east around Stanley were cut off from the forces holding the western end of the island and the main city districts. 1st Battery abandoned its guns and along with men from 1st and 2nd Companies pulled back to the Stanley area. An HKVDC platoon of warders from the local prison was part of the Stanley force. Japanese forces reached Deep Water Bay on the south coast. Bitter fighting raged in a seaside hotel at Repulse Bay with British and Japanese forces holding different floors. An attempt on 21 December by regular and Volunteer troops from Stanley to retake Wong Nei Chong Gap was defeated. Japanese forces began to press west towards the main city district while other units moved in on Stanley.

By 21 December most Volunteer infantry units had been driven from their original positions with substantial losses. 3rd Company had practically ceased to exist after losing 70 per cent of its men; 1st and 2nd Companies were holding out around Stanley on the south coast; 4th and 7th Companies were in positions around Mount Cameron in the western half of the island; 6th Company was doing anti-aircraft duty on the north coast around the main city. Only 5th Company, stuck at Mount Davis at the western tip of the island in case of a Japanese landing, had gone virtually untouched. Of the artillery, 4th and 5th Batteries had been written off; the remnants of 1st and 2nd Batteries were in the Stanley perimeter; and 3rd Battery was on Aberdeen Island on the south coast.

The final days of the siege were a blur of dozens of desperate little fights as the bedraggled and dazed defenders fought on. Harry Wood, a regular sergeant serving as an HKVDC instructor, remembered how swiftly things fell apart. 'When you put all these bits together, you get a composite picture of being ineffectual as a garrison. It was left to the individual who did this and that. There was no direction. Everybody was doing their own thing, especially towards the end.'[39] Harold Yates, a gunner with the Royal Artillery's 24th Coast Battery, said attacks and sniping by Chinese fifth columnists inflicted serious losses on the defenders:

> 'We had orders, actually, during the last three days or so to shoot any Chinese we saw around the Mount Davis area whether they were in uniform or not. That's how bad it was. But I assume that the Chinese who were loyal to us such as the Volunteers were told to keep away from this area.'[40]

There is no indication any such warning was ever issued.

Japanese forces regrouped during 22 December, giving the defenders a chance to repair the defences. 1st Company, promised a rest at Stanley after the failed attacks on Wong Nei Chong Gap, instead was ordered to dig trenches and latrines. It had about 40 men left. Positions at Repulse Bay were abandoned and a few surviving members of the Volunteers escaped through the Japanese lines to reach Stanley.

Japanese forces took Stanley's outer defences on 23 December and pushed toward the peninsula where what was left of the garrison manned a series of defensive lines. Troops from at least seven Japanese battalions were deployed to take the shrinking British position. A scratch force of about 70 men of 1st Battery HKVDC, fighting as infantry, and 30 men of the Middlesex Regiment held a ridge in front of Stanley. An attack by more than 2,000 Japanese troops overwhelmed the ridge just hours before General Maltby decided continued resistance was pointless. At least 35 Volunteers were killed and berserk Japanese troops drove their bayonets into the dead and wounded bodies of fallen defenders on the ridge. British troops were still holding Stanley and the west of the island when the battle ended.

Hong Kong's garrison surrendered on Christmas Day after military commanders told the governor the troops could only fight for one more hour. Many HKVDC survivors could not believe the battle was lost. The corps lost 227 men killed or missing. Many more HKVDC men were wounded. At least 78 Volunteers were to perish in Japanese prison camps. HKVDC men were among the dozens of defenders killed in a series of massacres after being taken prisoner or when military hospitals were captured.

Maltby praised the Volunteers in a post-war dispatch as 'stubborn and gallant soldiers'.[41] Regretting that his official report was too short to recognise the HKVDC fully, he singled out the corps' Z Force or reconnaissance platoon. This 20-man unit, trained to operate behind enemy lines, blew up a park of Japanese ammunition trucks on the night of the surrender.

An apt epithet on the HKVDC's part in the battle for Hong Kong came from a regular officer, Lieutenant-Colonel R. J. L Penfold:

'To fight where he dwells is probably the most distasteful task a soldier faces. It was in these daunting conditions, in the few days' bitter fighting among the ruins of their homes that the HKVDC fully confirmed the right to their proud motto – *Nulli Secundis*.'[42]

Volunteers were rounded up with the rest of the garrison and marched to captivity. Some Volunteers, mostly Chinese who could blend into the population, shed their uniforms and slipped away. HKVDC officers feared non-European Volunteers would be singled out for reprisal and encouraged them to escape. Other Volunteers escaped from the camps in the early days when security was lax. Corps records indicate between 400 and 500 Volunteers evaded captivity, mostly Chinese and Eurasians. Japanese officials later released 123 Volunteers, mostly Chinese, but also a few men with Indian and European names. Details are sparse and it appears to have been an attempt to win local support.

A few of the Volunteers and regulars escaped and trekked hundreds of miles across China to contact British forces. Some joined the newly-formed British Army Aid Group at Kweilin. It gathered intelligence and had intermittent contact with prison camps in the colony. Other survivors went on to India by air or on foot.

Men still capable of serving were formed in India into the Chinese British Unit. It was later renamed the Hong Kong Volunteer Company. All the officers and most of the NCOs were British. Nearly all of the other ranks were Chinese. Local British military commanders disparaged the force and the men were 'treated like coolies' until Brigadier-General Michael Calvert, who had served in Hong Kong, heard about them. He parcelled about 120 men out to various Chindit units for operations behind Japanese lines in Burma. Hong Kong troops helped to defend a Chindit base against Japanese attacks and took part in other actions.

Subsequently they were reassembled as a company to train for operations in Malaya. A parachute platoon was formed and some men qualified as paratroopers but most of the company's time was taken up with routine duty enlivened by occasional sports days. A rare bright spot was a party put on for the Chinese New Year in February 1945 by a British Army entertainment group. Miss Daphne Ray, one of the performers, was 'acclaimed as the company's Pin-Up Girl'. Japan collapsed before the British invasion of Malaya. The company finally returned to Hong Kong in 1946.[43]

The Final Decades

Hong Kong faced new fears of invasion in 1949 when communist forces took control of China. Officials in London and Hong Kong worried the communists would annex the colony. A large military force was kept in the territory to deter an attack. Local officials suggested reviving the virtually moribund HKVDC as part of a new voluntary defence force. The War Office simultaneously backed the plan and declined to pay for it, a point it frequently reiterated. Discussions on the make-up of the force almost collapsed after the colony suggested forming a commando unit. The War Office tartly questioned the plan's wisdom and said the Navy would have to train such a force. Hong Kong explained there were no plans for an amphibious assault unit. It had just been toying with using commando as a name because its cachet would aid recruiting. Reassured, the War Office spent months happily outlining ambitious plans for an infantry force with armoured-car and heavy anti-aircraft units. Each evolution in the plan came with a reminder that London would not pay any costs or lend any equipment.

Hong Kong was not deterred by the Army's miserliness but former Volunteers were less enthusiastic about taking up arms again. Many complained they had been badly treated by the British military authorities during the war. Captain A. R. Morrison, a HKVDC veteran, told a 1947 commission that Volunteers who escaped after the colony's fall were not recognised by the Army as soldiers. Volunteers' families had been poorly treated and denied recognition and aid, Morrison said. Disabled survivors had not been cared for by the government and pensions for widows and orphans were derisory, he added.[44]

Old and new residents believed the 1941 battle proved that the enclave was indefensible. Officials blamed initial reluctance to volunteer for the new force on a 'certain cynicism' over the feasibility of defending the colony after the experiences of 1941.

The HKVDC was formally dissolved in February 1949. It was replaced the next day by the Hong Kong Defence Force, with land, sea and air units for local defence. Ambitious plans called for a force of some 6,000 men and women. Its land arm, the Hong Kong Regiment, took over the functions of the HKVDC. All nationalities could enlist although old colonial habits of separate ethnic units lingered on. An official report defended it as 'racial grouping – though not racial discrimination'. Segregation soon crumbled and by 1953 Chinese made up 45 per cent of the regiment, Portuguese were again second with 23 per cent while British whites accounted for 16.5 per cent. Eurasians were still classified as a separate group making up 5.3 per cent of the force. Racial separation eventually collapsed as the colony's government focused increasingly on Chinese recruitment. Some British residents complained in later years that they could not get into the force. At the end, the regiment was 97 per cent Chinese.

In the early 1960s, the now Royal Hong Kong Defence Force was disbanded. The Hong Kong Regiment continued, changing from an infantry battalion to a reconnaissance regiment to support the regular garrison. It was frequently called out to help police the border and assist in handling occasional unrest in the colony. Volunteers patrolled the streets as the chaos of China's Cultural Revolution lapped over the border in the 1960s. Recognition for its services came in 1969 when it became the Royal Hong Kong Regiment. Training and occasional deployments continued until the end of British rule. It ended active operations on 1 July 1995 on the eve of Hong Kong's return to China.

The regiment appeared for the last time at a disbandment parade on 2 September. It mounted guard for the final time the following day at Government House. Sentries presented arms at midnight as the Last Post was sounded. As the stark bugle tones died away, the regiment marched off for the last time.

Chapter 8

OUR VERY OWN

The Hong Kong Regiment

A THOUSAND YOUNG INDIAN SOLDIERS crowded the decks of the SS *Bombay* as it sailed into Hong Kong on a May morning in 1892. Many had been recruited just a few weeks earlier from the farms and villages of northern India. Virtually all of the men were seeing a foreign land for the first time. It was the start of an experiment in raising a new type of regiment to garrison Britain's Asian outposts. No accounts seem to have survived of the soldiers' first or subsequent impressions of their new home. Hong Kong's rulers, for their part, were not at all pleased.

*

It had been a very different story a few years earlier. London had suggested adding a second battalion to the colony's garrison in 1888. Hong Kong welcomed the plan as recognition of its growing commercial and military importance. Agreement quickly ended at that point. Officials in Hong Kong had assumed the plan entailed sending a second British battalion. The War Office said it could not spare any British troops. Somebody suggested raising Indian troops for a new type of unit that could transform imperial defence. It would be modelled on the regiments of the Indian Army, but be part of the British Army and financed with imperial funds. Levies of Indian troops, usually recruited informally by contractors, had been used in Hong Kong and other colonies in the past. Such haphazardly raised units were often badly trained and led. London now suggested emulating the success of the Indian Army to mine India's vast manpower resources to create a new imperial force. It was a beguiling plan that could solve the perennial challenge of garrisoning an expanding empire without depleting the small British Army. It would also be significantly cheaper than using British regiments.[†]

† Regular units of the Indian Army had participated in various wars in Asia by the late 19th century, but invariably returned home as soon as possible. Indians were being raised at the same time for the Hong Kong artillery, but these were still essentially levies and their make-up and organisation were far less ambitious.

Hong Kong's bureaucrats were mortified at the suggestion of Indian troops. Disquiet turned to indignation when London suggested raising 'a native battalion of Madrassees'.[1] Hong Kong insisted that it wanted British troops. Anything less would be taken as a slight on the colony's prestige. Swarthy south Indians were completely unacceptable. 'Sending a battalion of Madras troops here would be regarded with much disfavour by the community, the "Madrassees" being looked upon as the most unwarlike and the least efficient among the soldiers of the Indian population,' the colony's government wrote.[2] News of the planned regiment spread in the colony and was widely discussed. A few wry commentators suggested any Indian might be superior to the often weak, sickly men of the British garrison. But local opinion mostly echoed the administration's outraged reaction to the idea of Madras sepoys. Bureaucrats in London, Hong Kong and Calcutta launched into a protracted duel over the composition of the proposed unit. Memos leisurely wandered back and forth between the three centres. Rival proposals were offered on everything from the type of men to be recruited to their pay and allowances. India's officials insisted they would decide on the type of men to recruit for the regiment, but there was no rush in the higher echelons of the Indian Army to make a decision. Hong Kong said that Madras men used as artillery levies in the colony years earlier had been unsatisfactory. If Indian troops were unavoidable, officials pleaded, could they at least be dashing, warlike Sikhs like those recruited for the colony's police? 'I would strongly urge the sending of Sikhs in preference to any from Madras, the colony having had some experience of the former, and possessing, I understand, confidence in them,' an official explained.[3]

The concept of martial races was spreading across the Empire by the late 19th century. Hong Kong's merchants and bankers were as convinced as the most doctrinaire Indian Army recruiting officer that the paler men of north-western India were far superior to the short, dark inhabitants of the south. India saw Sikh soldiers as a valuable commodity, however, and was not inclined to diminish its own supply by sending a force to another colony. London eventually decided in 1891 to raise a battalion of 'Mohammedans of Upper India'.[4] Hong Kong glumly accepted what seemed likely to be the best offer it would get. ' These Mohammedans of Upper India, if not actually Sikhs, will at any rate presumably be more warlike than the southerners from Madras,' an official grumbled.[5]

It had taken years of bickering and gallons of ink to agree on the make-up of the regiment. It was formed with astonishing speed once the decision was made. Major Edmund George Barrow, of the Indian Army's 7th Bengal Infantry, was given the task. Barrow, an inspired and highly intelligent officer, recognised his new command was a formidable challenge. Indian Muslims, most of them uneducated peasants, were being sent thousands of miles from home to uphold the rule of alien masters over an equally foreign Asian race. There would be tremendous social, cultural and religious pressures on the men. Success depended on forging a force capable of upholding British rule anywhere in the Empire. Barrow appealed to the men's honour and even their faith to ensure success. A new identity was spelled out in the regiment's first standing order:

> 'The Hong Kong Regiment, the first Corps raised in India for "General Service" under the War Office. It behoves all who may have the honour to serve the Queen Empress in this regiment to devote all their energies to rapidly raising it to such a state of efficiency as will fit it to honourably discharge all such duties as it may be called upon to perform. All ranks must remember that the position of the Corps is an exceptional one – a Class Regiment of Mussulmans, especially raised for Service beyond the Seas, so that not only have they in their keeping the reputation of the Corps to which they belong, but also the credit of Islam and the good fame of the Indian Army, who, in a sense, will be represented by this Regiment in the Far East.'[6]

Barrow was innovative and often unorthodox. He turned to the Prussian Army for training methods, particularly its use of theoretical instruction to train men in both military and political duty. Men were given daily lessons on a wide range of subjects. 'In the British service we do not usually appeal sufficiently to sentiment,' Barrow wrote. He added, '. . . discipline is the product of moral training combined with the force of habit'.[7] It was an unusual approach in a military culture that generally scorned anything that smacked of being intellectual or foreign.

Lord Roberts, Commander-in-Chief of the Indian Army, suggested the new regiment be raised at Jhelum in the Punjab. Barrow recruited NCOs and experienced sepoys from local regiments to form the backbone. Recruiting parties were then sent into the countryside to sign up young men. Barrow compared it to a shooting party for game – sending out 'small parties of old soldiers to beat up new recruits'.[8] Everything was meticulously planned. The regiment's ethnic and clan composition was worked out with the Indian Army's increasingly elaborate racial alchemy. It was decided that an ideal concoction comprised: 2 companies of Pathans from west of the Indus River; 5 companies of Punjabis from east of the Indus River; and 1 company of Hindustani Muslims recruited from Oudh and the North-West Provinces.

Barrow further broke down recruiting requirements within these categories. Twenty tribes or clans in the region were eligible for recruiting. Recruiters were instructed to shun seven other tribes. Tinkering or refinement in 1896 led to a new racial formula for the regiment's make-up: ⅛ Khattaks; ⅛ Yusuzais; ⅝ Punjabis – of which ⅘ Trans Ravi and ⅛ Cis Ravi; and ⅛ Hindustanis.

Barrow took an intense interest in the perceived racial and moral characteristics of the different groups he recruited. Pathans were 'practically the same as the Afghans' – temperamental and prickly, he noted. Most of the other enlistees were 'agriculturists' or peasants, the favourite recruits of the Indian Army: 'When recruited they are as a rule taken straight from the plough, and have never seen any really big town,' Barrow said.[9] Such men had no knowledge of the larger world. British officers saw them as the perfect recruit: sturdy, strong, trusting and dependent. Command was left to the regiment's 10 British and 17 Indian officers. Good pay, local traditions of soldiering and talk of adventure in foreign lands brought in hundreds of aspiring soldiers. Some 900 men were signed up in two months for a minimum of five years' service. Men united by friendships, family and village ties or clan were grouped in squads and platoons. Drilling and other training began as the men flowed into the temporary regimental depot. Tailors, cobblers and craftsmen were hired to help the Indian Army's clothing department outfit the formation. Plans to name the new unit as the Hong Kong Native Infantry Regiment were changed at the last minute and it became The Hong Kong Regiment

Barrow drew up elaborate and precise instructions for moulding the regiment. Training was to be based on discipline, marching and shooting. Bullying and threatening behaviour would not be tolerated. Officers and NCOs had to keep the men interested in the work by ensuring they were cheerful and content. Officers were told to cultivate their men's intelligence so they understood the reasons for training and orders and did their best. 'The soldier should be made to feel that he follows a noble profession and that in his humble way he is entrusted with the honour of the army,' the commander wrote.[10] Equally thorough attention was given to developing the ability and initiative of the British and Indian officers. Senior British officers were expected to give juniors broad latitude, only stepping in if there were problems. And at a time when whites expected deference from natives, Barrow issued a standing order that the men were not to salute

European civilians: 'A salute is only due to a person holding Her Majesty's Commission.'[11]

Barrow's far-sighted approach was unusual in an army addicted to hidebound rigidity. He did accept Army orthodoxy on one key point. Indian soldiers had shown countless times that they were capable of heroic endurance and bravery. Yet even innovative officers like Barrow believed their men could only be good soldiers if led by white officers or fighting alongside white troops. Barrow reflected this in a talk to British other ranks at the Soldiers and Sailors Institute in June 1892 aimed at getting them to see his men as fellow soldiers.

> 'Now that you are quartered alongside a Native Regiment I want to tell you that you must not think because you see a number of raw, wild, untrained boys that native soldiers are not worthy of being looked upon as comrades. In cantonments there is a vast difference between the British soldiers and the native soldier, but in the field I am proud to say the Sepoy, under British officers, has often done deeds worthy of the British soldier … [native troops] what brave, faithful, enduring fellows they are in any service, ever ready to starve or march or fight so long as they have a British officer to lead them or Tommy Atkins to set them an example of fortitude and discipline … I hope then … you will always look upon the Sepoy as a fellow soldier.'[12]

Hong Kong's Chinese population did not welcome the colony's new guardians. Local newspapers reported the Chinese were terrified of the Indians, and some believed the sepoys were cannibals. Indian soldiers traded insults and blows with Chinese in a street brawl just days after the regiment arrived. Police reinforcements had to be called out to end the mêlée. Reports of growing Chinese fears of the Indians spread in coming weeks. A Chinese servant told her mistress she met a sepoy in a shop and ' … was afraid he might want to eat her as these soldiers did eat Chinese when they could get the chance,' the *Hong Kong Daily Press* recounted.[13] Initial European mirth at the antics of the Chinese changed when some colonists said British integrity was being questioned. Newspapers now said it was monstrous that anyone should think Britain would employ cannibals. One editorialist fumed:

> 'The Pathans are some of them rather wild and fierce looking in mufti, but it is hard that they should be credited with cannibalism and that the civilized British Government should be deemed capable of employing monsters.'[14]

Chinese fear of the regiment did it no harm in the eyes of British residents. Keeping the Chinese majority subdued was the garrison's main task, as far as many civilians were concerned, and the sepoys were clearly effective at that. Attitudes towards the regiment softened, gradually turning to pride. Hong Kong newspapers began referring to the unit as 'our very own' and a group of leading local ladies stitched a set of regimental colours.

It was agreed the regiment was a splendid sight. Regimental parades became a popular diversion for the colony. Sumptuous uniforms designed, or at least approved, by Barrow, were widely admired. Ceremonial dress consisted of magnificent scarlet blouses with yellow facings, gold cummerbunds, blue trousers with red stripes, white gaiters and a turban of indigo and gold cloth. Marching order dress was blue serge blouse and knickerbockers in winter and khaki during the summer. British officers wore white foreign service helmets with a *pagri* or binding of the regiment's indigo and gold cloth. Such sartorial magnificence seems to have been a ploy to persuade Hong Kong's rulers they were getting as good as Sikhs, if not better. A regimental band was formed and became a favourite fixture at the colony's cricket ground.

Hong Kong's disdain for Indian soldiers seems to have evaporated by April 1895. A special parade attended by the colonial elite was held to present the regiment's new colours. Press reports praised the regiment's appearance and marching:

> 'All credit is due to those fine swarthy fellows for this magnificent display they made and to the officers of the Regiment for training what was formerly a "rabble of raw recruits" to use Colonel Barrow's expression, in such a praiseworthy manner.'[15]

Barrow and the regiment settled into the dull routine of garrison life. Its main task was sentry duty. Detachments guarded the forts, the magazine, government laboratory, docks and other key locations. Men were warned not to touch the coastal guns after a complaint that the brass fittings had been soiled by fingerprints. Severe retribution was also promised after a complaint that bored sentries were defacing roster books.

Humdrum routine was enlivened by occasional dangers such as the typhoons that sweep the China coast. In such an event the men were trained to pack their gear away and take shelter in the docks' warehouses. Efforts were made to make the soldiers comfortable in their new home. A mosque fund was started after the colony provided free land for a building.

Petty misdemeanours or crimes sometimes marred regimental life. Men who contracted venereal diseases were warned they faced court martial if they tried to conceal the illness. Several men lost good conduct badges after being caught in a 'common gambling house'. A ban was imposed on keeping cows, pigs, goats and poultry in the barracks or married quarters. Officers were chided for occasional lapses such as failing to contribute to the band fund. Native officers were censured for not looking after their service pistols. British officers were expected to improve their abilities rather than loll around like those in most garrison units. Any officer passing the government exams in colloquial Chinese was awarded £50.

More serious crimes sometimes shook the regiment. Several men were punished in June 1896 for pilfering the regimental funds. The reading room, sports, mosque and school funds were moved to a Hong Kong bank to remove temptation. A rash of fake school certificates submitted by men studying to be NCOs prompted an order that only regimental school documents would be accepted. Officers and NCOs were warned in a regimental order not to accept gifts from subordinates:

> 'The Native Soldier rarely makes a present without expecting some return, usually promotion for himself or a friend – and consequently the offer of a present is usually nothing more than a bribe and should be regarded as such.'[16]

Petty corruption appears to have been the one dark stain during Barrow's command. There were unusually harsh words when he left the regiment in October 1895 as well as the usual praise and sentimentality of farewell speeches. 'The great faults of Indian soldiers, whether Officer or Sepoy, are love of intrigue and favouritism,' Barrow warned the assembled formation. Such traits must be avoided, he added: 'They only bring trouble and shame and lead to bad blood and enmity.'[17] He also warned the men against drinking, reminding them it was a cardinal sin in their religion.

Barrow's greatest regret was never leading the regiment he created into battle. It was not to see action until April 1899 after Hong Kong had leased additional territory on the mainland. Local Chinese villagers were not happy at coming under foreign rule. Thousands of Chinese armed with cannons, matchlocks, swords and pitchforks turned out to resist the impending British occupation. Men of the Hong Kong Regiment were deployed with other British units to secure the territory. A company of the regiment under Captain E. L. C. Berger confronted a mob of some 1,000 Chinese. It opened fire, driving the Chinese back with numerous casualties. Chinese fighters bombarded the Hong Kong Regiment detachment with some old cannon, causing little damage. A few days later the regiment dispersed an armed crowd reported to number at least 3,000 men, again inflicting extensive casualties. While skirmishes with untrained peasants hardly deserved to be called battles, British officials grandly praised the regiment's performance. Hong Kong's very own had passed the most important test.

Two companies of the regiment were dispatched a year later to the relief force sent to fight the Boxer Rebellion in China. A multi-national force attempting to relieve their besieged embassies in Peking was bottled up at Tientsin. The Hong Kong detachment joined a British force in bitter fighting around Tientsin. Reinforcements arrived from the regiment in Hong Kong and the enlarged detachment took part in the subsequent bloody advance to Peking. Fighting trained Chinese troops and fanatical Boxers was far more dangerous than chasing ill-armed peasants. At least 11 Hong Kong Regiment men were killed and another 31 wounded. Reports on the Hong Kong Regiment's performance were complimentary.

It was not allowed to enjoy its triumph for long. Success had created envy, and its reward was to be disbanded. Military commanders in India saw the regiment as a potential threat to the primacy of their own forces. There had been complaints about the effect the Hong Kong Regiment allegedly was having on Indian Army recruiting. Its higher rates of pay were claimed to be attracting some of the best recruits. Reports of the regiment's comfortable life in Hong Kong were supposedly drawing recruits away from Indian Army units. India's military establishment also realised the advantages of expanding its role outside the country to become the main guardian of British Asia. It would boost the importance of the Indian Army, increase its status in the old rivalry with the British Army and enhance career prospects. India offered to raise five new regiments to garrison the Far East. Its offer was accepted by London, changing the face of imperial defence in Asia. There was no longer any need for independent Indian formations and the Hong Kong Regiment paraded for the last time on 10 October 1902. It sailed two weeks later for India to be disbanded, after which many of the men enlisted in other regiments.

Chapter 9

SOBER GUNNERS

The Hong Kong–Singapore Royal Artillery

THE HONG KONG–SINGAPORE ROYAL ARTILLERY is rarely mentioned in the military annals of the British Empire even though it was one of the largest colonial units. As a unit of Indian gunners serving in the Far East it tends to be forgotten because it does not fit neatly into the military heritage of either region. From subservient origins as labourers and support troops, the regiment evolved into an elite fighting formation. It garrisoned the two colonies that gave the regiment its name and manned outposts dotted across the Indian Ocean for more than a century. Its greatest moments came in the doomed defences of Hong Kong and Singapore. While those battles blemished the reputations of far more famous units, the HKSRA won praise for its dogged bravery, often fighting to the end against unbeatable odds.[1]

*

Little is known about the regiment's early years. Fragmentary records trace its origins to a formation called the China Gun Lascars that was raised in Madras in 1841 for service in the 1st China (Opium) War. Lascars were here essentially labourers for the artillery: one of the definitions of the term is tent-pitcher. Lascars set up camps, dug entrenchments and carried heavy loads, especially barrels of gunpowder and cannon balls, while Europeans manned the guns. The unit was disbanded in 1843 after returning to India.

A Royal Artillery company was based in Hong Kong for the first time in May 1842. Its ranks were rapidly decimated by disease and the climate like so many British units stationed in the Far East in those early years. It was suggested native auxiliaries be recruited to spare the British gunners the enervating labour of moving guns and ammunition. A plan to use Malay soldiers serving in British colonial units fell apart because Malays refused to do what they saw as coolie labour. Somebody recalled the pliant and willing lascars from Madras and recruiting was shifted to India. Recruiters had no difficulty in finding suitable enlistees. About 90 Madras recruits arrived in Hong Kong in 1847 and the new formation was approved by a royal warrant the following year.

Records for the next few decades are scanty and often confusing. Lascars appear to have been employed by the resident Royal Artillery garrison throughout the period as labourers and guards. The auxiliaries were commanded by a British officer seconded from the garrison's Royal Artillery unit, assisted by a British NCO and an interpreter. Lascars were seen as a success 'for reasons of economy and to enable the British artillery of the garrison to be reduced in number'.[2]

Contemporary accounts refer to auxiliaries being recruited from across Asia for service in Hong Kong. A report in the *South China Morning Post* in 1905, claiming to be based on interviews with veterans, said that from 1865 'men of all Asiatic nations' were recruited for the lascars.[3] By 1880 the unit was a foreign legion, it said, with Madras Christians, Madras Muslims, Portuguese Eurasians, Jews, Punjabi Muslims and Malay Muslims filling the ranks. Indeed recruiting in Madras appears to have ended in the late 1880s. The martial races concept had captured the heart and mind of the Indian Army and most southern Indian soldiers were universally looked down upon.

A War Office directive of 1881 approved the creation of a second lascar company for Hong Kong. Colonel Hall, the colony's Royal Artillery commander, suggested the new company be made up of Sikhs. Hong Kong had something of a mania for the burly warriors of northern India. Local officials favoured their use over all other Indians for military and police formations. A local Sikh police officer was given the task of returning to India to raise the new company, which arrived in the colony in July 1881. The Sikhs were designated as B Company, China Gun Lascars. The Sikhs were unhappy at being called lascars, but their request for the unit's name to be changed went unanswered.

Two double companies of lascars were formed in an 1891 reorganisation, each composed of a company of Sikhs and a company of Punjabi Muslims. This set the pattern for future recruiting and men from other races and religious groups were weeded out. The formation was renamed the Hong Kong Asiatic Artillery. That year also saw the formation in Singapore of a local artillery company with Indian troops. A detachment from the Hong Kong force formed its core with drafts from India filling the ranks. Its men were used mainly as labourers for Royal Artillery coastal batteries.

Singapore's military authorities, lacking experience of Indian soldiers, had little idea of how to handle the new unit and there was a near mutiny shortly after its formation. 'From the very time these soldiers arrived in Singapore they seem to have been treated in a most unfortunate and ill-advised manner,' reported the *Free Press*, a local newspaper.[4] Muslim soldiers were put under Sikh officers and a young British subaltern who had no experience of Indian troops '... and is ignorant of the meaning of a single word of their language'. When four men were sent to the guard house over a minor dispute, 45 of their comrades volunteered to go with them. Fearing a revolt, the authorities issued live ammunition to British gun crews. Experienced officers intervened and restored order. The company was put under seasoned commanders and the upset quickly forgotten.

By 1892 there were Asiatic Artillery Companies in Hong Kong, Singapore, Ceylon and Mauritius made up of Indian soldiers. A series of reorganisations followed over the next few years. In 1893 the Hong Kong unit became the Hong Kong Company, Royal Artillery, and the Singapore unit was renamed the Singapore Company, Royal Artillery. In 1898 the Hong Kong and Singapore companies were grouped as the Hong Kong – Singapore Battalion. Companies in Ceylon and Mauritius were combined the same year as the Ceylon Battalion Royal Artillery. Further changes in 1899 saw the two units renamed as the Hong Kong – Singapore Battalion Royal Garrison Artillery, and the Ceylon – Mauritius Battalion Royal Garrison Artillery. However, the Ceylon battalion was dissolved in 1907 and Muslims from the disbanded unit were transferred to the Hong Kong – Singapore Battalion to form a fifth company. Three companies of the Hong Kong – Singapore Battalion Royal Garrison Artillery (HKSRGA) were based in Hong Kong with single companies in Singapore and Mauritius. Companies rotated between the three bases. Imperial policing was part of the regiment's regular duties. A company on garrison duty in Mauritius helped suppress a riot in 1911. A final organisational change would come in 1924 when the unit was renamed the Hong Kong – Singapore Royal Artillery (HKSRA).

Moves in the 1880s to use lascars as part of gun crews for the first time marked the start of the force's transition from an auxiliary labour formation into a regular artillery unit. Lascars began to act as loaders while British gunners laid and fired the weapons. This change followed complaints by British officers that the Indians were being overworked with petty fatigues and their military potential wasted. Indians played a progressively greater role until they were allowed to take over servicing and firing weapons in the 1890s. Another key change was an 1889 decision to create a permanent European officer corps and no longer use Royal Artillery officers on temporary assignment. A small number of European NCOs continued to serve with the force in addition to Indian officers and NCOs. Thus, by the end of the 19th century, the unit had been transformed into one of a handful of native colonial artillery regiments dotted around the Empire.

There was strong competition in India to enlist in the force because of its new prestige – Indian Army troops had not been allowed to man heavy artillery since the Indian Mutiny. It also helped that rates of pay were higher than in the Indian Army. 'The men are the pick of the Punjab [the prime recruiting area in India]' the regiment boasted in its internal reports, with most men serving for 21 years. 'Men are very smart and any stigma which may formerly have been associated with service with Gun Lascars or Asiatic Artillery has entirely disappeared,' declared another regimental report.[5]

The regiment first saw action in 1899 when Chinese irregulars and villagers tried to block Britain's take-over of Hong Kong's New Territories. Its field guns supported infantry of the Hong Kong Regiment. Far more serious fighting came a few months later in the Boxer Rebellion. No. 2 Company, equipped with Maxim guns, and No. 4 Company, with mountain guns, helped to defend the besieged international settlement at Tientsin. Both companies took part in the subsequent march on Peking. The detachment's mountain guns supported Russian and French troops in the assault on the Chinese capital. Some HKSRGA men were used as stretcher bearers. British commanders commended the regiment for its fine performance and bravery.

An HKSRGA mountain gun battery formed with drafts from several companies was sent to the Middle East in 1915 during World War I. Volunteers clamoured for the 200 vacancies. It was assigned to the Imperial Service Camel Brigade and helped guard the Suez Canal before seeing action in 1916 against Senussi tribesmen in western Egypt. Later that year the battery was in action against Turkish troops at El Mazar and Bir el Mageibra. Mules were replaced by camels for desert fighting and the battery was assigned to the Desert Mounted Corps. It saw more fierce fighting during 1916 and 1917, in the battles around Gaza and in the fall of Jerusalem, before taking part in the final attacks of 1918. The HKSRGA company based in Singapore helped suppress a revolt by the Indian Army's 5th Light Infantry in 1915, as described previously.

The regiment returned to the placid routine of imperial garrison duty after the war. Hong Kong was its main base, with a company stationed in Singapore and occasional deployments elsewhere. Life was pleasant if often stultifying. The British in Asia did not want to believe that their ascendancy would be touched even as the international situation deteriorated in the 1930s. Delusion and complacency persisted right up to the eve of war. A history of the HKSRA's part in the battle for Hong Kong commented: 'The whole atmosphere of the colony gave the impression that no war with Japan was to be expected in the near future.'[6] An Indian HKSRA officer returning home in April 1941, was asked about the colony's readiness for war: he replied there was 'too much jollity' and few thoughts about fighting.

Britain belatedly began to bolster its Asian defences in the late 1930s. Singapore's naval base, the lynchpin of regional defence, was finally completed. The HKSRA was expanded to augment the defences of Hong Kong and Singapore. Asian troops were still much cheaper than British soldiers. In the early 1930s the regiment comprised a mountain battery and three heavy batteries in Hong Kong and a single heavy battery in Singapore. Plans were drawn up to transform the regiment from a mainly coastal defence unit into a much larger, more modern force with coastal, field artillery, anti-aircraft and searchlight batteries. Three new heavy batteries were formed in 1938, with one each allotted to Hong Kong, Singapore and Penang, but the biggest change came with the raising of anti-aircraft units for the first time. Some British officials had questioned the ability of Indian troops to handle anti-aircraft guns. It was claimed that experiments had shown most Asians lacked the mental and physical dexterity required to operate quick firing anti-aircraft guns and track aircraft. Chinese and Tamils 'were completely unsuitable to perform the duties of higher gun members and were graded as Category III personnel, only fit for unskilled labour', a post-war history of coastal defence commented.[7] Trials with HKSRA men were judged more successful and the regiment was made responsible for the anti-aircraft defence of most of Malaya and Singapore. 'Though it was at first considered doubtful whether the Indian gunners could handle the more complicated equipment required by such units, this experiment was justified by results,' commented a senior artillery officer.

While Indian gunners were to prove second to none in engaging Japanese aircraft and other targets, the HKSRA's expansion in the late 1930s was far too rapid. New batteries were created overnight after war broke out in Europe. Training that normally lasted years was telescoped into months and then weeks. Its strength in Singapore and the Straits Settlements went from a single heavy battery in the early 1930s to 14 existing or forming units, including nine anti-aircraft batteries and three coastal batteries, by 1941. Some units were created in the last days of peace in Asia. Some HKSRA batteries were diverted to the Middle East even as new units were being formed to face the Japanese despite warnings that they could not be spared. The 20th Heavy Anti-Aircraft Battery was formed in Malaya on 11 March 1941, while regimental records give 19 November 1941 as the formation date for the 25th Medium Battery in Hong Kong. Some units were never more than plans on paper and virtually nothing is known of them. A post-war HKSRA survey says of the 19th Light Anti-Aircraft Battery in Hong Kong that there was 'no record that this bty [battery] ever formed. Had not been formed up to late 1941'.[8] The same record says it could not find dates for the formation and other basic details for at least five batteries. Most records were destroyed in Hong Kong and Singapore along with the units and most of their personnel.

Up to the late 1930s recruiting had been confined to a few Sikh and Punjabi Muslim groups regarded as the cream of the Indian martial classes. Rapid expansion forced the regiment to turn to men of 'inferior quality and to extend their recruiting to Jats and other Hindu classes'. A War Office memo, defending the dilution of the regiment's martial gene pool, tried to excuse the recruiting of new castes and races as a purely 'temporary war time measure'.[9] Non-Indians were among those recruited. Eurasians were enlisted in Singapore and Chinese, recently excoriated by the regiment as suitable only for manual labour, were recruited as drivers in Hong Kong, and, finally, as gunners on the eve of the Japanese attack. Experience with Indian troops during the war would demolish the theory of martial races as men traditionally spurned as inferior performed as well as any others. Some British officers, nonetheless, clung to the belief even after the war that only a few, select Indians were suited to be artillerymen. The post-war history of coastal defence bemoaned the recruiting of even Punjabi Muslims and Sikhs of 'inferior quality' let alone other Indians such as Jats.

Hasty recruiting and poor training meant many new gunners lacked the most basic skills. Many men were still adjusting to the realities of the army and life in a foreign land when war started. New batteries that had existed for just a few months were not ready for active service and the whole regiment lacked knowledge or experience of modern warfare. Roughly 10 per cent of the HKSRA men in Hong Kong were new recruits with less than six months' army experience. All of the new men had been in the colony for just one month when the war began. Most batteries were under-strength despite the frantic efforts to expand. There were serious questions about the fitness of some of the veterans, particularly Indian officers and NCOs. Promotion was by seniority rather than ability and some of these men had been worn out or grown lazy after years of idle garrison life in the tiny colony. Many of the senior Indians, knowing only parade-ground routine, stumbled in combat, unable to deal with the reality of war. Before

1939 Indian officers and NCOs were not allowed to act without the supervision of British officers. Last-minute changes giving Indian officers greater responsibility overwhelmed men who had spent up to 30 years turning to British officers for permission to do even the smallest things. 'In those cases where the morale was not quite so high as it might have been, it could be attributed to the fact that most of the senior ranks had served for too long in Hong Kong,' an assessment concluded later.[10] Some young Indian NCOs proved far more effective, some taking command of guns at critical moments in the battle for Hong Kong.

Most of the regiment's newly-formed units in Singapore and Malaya obviously did not suffer from the inertia of peace-time soldiering, but their inexperience often meant they were just as unprepared to fight, as noted in an official post-war report:

> 'This tremendous enlargement meant not only a steep drop in the standard of the rank and file but also in the quality of the Indian officers and NCOs which together had the most disastrous results on morale, efficiency, discipline and loyalty of the unit. It was a short sighted policy which ruined this fine corps of Indian artillery by such reckless and improvident expansion,'[11]

Some of the British officers were equally unready for war. Too many of the British commanders had little experience or understanding of leading Indian soldiers. While Indian Army units prided themselves on British officers using the men's native tongues, standards had slipped in the HKSRA. Most officers 'had but a slight knowledge of Urdu', the regiment's working language, and had to rely on English-speaking Indian NCOs to issue orders and talk with the men. 'There is no doubt that a great deal more could have been done before the war to make officers proficient in the language,' a regimental report said. 'The standard aimed at was far too low to be of any practical use, and there was very little incentive for an officer to study the language at all.'[12] A shortage of British officers, despite their general shortcomings, compounded the regiment's lack of leadership when war came. Ten officers – five from Royal Artillery units and five civilians with artillery experience – were drafted into the Hong Kong batteries in the last days of peace. They could not speak Urdu, had no knowledge of Indian troops and no time to learn about their new commands.

There were occasional surreal moments as the HKSRA prepared for war. Sikh gunners in Hong Kong refused to be issued with steel helmets in 1940. The men insisted that for religious reasons they could only wear turbans. Most of the battery warned they would boycott a parade to be issued with helmets. All of the men were confined to barracks as Indian officers and NCOs urged them to relent. The spat was defused after a few hours – 'although some personnel of the battery wavered no actual disobedience occurred and all was quiet by evening'.[13] Five ringleaders were sent home to be discharged. Officers from a Sikh infantry battalion came to talk to the men and persuaded them that helmets did not besmirch their faith. On 16 February 1941 the entire unit drew helmets. It went unremarked that a front-line combat unit only received such basic equipment less than a year before the Japanese attack.

Hong Kong's Fall

A remarkable account of the HKSRA's role in the doomed defence of Hong Kong was written after the campaign by the regiment's surviving British officers. The war diary of the 1st Hong Kong Regiment of the HKSRA was compiled in the colony's Argyle prisoner of war camp between April and May 1944.[14] Over several weeks the officers pooled their recollections of the battle, discussed and analysed what had happened and compiled a narrative account of remarkable detail. A generally unflinching assessment, it underlined the regiment's weaknesses as well as lauding its brave fight in the face of overwhelming odds. It was intended to be both a post-mortem and a primer for rebuilding the force after the war. Written in a set of school exercise books, it was buried in the POW camp and recovered in October 1945.

The HKSRA in 1941 mirrored Hong Kong's mostly dilapidated defences when Japanese forces poured over the border. Its main force comprised two mountain batteries equipped with 3.7-inch and 4.5-inch howitzers and three medium batteries with four 6-inch howitzers apiece. Three anti-aircraft batteries, of which at least one existed essentially on paper, rounded out its field strength. HKSRA detachments also helped man the colony's larger coastal guns. Pre-war strategy postulated it would be 130 days before relief came if Hong Kong was attacked and ammunition for the garrison's artillery was rationed accordingly. This gave a laughable 80 shells a day for the 6-inch howitzers, 10 shells a day for 4.5-inch guns and 20 shells a day for the 3.7-inch guns. Japanese artillery and mortars fired scores of shells for each round the garrison managed to hurl back.

Shells were just one of many shortages noted by the surviving HKSRA officers. There were not enough army trucks to move the regiment's handful of guns. Civilian trucks and drivers pressed into service could not do the work of trained soldiers. Units did not have enough small arms to defend their gun positions. Each section had just one Thompson submachine gun and one Lewis gun. Only two or three men in each section could fire a Lewis gun and there was very little ammunition for the weapons. Almost nobody knew how to handle the newly-issued Thompsons. Pre-war rifle training consisted of an annual trip to a firing range, where the men fired their yearly allocation of 10 bullets.

On paper, the Hong Kong regiment of the HKSRA had a strength of 20 British officers, 20 British NCOs, 12 Indian officers and 970 Indian NCOs and other ranks. At least 100 men were on leave or away on courses when the war began. However, officers could still report on the eve of the battle that the batteries were mostly composed of veterans with 'high standards' in handling and firing guns.

HKSRA gun crews fought in the first battles on the mainland when the Japanese attacked Hong Kong. Guns from three batteries supported three British and Indian infantry battalions holding a straggling collection of half-finished positions called the Gin Drinkers' Line. The poor state of British training and inadequate equipment was soon apparent. Communications were erratic and British battery fire was rarely coordinated. Lack of transport made it difficult to move guns. Civilian drivers signed up at the last minute often abandoned their vehicles. Vital equipment and all of the pack mules for the mountain guns were left behind when the defenders withdrew to Hong Kong island on 12 December. Colonel J. C. L Yale, the HKSRA regimental commander, was taken to hospital, apparently overcome by strain. Major W. T. Temple took over command.

Surrounded on Hong Kong island, the gunners of the HKSRA, Royal Artillery and the Hong Kong Volunteer Defence Corps were soon overwhelmed by the much more numerous and experienced Japanese artillery. British batteries struggled to pinpoint enemy artillery positions on the mainland. Ammunition was rapidly depleted. Guns were ordered not to fire at night unless they received emergency calls for help from embattled infantry units. British artillery was unable to stop the Japanese landing on Hong Kong island on 18 December and the invaders soon began to overrun British gun positions in different parts of the island. Gun crews fired over open sights at attacking Japanese infantry in often vain attempts to save their weapons. Just seven men survived when a section of 4.5-inch howitzers was over-run on Tytam Hill. There was desperate hand-to-hand fighting as crews tried to defend weapons that could not be moved to safety. Some of the gunners did not have rifles by this point, using spades or whatever clubs they could find. A charge by gunners to take back a lost 3.7-inch gun on the first day was shattered by Japanese fire. Angry artillery officers complained that infantry units often failed to defend the gun positions. When there was time, guns were disabled by the crews, their sights buried or smashed, to prevent the Japanese turning them against the defenders. 'Our small number of guns was quite unable to silence the enemy batteries,' the HKSRA war diary records with cutting simplicity.[15]

HKSRA survivors who had lost their guns were formed into impromptu infantry units. A group of about 100 officers and men, only half of them armed, took part in a night attack with armoured cars of the Hong Kong Volunteer Defence Corps to clear the main road south of Wong Nei Chong Gap. What was supposed to be a surprise attack became a disaster as the entrenched Japanese heard the tramp of the approaching attackers and mowed them down. 'The men were untrained in the infantry tactics necessary for a night counter-attack, and ... their hobnailed boots gave away all attempts at surprise,' the unit's diary said.[16] Three officers and about 30 men were killed, and twice that number captured. Just 13 men returned to the British lines. Colonel Yale, the HKSRA commander who had discharged himself from hospital to take part in the attack, was among the dead.

Sections of the regiment, cut off and surrounded in different parts of the island, fought to the end or were butchered by the Japanese. A detachment under Jemadar Mohammad Ali was ordered to reinforce an anti-aircraft gun position at Wong Nei Chong Gap. It kept the guns firing until the last moment, engaging planes and other targets, while some of the men with machine guns and rifles held off Japanese infantry attacks on the post. Many of the gunners were captured after the position fell. The war diary laconically recorded the fate of Ali and other survivors: 'Unfortunately, he and the majority of his party that were captured alive, after being made to carry stores and ammunition for days, were either shot or bayoneted into trenches.'[17]

Singly or in pairs, the HKSRA guns were over-run or abandoned. Failing communications, confusing reports and the breakdown of command made the defending artillery's fire less and less effective. Lieutenant F. H. Fairclough, serving with the regiment's anti-aircraft guns, on Christmas Eve told 50 Chinese gunners, who had been recruited just before the war, to discard their uniforms and slip away. He and the remaining Indian gunners held off Japanese infantry attacks for three hours on Christmas Day, firing their 3.7-inch weapons over open sights. Eventually a Japanese bayonet charge overwhelmed the position. Fairclough and most of the other defenders were shot or bayoneted in hand-to-hand fighting. Regaining consciousness, he found himself 'looking up straight into the eyes of a Jap soldier who, realising that I was still alive, took careful aim and shot me again'. Fairclough survived and eventually escaped to India after being briefly held as a POW in Hong Kong.[18]

HKSRA units sustained heavy losses in the battle: 11 officers were killed or missing with 146 NCOs and other ranks killed, 45 missing and 62 wounded. Virtually all of the survivors, 710 men, were taken prisoner. A few Indian gunners slipped away and reached British officials in China after long and dangerous treks across the mainland.

Malaya: Idyll and Panic

If it was tacitly accepted that Hong Kong would not hold out against a major attack, Singapore was seen as an invincible bastion. The fall of the 'Gibraltar of the East' was inconceivable. Batteries of the HKSRA played a major role in the battle for Singapore and Malaya and formed the backbone of the anti-aircraft defences. Its performance demolished any doubts that lingered from ignoble pre-war debates about whether Indians could handle anti-aircraft guns or anything else.

The battalions of the HKSRA in Singapore and Malaya had less experience than the regiment's Hong Kong contingents. Many men had been in the army for just a few months. Most batteries were newly formed with officers and men still learning basic skills. There had been little time to learn higher skills such as cooperation with other batteries and units. Gun crews rarely practised with live shells because munitions were in short supply. Communications were poor with the primitive radios rarely working in the tropical conditions. All too often there was no effective way to alert gunners of approaching air raids.

The high performance of the Japanese planes and pilots stunned the defenders. British troops had been fed the old pre-war colonial stories ridiculing the Japanese as comical throwbacks who could not fly modern planes. HKSRA gunners struggled to engage Japanese aircraft that easily exceeded the speed and manoeuvrability of the outmoded British planes they were familiar with. British airfields were shattered by incessant Japanese attacks that smothered the anti-aircraft defences.

Most of the HKSRA's rapid pre-war growth was in Singapore and Malaya. It ballooned from a single heavy battery in Singapore in 1934 to three regiments with 14 batteries by 1941. Most of the growth was packed into the four years before the Japanese attack. The first HKSRA anti-aircraft battery in the colony was only formed in October 1937. Nine anti-aircraft batteries existed by late 1941, of which six were claimed to be fully operational. Other HKSRA units included coast defence batteries at Singapore and Penang. Several anti-aircraft batteries were still being assembled, including the 20th Heavy Anti-Aircraft Battery formed on 11 March 1941. Regiments and higher formations to provide command and control for the batteries were formed even later with the 3rd Light Anti-Aircraft Regiment becoming operational on 1 September 1941. Plans for additional regiments and batteries were swept away by the Japanese deluge.

Expansion forced the regiment to speed up recruiting dramatically in India. Recruiting had traditionally been confined to a few Sikh and Punjabi Muslim groups identified by the regiment as the finest sources of military manhood. Recruiting had been an unhurried, almost ceremonial event that took place once a year before the war. A party of officers and NCOs leisurely toured the Jhelum area in the Punjab to hand-pick a few recruits. Much of the recruiting tour consisted of social events and gatherings that were a hallowed regimental tradition. Recruits routinely came from families that had provided men to the regiment for decades. Aspiring youngsters were inspected as recruiters mingled with veterans and families with long ties to the regiment.

That all changed with the forced expansion of the regiment. Recruiting soared from a few dozen men once a year to 50 men a month. While the enlarged intake was small by the standards of the looming war, it swamped a regiment accustomed to handling a few men at a time in a pattern honed over decades. Recruiting areas were expanded and a depot opened at Ambala in northern India to handle the influx.

Work began in 1938 on a massive new cantonment at Nee Soon on Singapore island to house the multiplying batteries and training facilities. It comprised barracks, family accommodation for British and Indian personnel, sports fields and temples. It was largely completed when work was suspended in 1939. Like other units in the last years of peace, the regiment seemed at times preoccupied with social and sporting amenities rather than what was necessary for war. 'The officers' mess was probably the largest that has been built as a permanent establishment outside Great Britain. Its dining capacity was 90,' boasted a regimental history.[19]

British military thinking stipulated that recruits had to be trained and led by men from the same religion and caste. Jats and other Hindus were recruited for the first time in addition to the regiment's traditional intakes of Sikhs and Punjabi Muslims. There was a desperate scurry to find Hindu NCOs and officers to oversee the new class of recruits. Candidates were snapped up from Indian Army units, the Burma Police and anywhere else they could be found. It was not surprising that some officers, new and old, were not up to the changing demands on the regiment. 'Not all these transferees were suitable, and a few had to be discharged or returned,' a regimental report concluded. Some of the regiment's veteran Indian officers, including many with 20 years or more of service, were overwhelmed by the changes. 'A number of officers were found unsuitable for modern requirements and were discharged, a beneficial purge,' the report added.[20]

Pre-war recruits received 14 weeks of basic military training, when they were taught to march and use small arms, followed by up to 12 weeks of introductory artillery drill. It normally took at least a year to ready a recruit for basic duties in an anti-aircraft battery. Advanced training took place when men were assigned to batteries. Basic training was cut 'drastically' as the threat of war grew. The HKSRA faced a growing shortage of experienced officers and NCOs to train the swelling stream of recruits. A decision in late 1939 to form a new battery for Aden forced the regiment to take experienced gunners from Singapore units. Subsequent demands for reinforcements for the Middle East cost the regiment more trained men. Further men were lost to HKSRA recruiting efforts in India and to provide trainers for new Indian Army artillery units. Experienced NCOs and gunners were taken from the field for the new training depot at Singapore. Soon NCOs and men halfway through training courses were being pulled out to train even rawer recruits.

New methods, new technology and constant changes continually set back training and preparation for war. The last-minute arrival of radar in Malaya forced the regiment to transfer experienced gunners to operate the sets. Light anti-aircraft batteries assigned to static defence in Singapore were converted to mobile units in the middle of 1941 for operations in northern Malaya. It was a major change with gunners having to learn to drive and master the skills of handling mobile guns in a few months. One battery was converted to a mobile role after the Japanese attack and hurled into the battle without training.

Civilians and British Army personnel were recruited to make up the shortage of British officers. Few of them had any experience of commanding Indian troops. They struggled to learn Urdu, the regiment's working language. Hasty classes purportedly gave the new arrivals 'a reasonable smattering', but it was hardly enough to command troops in battle. Officers who joined in the last days of peace had little time to learn anything before being sent into the field. Belated attempts to teach English to the Indian rank-and-file had limited success. Men who made enough progress were awarded badges consisting of a large 'E' to denote English proficiency and presumably advertise their presence to dumbstruck officers looking for help. While some Indian officers and NCOs spoke English well, the regiment later admitted, 'the language problem was always a difficult one'.

Singapore's war plans called for close-quarter anti-aircraft defence of the naval base and the military airfields. The anti-aircraft defences consisted mostly of outmoded 3-inch guns of little use against modern aircraft. Some HKSRA light batteries were armed initially with First World War-era Lewis guns of even less use. New batteries were being formed more quickly than guns could be found to arm them. Some of the new units had to borrow anti-aircraft guns from established batteries to train recruits while they waited for weapons. Guns temporarily went missing as they were informally handed around between units for training. One set of guns was tracked down after being passed around between five separate batteries. A limited quantity of modern Bofors guns finally arrived in 1940 and some modern 3.7-inch anti-aircraft guns reached the colony on the eve of the Japanese attack. There were never enough modern guns for all the imperial anti-aircraft units and some old HKSRA 3-inch guns were passed on to the Indian Army's 1st Anti-Aircraft Regiment, which reached Malaya in May 1941.

A false alarm in early 1938 gave an ominous insight into the inadequacies of Singapore's defences. An alert was issued after British intelligence lost track of the main Japanese fleet. Fearing Japan might be about to attack, British naval and air reinforcements were rushed to Singapore. An HKSRA officer was summoned to the island's military headquarters at Fort Canning. He was brusquely asked why he had not reported for duty as the island's Air Defence Commander. The startled man said he had never been given such a post. 'I here and now appoint you Air Defence Commander,' the head of Singapore's artillery barked. Asking for a staff to carry out his new duties, the unnamed HKSRA officer was told to '****ing find his own'.[21]

Summoning men from his regiment, the new anti-aircraft chief swiftly discovered that his command was little more than a footnote in the island's exceedingly vague defence plans. Nothing had been done to set up an anti-aircraft defence command system. There was no way to communicate with the anti-aircraft batteries from central headquarters at Fort Canning. No system had been planned to deal with air raid warnings. A portable telephone exchange with 12 lines was set up on a veranda at the head-quarters. By the end of the three-day flap signallers had managed to establish contact with most of the gun positions.

Getting information about possible Japanese movements was hindered by petty inter-service rivalry. RAF officers, handling reports on Japanese movements and manning a plotting table, either declined to share intelligence or insisted on sending handwritten messages. Each message had to be recorded in a register in the RAF room before being carried to the artillery staff on the nearby veranda, where it had to be signed for and a receipt sent back so a record could be kept. It sometimes took hours for messages to journey the few yards from the RAF room to the veranda. Some messages arrived long after their contents had turned out to be untrue or had been forgotten. Things did not improve when the artillery's switchboard was moved to the corridor outside the RAF room with artillery runners waiting inside the room to take messages. Annoyed RAF officers eventually were forced to accept the switchboard in the plotting room and to let an artillery officer stand with them at the plotting table.[22]

The 1938 incident at least led to the creation of an integrated warning and control system for the island's anti-aircraft defences by the time war came. An inter-services conference in October 1941 called for a major expansion of the anti-aircraft defences. Plans included 12 guns manned by the HKSRA to bolster Penang's defences. Work on building positions began with meticulous plans specifying completion by 30 January 1942. Plans also called for more British and Indian Army anti-aircraft reinforcements. HKSRA units were designated to support a planned British strike into southern Siam to forestall any Japanese landings in northern Malaya.

All HKSRA units were in their assigned positions when Japanese forces attacked on 8 December 1941. Many officers and men were still struggling to master their roles, new guns and equipment were being broken in, and the training depot at Changi was full of newly arrived recruits. Nonetheless, there were enough trained and partly trained men to man the guns. Despite shortages of everything from radios to experienced men, the regiment reported it was ready for war.

The Doomed Campaign

HKSRA units were among the first British troops to engage the Japanese forces that invaded Malaya. Around 4 a.m. on 8 December word reached the gun control room at Fort Canning that war had broken out. Moments later RAF fighter control detected two formations of aircraft approaching the colony. Anti-aircraft radar picked up the planes minutes later and it was assumed they were Japanese bombers. Some of the aircraft were caught by searchlights as they crossed over the island. Anti-aircraft batteries opened up with a furious barrage, and failed to hit anything. 'Shooting was for the most part indifferent, probably due to intense excitement on the part of the young Indian gunners,' a regimental report said.[23] A second formation of planes was spotted and a 4.5-inch gun reported hitting one aircraft. Radar trackers said the plane plunged into the sea.

Dawn brought a wave of fierce Japanese air attacks on the string of British airfields defending northern Malaya. Gunners of the 9th Battery of the 1st HKSRA Regiment at Khota Bahru and Alor Star struggled to protect the landing strips gouged out of the jungle. Khota Bahru was attacked repeatedly by Japanese bombers and fighters covering infantry landings on the nearby beaches. Anti-aircraft gunners tried to protect the aged British bombers as they took off to attack Japanese troopships disgorging men and equipment. Again the young gunners struggled to control their excitement and settle down to the calm, meticulous work needed to target and bring down attacking planes. Japanese planes frequently bombed from high altitudes and the guns failed to make any hits. A lull around midday allowed the airfield's defenders to clear some of the damage and reorganise. Japanese planes resumed the onslaught with low-level attacks, repeatedly singling out the anti-aircraft positions. Three HKSRA gunners were killed and eight others were wounded, but the crews had recovered from the first shock of combat and downed two aircraft. Their old 3-inch guns frequently malfunctioned and a solitary British fitter went from position to position during the attacks to clear jammed weapons.

With most British aircraft lost or out of action, the RAF began to abandon the airfield around 5 p.m. The HKSRA unit did not receive orders to withdraw and went on fighting until just before midnight. Lieutenant J. C. Close, the HKSRA commander, suddenly realised that infantry guarding the airfield had left without warning. Japanese troops were closing in on the HKSRA positions. Close ordered his men to leave with whatever stores they could carry. He and a small party stayed behind to destroy the guns. Close, who was captured by the Japanese, received a Military Cross for his leadership. Most of the battery reached the railway line at Kuala Krai where they briefly took over two 3-inch naval guns. Forced to abandon the weapons and fall back with the retreating infantry, the gunners found four more 3-inch guns and manned those until British forces abandoned the area. It would not be the last time in the campaign that HKSRA detachments would complain of being left virtually alone to defend airfields when RAF and Army troops left without warning.

Things were no better at the Alor Star air base where the rest of 9th Battery was deployed. A formation of 27 Japanese planes bombed the strip in mid-morning, destroying several aircraft on the ground and a supply dump containing 300,000 gallons of petrol. An HSKRA radar set, one of a handful in northern Malaya, was destroyed. There was now no way to warn of Japanese attacks before they reached the airfield and it was abandoned on 10 December. Its HKSRA battery was ordered to move south to defend the air base at Butterworth, but that too would be abandoned before the gunners could reach it.

A dismal pattern of retreat, chaos and hopeless rearguard actions followed as British forces were pushed 500 miles back to Singapore. The 9th Battery section from Alor Star was sent to defend six different places during the retreat. Each time it was compelled to abandon positions soon after reaching them. Its guns were not designed for frequent movement, their solid rubber tires soon wore out, and there were very few spares. Only a fraction of the tractors and trucks needed to move a mobile battery were available. Frequent, heavy rain made movement on dirt roads impossible. The skill of the gunners increased, nonetheless, and the battery inflicted a rising toll on the attacking Japanese planes.

An epic rescue was mounted to save the guns of the HSKRA's 13th Battery from being captured. It was at Sungei Patani when British defences in the region began pulling back. Battery commander Major P. E. White had just a single gun tractor that could extricate the guns down the dirt track linking their emplacements. Japanese forces were closing in and the solitary tractor could not move all of the guns. Malaya Command had only three other gun tractors, including a makeshift one assembled from other vehicles, and they were in Singapore. It was decided the guns had to be rescued and all three tractors were sent north. Three drivers were assigned to each tractor so they could be driven day and night to beat the Japanese to Sungei Patani. It took 36 hours of non-stop driving for the tractors to reach the guns. Half of the guns were saved while breech fittings were removed to make the others inoperable. Moving south, the battery was ordered to defend Butterworth airfield and had one gun ready for action by 15 December but RAF ground crews abandoned the base without warning the same day, leaving behind a great deal of equipment. Discarding two more guns, because there was not enough time to move them from their fixed emplacements, the battery headed south for the air base at Ipoh. White and some men returned to Butterworth and rescued the two abandoned guns as the Japanese closed in. With the battery reunited at Ipoh, it soon became clear the area could not be held. Resuming the retreat, the remnants of the battery reached Singapore and were in action on the island by 21 December.

Other HSKRA batteries had similar experiences as British defences crumbled. The 14th Battery was rushed north from Singapore to defend the air base at Ipoh against daily air raids, and shot down five Japanese planes with five more claimed. A gun put out of action by a tide of burning petrol that spilled from a bombed supply depot was repaired and returned to service. Part of the battery pulled out on 24 December. Rioting and looting broke out at Ipoh on Christmas Day and an HKSRA sentry was knifed by a looter. What remained of the battery left Ipoh on 27 December. Several of the trucks were handled by Indian officers who had never before driven a vehicle. British personnel turned on the engines and engaged gears before handing over the steering wheels to the officers. All of them reached Kuala Lumpur.

Guns of 16th Battery were assigned to cover the retreating III Indian Corps. Most of the battery's guns were deployed to protect bridges and key crossroads on routes clogged with retreating British columns. Japanese aircraft began to single out the guns and several were damaged. B Troop was caught up in one of the most critical moments of the Malayan campaign. Japanese tanks sliced through retreating British units and reached a vital bridge over the Slim River that was defended by HKSRA guns. The first word of the breakthrough came when a speeding British truck roared over the bridge with the driver yelling that Japanese tanks were right behind. The gunners and other troops defending the bridge had no idea the enemy was so close. Two Bofors guns were swung around to cover the bridge, their sights adjusted to 'near' – the shortest range. The guns were not designed to engage armoured targets and there was not a single anti-tank shell in Malaya suitable for anti-aircraft guns. Three Japanese tanks charged on to the bridge as the guns fired at them. Several shells hit the tanks only to explode harmlessly on their armour plating. Two tanks roared across the bridge while the third engaged the anti-aircraft guns and drove off the crews. Five more Japanese tanks appeared and the British defenders fled. B Troop lost all of its guns and stores and most of its vehicles. Almost half of the troop was missing. Dazed and exhausted, three officers and 35 men reached the battery's A Troop after trekking through the jungle. The capture of the bridge cut off a major British escape route.

British commanders tried to form a unified anti-aircraft command half way through the campaign for Malaya. It was the usual story of too little too late. Lieutenant-Colonel H. V. Allpress, commander of 2nd HKSRA Regiment, was named commander of anti-aircraft defences for Malaya. He was based at Kuala Lumpur with a small staff. There were no telephone links to some units and Allpress's deputy had to drive miles to deliver messages to them. Intelligence about impending air raids and the position of Japanese forces was scanty. Allpress's first task was to pull together air defences for virtually unprotected Kuala Lumpur and the nearby airfield. Guns from three batteries were deployed at the airfield. Alternate positions were constructed so guns could be moved between raids, defeating attempts by Japanese pilots to plan attacks that evaded the defending guns. The defenders shot down five Japanese planes and claimed seven probable kills. After several days the Japanese planes started bombing the airfield from high levels, reducing their effectiveness. But the handful of guns in Kuala Lumpur could not defend an entire city as wave after wave of Japanese aircraft attacked. Kuala Lumpur was abandoned as Japanese forces neared, the anti-aircraft batteries pulling back to new positions. Some of Kuala Lumpur's guns were sent to Port Swettenham on the west coast to cover Royal Navy light boats operating from the harbour. A section of 14th Battery suffered losses from repeated low-level Japanese air attacks.

The Malayan campaign was a blur of confusion, incompetence and exhaustion for the British forces. Attempts to stop the Japanese were abandoned time and again as the enemy outpaced or flanked the defenders. Lack of intelligence, demoralising rumours and bursts of panic bedevilled the retreating British. Japanese forces dominated the air battle from the start. Often there was only a handful of anti-aircraft guns to defend airfields, infantry units and vital communications links. The ground defences were too weak to halt incessant air attacks as the retreat went inexorably on. Many of the HKSRA's guns were worn out in the fighting and the crews were exhausted. During the long withdrawal down the Malayan peninsula the HKSRA shot down 51 planes and claimed another 30 probable kills. They accounted for most of the 72 planes reported shot down by British forces during the campaign. Fourteen of the regiment's guns had been destroyed or lost and dozens of its men killed, wounded or posted as missing by the time Malaya was abandoned.

A high priority was placed on saving as many anti-aircraft guns as possible for the final defence as the battered British and imperial forces pulled back to Singapore. Mobile anti-aircraft batteries covered the infantry units trudging down the two main roads to the Johore causeway linking the mainland to Singapore. A major Japanese air attack was anticipated as British forces crossed the causeway: 90 guns were deployed to defend the highly vulnerable bridge. In a rare stroke of luck for the defenders, the Japanese never attacked and the British rearguard cleared the causeway on 31 January.

HKSRA batteries had been in action on Singapore island since the start of the war. Some units did not have a full complement of guns and emplacements were still being built when the first Japanese bombs hit the city. A few guns intended for Hong Kong and Burma were found in the island's warehouses and turned over to the garrison. Japanese planes regularly released their bombs at 20,000 feet, beyond the range of most of the island's anti-aircraft guns. Japanese squadrons of up to 27 planes attacked in formations spread out over a mile that further frustrated efforts to shoot them down. Fire from the 3-inch guns that made up most of the air defences was admitted to be 'practically useless'. While the raids damaged the naval dockyard, airfields and other key military targets, bombs also killed and wounded hundreds of civilians. Gun crews were demoralised after only shooting down a few planes. Efforts were made to boost confidence by spreading reports that RAF radio interception had picked up conversations between Japanese pilots complaining of serious damage and losses after raids.

It is very difficult to establish how many Japanese planes were shot down by the British defences. Japanese records of losses are far lower than the figures claimed by the defenders. Just as British success against the Luftwaffe was overstated during the Battle of Britain, it seems certain, and equally understandable, that the beleaguered garrisons of Malaya and Singapore made inflated claims. One small victory came during a daylight raid when an anti-aircraft shell scored a direct hit on one plane and detonated its bomb load. A huge explosion consumed the plane and destroyed aircraft flying on either side. Dozens of onlookers reported seeing the wreckage of the three planes plummeting to the ground. Despite such occasional successes, the number and intensity of raids increased as the Japanese put captured British airfields in Malaya into service. Bombers that had to fly hundreds of miles from Saigon and other distant bases at the start of the campaign could now reach Singapore in an hour or two.

The Final Defence

All of the surviving HKSRA guns were deployed to face the coming invasion of Singapore island. The HKSRA had few illusions about what kind of battle it would soon be fighting. Gun positions were cleared for all-round ground defence. Extra rifles and light machine guns were issued to defend positions against infantry attacks. Orders were given that guns had to be defended against ground attack for as long as possible. Crews were told they could only withdraw if the covering infantry had pulled back, and only after wrecking the guns. Crews who lost their guns were ordered to attach themselves to infantry units and continue fighting.

Japanese troops began landing on the night of 8–9 February. HKSRA and other anti-aircraft units suffered heavy losses as their positions were singled out by Japanese aircraft and artillery. 1st HSKRA Regiment crews holding the Dairy position reported hearing Japanese infantry in their rear shortly after the first landings. There was no sign of the British infantry who had been positioned nearby so the gunners destroyed their guns and retreated. A growing toll of lost guns followed over the next few days as they were destroyed by Japanese fire or abandoned as enemy troops surged through the defences. A troop of 9th Battery lost all of its guns to Japanese mortar fire. Often there were was no transport to move guns as the Japanese over-ran the defences and they were abandoned. 20th Battery was forced to destroy its guns and retreat when its commander discovered the nearby headquarters of the 22nd Australian Infantry Brigade had withdrawn without warning the gunners. Surviving batteries were pushed back to Singapore City but gun crews still tried to give some defence against Japanese air attacks on the city.

A handful of HKSRA guns were kept in action until British forces capitulated and an *ad hoc* infantry battalion was created on 12 February with almost 500 British and Indian gunners from 2nd HKSRA Regiment. It suffered heavy losses with 17 killed, 49 wounded and 43 missing presumed killed while fighting as infantry. Some of the men sent to the force did not have rifles and were returned to the HKSRA depot.

It is not known how many HKSRA personnel were captured in Hong Kong and Singapore, but the figure probably numbered up to 5,000. Captivity was as difficult for the survivors as the lost battles. Indian officers and gunners were pressured to join the pro-Japanese Indian National Army (INA). Some men joined the INA willingly, some only after being threatened or tortured. Some turncoats helped guard the prisoner of war camps in Hong Kong. The Hong Kong HKSRA war diary sombrely records the suffering of Indian prisoners who did not want to serve the Japanese:

> '... to break the loyalty of these prisoners ... [the Japanese] used every conceivable means to accomplish this; terrorism; torture, harsh treatment, good treatment (or more usually the promise of it) spying and supervision by renegade prisoners within the camp, and continuous propaganda'.[24]

Some gunners refused to renounce their allegiance despite repeated mistreatment. 'Gunner Mohammad Afsar was suspended by his ankles until senseless,' the war diary states. He and other prisoners had refused to obey Japanese orders and were beaten and starved. A group of about 100

HKSRA men were sent to Canton as labourers, where they were beaten after refusing to carry rifles and serve under Japanese commanders. British commanders in Hong Kong advised Indian soldiers to cooperate with the Japanese to avoid cruel treatment. A few still refused to submit and some HKSRA men were reportedly killed by the Japanese and INA renegades. There is no hint of bitterness in the diary towards men who joined the INA. 'Hunger was their [the Japanese] most potent weapon.'

What survived of the regiment fought on in other theatres. One battery was retained in India and sent men to fill out the HKSRA force in Aden. Two batteries served elsewhere in the Middle East, one in the Suez Canal Zone and the second at Mersa Matruh. These three survivors, the 15th, 23th and 24th Heavy Anti-Aircraft Batteries, were reorganised as 1st Heavy Anti-Aircraft Regiment, HKSRA, in Egypt on 28 February 1945.

A small HKSRA detachment on Christmas Island in the Indian Ocean left a less glorious footnote in the regiment's history. A single British officer, an Indian officer, three British NCOs and 27 Indian NCOs and other ranks with a single 6-inch gun made up the island's tiny garrison along with a few police. A squadron of Japanese warships bombarded the island on 4 March 1942. Concluding resistance was futile, the HKSRA commander, Captain L. W. T. Williams, ordered the gun dismantled, collected his unit's small arms and ran up a white flag. For unknown reasons, the Japanese ships continued to shell the island and made no effort to land before sailing away. Williams ordered the white flag taken down on 9 March and the gun reassembled. Some of the gunners, no longer willing to serve the British, broke into the armoury the next day, seized weapons and shot the British soldiers in their beds. Other Indian gunners protested and refused to side with the mutineers. Japanese forces finally landed on the island on 31 March. Japanese officers praised the mutineers for resisting British imperialism, but still made them prisoners of war along with the men who had not taken part in the killings.

Details of the revolt were not discovered until Allied forces retook the island after the war. The mutineers and the loyal gunners had been removed by the Japanese during the war. A hunt eventually tracked down some of the mutineers. Seven were charged with mutiny and tried in Singapore in December 1946. Defence lawyers claimed the men were innocent because Williams, by surrendering, had forfeited his claim to military authority. Rejecting the argument, the court found six of the men guilty and five were sentenced to hang. An appeal against the sentences came from the new government of Pakistan, which regarded the men as its citizens. Britain did not want to antagonise the new Karachi government. After a review, the punishments were reduced to life sentences of penal servitude, and the convicted men were jailed in Singapore. All of the men were returned to Pakistan in the mid-1950s following appeals for clemency and no more was heard of them.[25]

Peace and the rush to end British rule of the Indian subcontinent raised questions about the HKSRA's future. It was thought initially that the unit would be dissolved along with Britain's other Indian military formations. Re-forming the regiment from the survivors did not seem feasible. Some 3,000 Indian NCOs and soldiers who returned from Japanese POW camps were shattered by years of captivity. 'Few were in a physical condition for further service,' a regimental assessment said. Men who defected to the INA could not be trusted again to serve in the British forces. The regiment was not represented in the victory march in London because War Office officials assumed it would be disbanded. It was a shameful snub to men who had fought loyally for Britain in one of the most desperate moments of the war. Equally it insulted the memory of all the HKSRA men who had served Britain for decades in war and peace.

A few months later there were second thoughts on disbanding the regiment. It was clear that Britain would continue to rule Singapore, Hong Kong and other key Far East colonies. Concerns about the cost of garrisoning colonies in the economic austerity of the post-war period led to proposals to keep the HKSRA alive. Indian soldiers were still far cheaper than British troops. 'The employment of HKSRA helped us to economize in British manpower requirements for Hong Kong, Singapore, Penang and Aden garrisons,' an anonymous bureaucrat noted in a memo. A bureaucratic debate occupied the next few months, with memos passing between London and New Delhi. For a time it seemed that the regiment would be saved. Just as suddenly as it was first suggested, the idea was dropped when a bureaucrat pointed out what should have been clear from the start: India and Pakistan were unlikely to countenance the recruiting of their citizens to uphold British imperialism in Asia. And with that rueful comment a proud regiment passed into history.

Chapter 10

GHOST FORMATIONS

The Hong Kong Chinese Regiment
And Other Local Units

CHINESE WERE SHUNNED AS SOLDIERS in Hong Kong for many decades. It was taken for granted that the colony could never be absolutely sure of the loyalty of such men. For many years the only exception was The Hong Kong Submarine Miners. Little is known about this force raised in 1891. Its role was to handle the mines that formed part of the port defences. Faded photographs show its men clad in blue tunics with conical Chinese straw hats. A newspaper claimed the men were the only unit in the British forces to wear silk uniforms.[1] Men from the force were sometimes included in the Hong Kong detachments sent to London for coronation parades and other grand imperial events. It ceased to exist as a separate force in 1905 when it merged with the colony's Royal Engineer detachment. Chinese soon proved their worth as sappers and more were recruited. 40th Fortress Company RE had 87 Chinese other ranks and 38 British other ranks in the mid-1920s. British commanders, while valuing the Chinese, worried about their loyalty if there was conflict with China. 'It is however extremely doubtful whether they could be relied upon in case of emergency for frontier defence work,' a 1926 RE report said during one of the regular bouts of border tension with Chinese forces. Chinese sappers formed one of four RE sections in the colony in 1941.[2]

The threat of war with Japan in the 1930s finally overcame the opposition to Chinese troops. Chinese were recruited for the local Royal Artillery batteries, starting in 1937, to supplement the British gunners. An initial batch of 23 men was given a 14-week training course. Further batches of recruits followed over the next few years and Chinese became NCOs for the first time in mid-1938. Most of the Chinese recruits initially were assigned to 8th Coastal Regiment. A large batch of 150 men was signed up in 1941 for the 5th Anti-Aircraft Regiment. The Chinese gunners fought through the battle for Hong Kong and suffered casualties.[3]

Chinese were also employed over the years by logistical formations that supplied regular British Army units. The Hong Kong Mule Corps, which provided pack animals for the garrison's artillery and supply units, was an Indian unit with 3 British officers and 250 Indian NCOs and other ranks in 1941. Chinese recruits were reluctantly taken into the Hong Kong Volunteer Defence Corps in growing numbers in the late 1930s as has been seen. A scratch unit, the Hong Kong Engineering Corps, was also formed after the start of the Asian war with some 200 men under the direction of the HKVDC's engineers. It built installations for a few days, and seems to have been little more than an improvised labour force.

A Chinese machine-gun regiment was formed in the final weeks of peace in one of the many frantic, often futile attempts to bolster the defences. Its raw Chinese recruits had almost no chance in the coming battle: in its brief history it suffered one of the highest casualty rates of any unit that ever served in Britain's colonial forces. A typed three-page report is virtually all that survives of a unit that existed for seven weeks.[4]

The Hong Kong Chinese Regiment (HKCR) was formed on 3 November 1941. It is not clear who sanctioned the force, although it appears on the Hong Kong garrison's final order of battle three days before the Japanese attack as 'one Chinese M. G. [machine gun] Battalion being formed'.[5] Captain R. D. Scriven, an officer of the Indian Medical Service, who wrote the skimpy report, helped picked men for a 'training cadre for a future machine gun regiment'. It was made up of 6 Chinese NCOs and 46 Chinese other ranks. Its two British officers were seconded from other units: Major Mayer of the Middlesex Regiment and 2nd Lieutenant Pigott of the HKVDC. Three NCOs came from regular British regiments: Sergeant-Major Riches and Colour Sergeant Bond of the Middlesex Regiment and Sergeant Chu Chan Mum of the Royal Engineers.

Somehow the men learned to use their weapons and a few other military basics in the month between enlisting and the Japanese invasion. The unit suffered its first casualty when Japanese planes dive-bombed its barracks on the first day of war. This was followed by several days guarding the Kowloon Brigade HQ during which Riches and a party of men were sent to round up Indian soldiers who had fled the front line and abandoned their weapons. British officers praised the little force's calmness when it retreated under Japanese fire to Kowloon City on 12 December and was evacuated with other troops to Hong Kong island. Four men were sent to act as interpreters for other units and the rest of the HKCR guarded a ration dump at Deep Water Bay. It was then deployed at Wong Nei Chong Gap after Japanese forces landed on the island.

On 19 December the unit was guarding an ordnance depot when Japanese troops were seen scaling a nearby hill. Fire from the HKCR inflicted several casualties before an officer ordered a halt because he thought the men climbing the hill were Canadians. The lag allowed the Japanese to get to the top of the height, unfurl a large flag and start firing down on the Chinese. Fighting followed for most of the day with the Chinese pinned down in a house and suffering a steady stream of casualties.

Orders came the next day for the unit to support an attack by a Canadian infantry company. Mayer left eight men under Corporal Tong Po Hing to hold the position. The rest of the unit then followed the advancing Canadians. Mayer went forward to consult with the Canadian commander when the combined unit paused at a road junction. Japanese troops suddenly opened fire with rifles, machine guns and grenades, trapping the Chinese. Mayer survived, but nearly all of the Chinese 'were wiped out'.[6] Corporal Tong's little group and some stragglers from other units fought all through the next day.

Eventually an HKVDC captain told the Chinese to change into civilian clothing and slip away. One man died of wounds before the survivors reached British lines. There they were told to hide 'until further developments'.[7] At least three of the men later reached a British unit in China after a long, dangerous trek and volunteered for further service. Scriven, who interviewed Mayer and the few other survivors for his report, said 31 of the original 57 members were killed or wounded – a 54 per cent casualty rate in three weeks. Scriven ended his report with the hope that if the regiment was re-formed it would be awarded 'Hong Kong 1941' as a battle honour.

Chapter 11

TO OUR RESPECTIVE NATIONS

The Shanghai Volunteer Corps

A SMALL BAND OF ARMED EUROPEAN and American civilians gathered on a patch of waste ground on the edge of Shanghai's foreign settlement on a spring day in 1854. Unruly soldiers from a Chinese army camped outside the city had assaulted several residents of the city's tiny Western outpost. A diplomatic note had been sent by the British and U.S. consuls ordering the Chinese general to move his force away from the Western enclave. The consuls, having brusquely given the Chinese a few hours to withdraw, decided a show of force was needed to awe the insolent Orientals. The men of Shanghai's newly-formed civilian defence force were summoned from their offices and homes.

The Battle of Muddy Flat

The Shanghai Local Volunteers had been formed less than a year earlier. It had just a few dozen men, mostly British and American merchants and clerks who spent their days checking inventories and compiling accounts. Most Volunteers hurried to the assembly in the everyday dress of Victorian gentlemen and traders: frock coats and jackets, top hats and caps. Few had any military experience or had ever been in a fight of any kind. Old muskets and bayonets had been issued to the corps when it was formed. Some of the men carried swords, clubs and any other weapons they owned. There had only been time in the unit's brief history for some basic drill and occasional target practice. It had taken longer than expected to mobilise because most Volunteers were out on their daily walks when messengers rushed around the houses with the call to assemble. Struggling to keep in step, the minuscule force marched out to face a Chinese army of 20,000 men. Shanghai's handful of Westerners had no doubts about what they saw as their infinite superiority, even if they were surrounded by millions of Chinese and thousands of miles from home.

None of the Volunteers could have seen how Shanghai, then a middling port, would become the world's sixth largest city on the eve of the Second World War – an exotic mixture of the modern West and ancient China. It would evolve into a semi-autonomous city state, governed by a council of Western merchants, and driven by business and profit in one of the best examples of what later historians like to term informal empire. Nor could the Volunteers have imagined that their ragtag little force would evolve into one of the strangest military formations of modern times: a miniature army with men from more than 20 nations.

Shanghai's tiny Western settlement had only the most tenuous foothold in 1854. China was torn by civil war and unrest, foreigners were widely despised, and Shanghai's Westerners could have been swept into the sea. Britain and the United States did not keep troops in Shanghai apart from occasional visiting warships, so the little Western community decided in April 1853 to form its own defence force after rebel armies began occupying the region around Shanghai. 'The young and numerically insignificant community of Shanghai, afraid to fall victim to the raving rebels, called a meeting to devise means of self-protection,' a contemporary report stated.[1] Captain Tronson of the East India Company's Bengal Army, who was visiting the port, taught the Volunteers drill and other rudiments for a few months. It was a very informal organisation: one of the few rules stated, 'any gentleman enrolling cannot unroll himself without the sanction of the Consul'.[2] As in many early colonial Volunteer units, initial enthusiasm soon evaporated. Men had come to China to make fortunes, or at least a living, and had little time to spare. Trudging up and down and learning to form ranks was a long way from the recruits' daydreams of battlefield heroics. After a few weeks 'afternoon exercises were discontinued on account of the dispatch of [business] mail,' reported the *North China Herald*.[3]

Rebels captured the old Chinese section of Shanghai in a surprise attack a few months later. An imperial Chinese army was sent to oust the insurgents. Clashes between the rival Chinese forces enthralled the Western community. Whole families went out to watch the carnage. Spectators clambered up the tower of the settlement's church for a better view, prompting a warning in the local newspaper:

'We have been requested to caution the community against ascending in large numbers on the Church Tower in order to watch the attack of the Imperialists against the city. The upper portion of the tower is very slightly built, and if it be crowded as on Wednesday night last, and again on Thursday, a catastrophe too painful to contemplate may result.'

Fairly cordial relations developed with the rebels, despite their blood-thirsty reputation, and the Westerners were soon complaining about the behaviour of their supposed protectors in the imperial army. A couple out for a stroll were attacked with swords and spears on 3 April by imperial soldiers, the gentleman reportedly suffering seven wounds. Scattered skirmishes followed between Chinese troops and British and American sailors from visiting warships. British Consul Rutherford Alcock and U.S. Consul R. C. Murphy demanded the Chinese army abandon its positions. A scratch force of British and American sailors and marines from three warships in the harbour was assembled along with Shanghai's volunteer corps to back the ultimatum. The force numbered some 300 sailors, marines and volunteers.

Contemporary accounts suggest just a few dozen volunteers took part in the ensuing battle. With flags flying and drums beating, the little column marched out, confident the Chinese army would flee as soon as it saw the Western force. Halting at the edge of the city, the men saw a Chinese courier approaching. Far from humbly apologising, the Chinese commander rejected the Western ultimatum and refused to pull back. The consuls promptly decided to attack.

Details of the battle are sketchy and contradictory. It appears the British and American forces attacked the Chinese positions in separate columns; the Americans mounting a frontal assault, the British making a flank attack. Some of the volunteers, who had set off so cheerfully, became increasingly uncertain and glum as they marched toward the Chinese posts. Most of the men had imagined they were going out for a stirring and symbolic display of might followed by a return home to dinner. Few of these temporary warriors had expected there would be any fighting. Their confidence crumbled further as the little army trudged across muddy fields. They could now see that the Chinese camp looming up ahead was a massive fortified position. Thousands of Chinese soldiers were rolling out cannons and lining the walls, as one volunteer, a Mr Wetmore, later wrote:

> 'There was a marked decline in the exuberance which had characterised the march out, and faces generally assumed a much more serious look, and I have no doubt most of the company wished themselves well out it.'[4]

Some volunteers were ordered to attack a sector where the camp was protected by a creek in front of the main wall, as Wetmore recounted:

'The order was given to Charge! And away we went at a round trot, hurrahing as if it were the greatest imaginable fun . . .

As we advanced with our glad hurrahs, the thought occurred to me that we could not reach the [Chinese] defences in front . . . without wading waist deep through the creek, and this prospect of a cold mud bath, with perhaps a taste of cold steel at last as we crawled up the opposite bank, was not particularly attractive.'

Some of the volunteers, accustomed to spending their days at desks, were already exhausted and struggled to keep up. Other men slowed or dropped back as cannon shot and musket balls hissed toward the thin line of Volunteers. Wetmore was horrified when business colleagues crumpled and collapsed around him. 'There was G. G. Gray of Russell and Co. being carried off with a bullet through each leg, and a marine close by with his face covered with blood.' Most of the Volunteers stalled at the creek as the attack came under intense fire. Suddenly the imperial troops began to run as thousands of rebels surged out of the old city and attacked the imperial positions. Dazed volunteers watched as the imperial force fled.

Shanghai's Volunteers soon persuaded themselves they had won what was dubbed the Battle of Muddy Flat. Others, like Wetmore, had some private doubts:

'My own opinion has ever been that to the unexpected cooperation of the rebels, of whom their besiegers had a mortal dread, we were chiefly indebted for our easy victory, and that had it not been for them the result for us would have been disastrous.'

The sober chronicler was not alone in questioning the whole affair, with some saying it had all been an over-reaction that needlessly endangered the settlement.

Alcock, the British consul, dismissed such doubts with an unflinching statement of how Britain ought to deal with lesser races:

'I am satisfied that under existing circumstances in China, there is less to be risked and lost by a firm and unhesitating resistance . . . then must inevitably be incurred by any temporising or timid policy.'[5]

Four Westerners were killed, including a single Volunteer, John Adolphus Brine, who died from wounds three weeks later and was buried in the tiny foreign cemetery. 'His untimely end proceeding from a wound received on the 4th of the same month in an attack by the combined forces of England and America and Shanghai Local Volunteers on the Imperialist Camps west of this settlement,' read the tombstone. His grave became a shrine of sorts for the Shanghai Volunteer Corps, and the date of the battle was later emblazoned on its badges.

The Early Years

Shanghai was a treaty port rather than a colony like Hong Kong or Macao. Britain, France and the United States had pressured China in 1843 to give their merchants the right to live and trade in the city. British settlement began with '25 persons'. Areas under informal British and American control were combined in 1863 to form an enclave that evolved into the self-governing International Settlement. A municipal council, elected by Western residents who paid the highest rate of residence tax, ran the settlement. France kept its zone separate. China controlled the remaining areas of Shanghai. Peking had no authority in the International Settlement despite retaining nominal sovereignty. Foreigners whose nations had sovereign status in the International Settlement answered to their own governments and were exempt from Chinese laws. A long list of nations gained special rights over the years for their citizens to live and work in the settlement: Austria, Belgium, Brazil, Denmark, Germany, Italy, Japan, the Netherlands, Norway, Portugal, Russia, Spain, Sweden and Switzerland. Shanghai's coat of arms featured most of the favoured nations' flags. Germany and Austria lost their sovereign status in the settlement during the First World War and Russia gave up its privileges after the Bolshevik Revolution. Chinese in the settlement came under the council's authority.

Western governments, with Britain as the first among equals, protected the enclave, some maintaining small garrisons, but the merchants and businessmen ran the settlement. British influence was very strong in the settlement with the British business community dominating local affairs and the council. Americans were the second most influential group on the council and in the settlement for many years. Over the next few decades, the council built up a large municipal infrastructure with everything from police and fire services to electricity and water systems, roads and hospitals. Hundreds of thousands of Chinese flocked to the city to escape their own country's turmoil. Shanghai offered a chance to survive and possibly get ahead, even if they were denied equality and banned from some city amenities. Shanghai's elite exuded a vaunting racism that matched anything in the British Empire. Still, major Chinese businesses were built up and Chinese businessmen were among the richest in the city.

Shanghai's Western residents developed a curious sense of identity over the years. Generally they saw themselves as patriotic citizens of their respective nations and only second as 'Shanghailanders'. In reality, they frequently put their own interests first, ignoring their governments when it suited them. Many British businessmen implicitly believed their government was beholden to them for the trade and financial returns it earned from Shanghai's vast wealth. 'The British merchants are an unusually self-satisfied race, who are confident in their own minds that they and their business count for everything in the future of the British Empire,' complained a British general in 1929.[6] Shanghai's leaders believed they only had to squeal, he added, and the British Army would pour in so that they could go on relaxing in the exclusive Shanghai Club undisturbed. The city's elite became merchant princes with enormous wealth, power and influence. Differences and even wars between the residents' homelands were often ignored within the settlement's boundaries. British and German members of what was by then the Shanghai Volunteer Corps (SVC) did not turn on each other in the First World War. Chinese and Japanese Volunteers served in the SVC even as their countries tore each other apart around the International Settlement in the 1930s. While soldiers of other armies drank a toast to monarchs, presidents and homelands, the SVC toast neatly summed up its hybrid roots: 'To Our Respective Nations'.

In the years after Muddy Flat, the volunteer corps followed the usual pattern of 19th-century colonial volunteer units. Recruiting soared when the settlement was under threat only to plummet as stability returned and men got fed up with juggling work and military training. The first Shanghai corps fell apart after the fight at Muddy Flat, although a nucleus of Volunteers appears to have limped on for several years.

Interest revived in 1860 when Taiping rebels threatened the city. A mounted Ranger unit was formed to act as scouts, but the Volunteers were not sent out to fight. Volunteers wore an outlandish uniform reminiscent of Garibaldi's Red Shirts, who were electrifying Europe at the time – voluminous red shirts, black or white trousers and black Tyrolean hats with cock feathers. Cavalrymen sported a mix of British and American uniforms with képis and pill-box hats.

A precarious existence was maintained by the force over the next decade as an independent unit run and funded by its members. Reports showing 200 members in 1865 complained that only a few men ever turned up for parades. Some of the settlement's biggest merchant houses refused to give employees time off for drill sessions. Most members were slow to pay the dues that financed the corps and it was always in debt to suppliers. Volunteers worried the corps might go bankrupt and they would be saddled with its large debts. Two auditors were appointed from the ranks, Sergeant Sutherland and Private Somerville, to try to trim the financial losses. Some equipment was handed over to the corps' main creditor and rented back in an ultimately unsuccessful attempt to solve the financial difficulties.

This precarious existence continued until 1870 when the Shanghai Municipal Council took control of the force and agreed to fund it. A public meeting on 2 July 1870 voted to re-form the unit, formally naming it the Shanghai Volunteer Corps. It was restructured with artillery, infantry and mounted units. New equipment was purchased – 500 Snider rifles, two 12-pounder howitzers, wagons, ponies and 50 swords for the mounted unit. The SVC had a strength of 333 men by 1872, including 11 officers and 16 NCOs but the enthusiasm inspired by the council's rescue did not last long despite the influx of public money. Volunteers began to skip drills once again and recruiting dipped. Some blamed the peaceful times and the lack of any clear threat to the settlement. 'Unless some steps were at once taken, the Volunteers as a body would soon cease to exist,' a council report warned.[7] An SVC sergeant, who had been a Volunteer in England, described a force hobbled by low military standards and patchy attendance in a letter to old comrades at home:

> 'The Volunteers here have no regular instructor and consequently do not know much about drill. My chief work is giving them squad drill, but the party that attends one night you perhaps do not see again for a week. They are all composed of merchants, shipping clerks . . .'[8]

Leading citizens backed a drive to invigorate the force and keep it alive. Public meetings were held to urge eligible men to do their civic duty and enlist. Pressure was exerted by the council on the settlement's trading houses and businesses to encourage employees to join the corps. The mounted unit was disbanded to boost the depleted infantry and artillery sections. Recruiting gradually increased and the crisis had passed by 1880. New uniforms helped, the council reported, by adding 'very much to the soldierly appearance of the men'. SVC membership reached 330 in 1881 and the mounted unit was revived. There was sufficient interest to start annual training sessions at a camp outside the city. However, recruiting would always be difficult in a city with so many pastimes and temptations. Shanghai had lavish sporting facilities, night clubs, casinos, brothels and

Development of the Shanghai Volunteer Corps

SVC Strength 1872		SVC Strength 1887	
Mounted Rangers	36	Staff	5
Artillery	33	Light Horse	35
Mih-Ho-Loong Rifles	79	Artillery	50
No. 1 Rifle Company	59	No. 1 Company (Mih-Ho-Loong Rifles)	65
No. 2 Rifle Company	60	No. 2 Company	54
No. 3 Rifle Company	66	No. 3 Company	41

Source: Kounin, Eighty-Five Years of the Shanghai Volunteer Corps.

many other distractions. Most Westerners had the money and the appetite to indulge in at least a few of the licit and illicit pleasures. Marching, kit inspections and taking orders at SVC drills after a long day paled when far more agreeable diversions were so easily had, as an 1896 council report admitted.

> 'In Great Britain one of the reasons for volunteering being so popular is that it is the principal pastime of a large majority of the volunteers. In Shanghai amusements are catered for on so extensive a scale that volunteering, to the majority becomes a duty attended by a certain amount of hard work.'[9]

SVC commanders had to increase the corps' social activities to attract recruits, providing plenty of sport, clubs, dinners and other events, even if they distracted from training and its military role.

British predominance in Shanghai saw the SVC adopt British military organisation, training and culture. Uniforms by the 1880s were recognisably British, with infantry clad in red tunics, blue trousers and white sun helmets. Cavalry wore blue tunics, white breeches and white sun helmets with metal spikes. Training and standards were slipshod in the early years. Officers and NCOs had little or no military experience and what passed for training was generally amateurish and inadequate. A note in the council accounts said that protective mounds had to be erected at the SVC rifle range after the 'unfortunate death of a Chinese' passerby. The council sought help from the British Army for instructors to train the Volunteers. Constable Garthwhite, of the Hong Kong Police and a veteran of the 80th Regiment, was the first permanent instructor.

Encouraged by the improvements that followed, council officials asked in 1903 for a regular British officer to act as commandant and oversee the expanding SVC. Since training was light at times, and the thrifty council was bearing the cost, it proposed the appointee also run the city's jail – 'a building wherein some 300 Chinese convicts are usually undergoing imprisonment with hard labour'.[10] Running the jail was later dropped from the officer's duties. Captain W. M. Watson of the West Riding Regiment, who had served with the 1st Chinese Regiment, was the first officer seconded under a system that continued to the Second World War.

A handful of British regular officers and NCOs eventually formed a small professional backbone, overseeing training and logistics. This encouraged military and civilian officials in London to assume that the SVC was under British control like any other colonial Volunteer force. Successive British regular officers sent to command the SVC often had to explain to London that the corps was under the strict control of the city council and its decidedly independent policies. Senior British officers nonetheless were regularly invited by the council to inspect the SVC. One early report praised the force's unique nature:

> 'Shanghai, not a colony, not even a [British] concession, but a fortuitous aggregate of self-governing English merchants ... furnishes a fine example of courageous independence and resolution, applied to self-defence without drawing one shilling from the Imperial Exchequer ... the merchants and settlers cheerfully devote time, money, and trouble to the improvement of the forces; and their measures are so well concerted that on a sudden emergency, so far from contemplating a rush on board ship, they are perfectly prepared to protect their lives, and property pending the arrival of succour from Hong Kong.'[11]

Subsequent inspections reported steady progress. 'Nowhere it appears to me is a Volunteer Corps so much needed,' wrote Major-General W. G. Cameron after an 1880s' inspection. A battery of four guns and 30,000 rounds of ammunition were donated to the SVC by the British government at Cameron's suggestion.[12]

Many Armies in One

The SVC developed and expanded as Shanghai thrived. Many of the settlement's foreign communities formed their own units in the corps. Italian, Portuguese, Austro-Hungarian, American, British, Chinese, Japanese, German, Scandinavian, Filipino and Russian detachments existed over the years. Some units flourished as long as the SVC survived, others withered or collapsed because of a lack of recruits or external politics. Men from smaller countries, such as Denmark or the Netherlands, who lacked the numbers to form separate sub-units, sometimes created amalgamated companies. Volunteers could also join the SVC's multi-national companies. China's huge state customs service, for example, was run by foreigners. Expatriate customs officials based in Shanghai formed an SVC Customs Company, the corps' most cosmopolitan unit. Its ranks included Britons, Americans, Australians, Germans, Italians, Norwegians, Portuguese, Russians, Swedes and others. Asian and mixed-race Volunteers were not welcome in most white units. Class snobbery and racism abounded in some units, where the costs of extra equipment and social events were kept high to discourage all but the city's elite.

British companies, which tended not to welcome outsiders, had the greatest social pretensions. Gaining admission to the haughtier units mirrored the ritual of joining a gentleman's club. Candidates were only accepted after being proposed and seconded by existing members of the unit who could vouch for applicants' social credentials. Many of the settlement's most eminent British businessmen and officials belonged to the Shanghai Light Horse, whose members needed deep pockets to meet the standards expected for equipment and entertainment. 'The Light Horse are on a totally different footing, they do what no other section of the corps does, and they do it remarkably well,' was how the unit smugly described itself. Run like an exclusive hunting club, the troop was noted for its dashing appearance on the city's polo ground. 'In those days this unit was armed with the Lance as a primary weapon, and very spectacular and awe inspiring that weapon, with its gay pennants, appeared,' wrote E. H. McMichael, who grew up in Shanghai in the 1890s.[13] He joined the troop after returning to Shanghai following schooling in England. Life in the unit was as much about sport as soldiering. 'Field Days held in the open country two or three times a year, were looked upon half seriously and half as a day of fun in the open air,' McMichael recalled.

A Company, or the Mih-Ho-Loong Rifles, was a British unit that banned non-whites and Eurasians, even those with British nationality. Non-British whites with a suitable Anglo-Saxon pedigree were admitted. 'A Company is the only unit which insists on their members being of full white parentage and that this rule has been in force since the formation of the company,' it informed prospective applicants.[14] Eurasians with British ties served in the SVC's B Company. All non-British members were asked to leave A and B Companies in 1915 following the outbreak of the First World War. Danes accepted an invitation to rejoin A Company in 1924. A Company traced its roots to a part-time European fire brigade, the Mih-Ho-Loong Hook & Ladder Company, which was formed in 1866, and doubled as a unit in the early military Volunteers. Fire-fighters and riflemen 'were one and the same body of men. They were firemen or soldiers as required. The foreman of the Hook and Ladder Company was Captain of the Rifles,' a company history noted.[15] Members were fined a silver dollar for failing to answer a summons to put out a fire. It merged in the 1870s with the SVC's No. 1 Company.

The Shanghai Scottish Company was the corps' other robustly British unit. It was formed in 1914 after the outbreak of war in Europe when the withdrawal of the regular British garrison made it necessary to boost SVC numbers. SVC commanders wanted to form several new companies, but only attracted enough men for a Scottish unit. Plans for an Irish company were dropped because of a dearth of recruits. The Scottish company's early days were racked by a dispute over whether it would be a highland or a lowland unit. Lowland Scots in the unit insisted they would never wear kilts. The Highlanders triumphed eventually and kilts were donned. There was then another protracted dispute over which tartan to adopt. Company members from various clans advocated their ancestral patterns. The Hunting Stewart sett was finally accepted as a compromise. It took several years to find enough bagpipers to form a band. A plan for a second Scottish company had to be dropped when it could not find enough men despite the many Scots working and living in Shanghai

A group of German residents in 1876 first put forward a plan to form their own unit; however, it took several years to find the necessary determination and numbers. German and Portuguese companies were raised in 1891. British Major-General Digby Barker, who visited Shanghai to review the SVC, singled out the German company's drilling as a pleasure to watch. Its high standards were not too surprising since half of the company had served in the German Army. It wore dark blue uniforms modelled on German Army dress, later adopting German-style colonial khaki outfits. It also used German drill and elected its own officers. Non-British companies usually adopted some aspect of their own national military traditions, such as drill or uniform, without breaching the corps' essentially British structure.

While Americans served in various SVC units from its earliest days, there were no separate American units for many years though a temporary American unit was formed for emergency service during the Boxer Rebellion. Embarrassed American residents eventually decided they had to form their own units after political unrest swept the city in 1905. 'The Mixed Courts riots ... presented a humiliating situation wherein Americans were required to depend upon other nations for their protection,' a history of the American company noted.[16] A public meeting in December 1905 voted to form an American unit, which was activated on 17 January 1906. Dr. S. A. Ransom, a city health official, was its first commander with some 60 men joining the company. It affected a colourful reputation in its early years. Several veterans of the American military were members, including a Sergeant Gillig, reputed to have been an orderly for Admiral George Dewey during the Spanish–American War. Another veteran was an ex-mule wrangler called Henkie, who claimed to have served as a British Army scout in the Boer War. A missionary, Rev. Thomas Meyers, predictably was nicknamed 'the fighting parson'. He declined to drill on Sundays, although a lurid newspaper account said, 'if there is any fighting to be done on that day he leaves his flock and is to be found in the thick of the action'.[17]

Other American units were soon formed with American-style uniforms and a distinctly American ethos. A cavalry troop established in 1922 wore khaki shirts, riding breeches and campaign hats modelled on U.S. Cavalry uniforms. Shanghai's thirst for sport and fun was a factor in its formation. The troop's founders admitted they were, at least partly, inspired by the prospect of challenging the haughty and British-dominated Shanghai Light Horse to polo, paper chases and other events. Insignia worn by the mounted troop featured an American eagle with a shield bearing the stars and stripes on its breast with crossed cavalry sabres. Badges of the infantry company were an eagle with crossed rifles. An American machine-gun troop followed in 1929 after the American business community donated two cars to carry Lewis guns. It welcomed all eligible residents and claimed to be the most cosmopolitan unit in the corps. An American reserve unit was formed in 1932 from older residents. A new Filipino platoon formed in 1922 was put under American command. It had attracted enough recruits to form a company by 1932. Washington struggled with the idea of its citizens serving in a foreign military unit. Still, instructors from the regular U.S. forces based in Shanghai helped train the American units and provided some equipment.

Shanghai's military force was not exclusively Western even though the settlement's white elite usually regarded Asians with withering contempt. Leading Chinese merchants offered to form a Volunteer company during the Boxer Rebellion because their community's wealth and Western connections made it a target for the rebels. Arming Chinese was rejected brusquely by the council, which tended to lump all Chinese in the same category as the Boxers. Refusing to give up, the Chinese community set up its own militia in 1905, calling it the Chinese Physical Recreation Association. Contributions from Chinese merchants provided a drill hall, gymnasium and parade ground. Everything that money could buy was lavished on this demonstration of civic pride and proffered loyalty. A battalion with four infantry companies and a light cavalry company was formed along with a brass band. Isolated and lacking qualified trainers, its enthusiasm trailed off after the first year and the unit floundered. Chinese community leaders asked the Municipal Council to integrate the unit with the SVC. With the Boxer threat gone, city leaders eventually agreed to accept enough men to form one company as long as it served under Western officers. Captain L. J. Cubitt, from the SVC Customs Company, was the commanding officer when the new unit was formed on 18 March 1907 with 83 men.

Cubitt and a succession of Western officers worked hard to raise standards and end prejudice against the Chinese as soldiers. Aware that many in the Western community wanted it to fail, the Chinese company was one of the SVC's model units. Chinese community leaders rigorously controlled admission to ensure that only the best candidates were admitted. The SVC history recorded how:

> 'A prospective recruit has to give a most minute account of himself and his antecedents and be guaranteed by men of standing in the community. Even then, he has to achieve a very high standard as a recruit before finally being accepted, and that standard must be maintained unceasingly so long as he remains in the company, for if any one man slacks there are dozens who will not, and who will be pining to take his place.'[18]

The company's smart marching and turn-out frequently outdid that of other units, and it routinely won corps competitions and prizes. A 1921 British Army report on the SVC lavished praise on the Chinese company in quite extraordinary language, holding it up as an example to military Volunteers of all races.

> 'Everything is undertaken in the most serious and practical manner in this Company and the number of parades attended by its members would open the eyes, I venture to think, of any volunteers in the world. The devotion to duty and determination of all ranks to do their best on all occasions are magnificent.'[19]

A ban on Chinese officers was dropped after repeated recommendations from successive SVC commandants. Sergeant T. A. Zee, one of the company's five original Chinese sergeants, was commissioned in 1915. Zee, who went on to command the Chinese company, was temporary corps commandant in 1934. Zee was hosted by the War Office on a visit to London, when he was described as 'a Europeanised Chinaman'.[20] Several Chinese officers rose to senior posts in the SVC headquarters staff.

A group of Chinese interpreters, formed during political unrest in 1932, was so successful that it became a permanent unit. The Chinese Interpreters Company was raised on 1 October 1932 with a strength of 125 men. Its members wore SVC uniform, underwent normal infantry training, and could be used for regular duties. Their main role, however, was to assist non-Chinese SVC units and regular Western military units based in Shanghai, such as the British Army and the U.S. Marine Corps. It won the corps' top award, the SVC Efficiency Shield for 1936–7, just five years after being formed.

An address (ornately decorated and written in Chinese characters) from the Chinese community to Colonel H. B. H. Orpen-Palmer, marking his departure as SVC commander in March 1931, touches on the prejudice the Chinese Volunteers faced:

> 'You have shown your intimate recognition of the importance of the unique position which the Chinese Company occupies in the history and life of the Volunteer Corps. Nay, you have demonstrated your firm trust in the ability and character of the members of the Chinese Company and you have done your utmost to afford them facilities, assistance, and comprehensive training of a very high order as becometh their natural enthusiasm for a cause affecting the leading commercial centre of their motherland; not to mention the many years struggle and sacrifice which they put into the work thus accomplished by them as a distinguished branch of the historic organisation that has made considerable advancement under your guiding hand.'[21]

Shanghai's Japanese residents formed an independent defence company in 1900. It is not clear if they were unwelcome in the SVC or preferred to be separate. Most of its early recruits were businessmen with no military experience. Captain G. R. Wingrove, a British SVC officer, was asked to be the company's instructor. It became part of the SVC in 1907. Britain's then alliance with Japan made it difficult to exclude Japanese from the corps even if few Western Volunteers wanted Asians in their ranks. Regular Japanese Army officers were later sent on temporary assignment to lead and train the company. Early photographs show Japanese Volunteers wearing British uniforms, including side caps and Australian-style bush hats.

Japan's war against China in the 1930s caused concern about the unit's loyalty, particularly of possible strains with the Chinese companies. Colonel N. W. B. B. Thomas, the regular British Army commandant, praised Japanese and Chinese Volunteers for their discipline and loyalty to the city during a major crisis. Such praise was intended, at least in part, to conceal growing differences with the Japanese. Strains at the end of the 1930s forced SVC commanders to keep the Chinese and Japanese companies apart on deployments and other activities. Japanese Volunteers resented the patronising condescension of the Western residents over the years. In a rebuke to the rest of the corps, the company's chronicler wrote that Westerners generally failed to accept that many of them owed their safety to the often maligned Japanese.

Despite its name, the Portuguese company was composed of Eurasians of Macao ancestry. It complained of having to endure the second-class status routinely imposed on Eurasians in Western outposts across the Far East. A history of the company claims its members had to make greater sacrifices than other Volunteers because they were unwelcome in European neighbourhoods and squeezed into less desirable areas outside the International Settlement. This meant their homes were left unprotected when the company reported for duty in the settlement during a crisis. Its chronicler noted the cost of one incident when rival Chinese armies clashed outside the settlement:

> 'When mobilisation so orders, the company is assembled quickly, leaving behind homes to be looted and burned or wrecked by shell fire. Personal belongings and all accessories of the home, which years of hard work had accumulated, had to be left behind to the mercies of the warring parties, in order that each might answer to the more noble call of assistance to the general public.'[22]

One of the more unusual SVC units was created when Shanghai's Scandinavian, Dutch and Swiss residents, too few to form separate units, decided to amalgamate. Dubious officials gave their consent as doubters, including some members of the new unit, predicted the different nationalities would never get along. It was an instant success, soon acquiring a reputation for pragmatism, versatility and cheeriness. A caption on a photo of the unit hails its members as modern-day Vikings. Initially an infantry unit, the company became a light artillery battery equipped with mountain guns in 1926. It had a howitzer battery of four 4.5-inch guns and a light battery of four 2.75-inch guns in the early 1930s. The aging guns were replaced by Maxim guns in 1936 when the unit became

C Machine Gun Company. It liked to see itself as hungry for innovation and change, unlike some of the more stuffy SVC units, suggesting it might form a chemical warfare unit.

A Jewish company formed in 1932 was the SVC's youngest unit. Jews had worked and lived in the settlement from its earliest days. Their ranks were swelled in the 20th century by successive waves of refugees from the Russian Civil War and Nazi Germany. By 1930, some 30,000 Jews lived in the International Settlement, often in great poverty. Jews had served in SVC units for many years. Talk of forming a separate Jewish unit during the First World War was overruled by Jewish community elders, who thought that integration was more important, but plans for a Jewish unit were revived in the 1930s. A Jewish platoon was raised on 22 September 1932 and attached to H Reserve Company. Noel S. Jacobs, an Englishman who served in the Hong Kong Volunteer Defence Corps before moving to Shanghai, was its first and only commanding officer. He had converted from Christianity to marry a Russian Jewish woman after arriving in the settlement. Jacobs ran a Shanghai Jewish boy scout group before taking over the new SVC Jewish unit and many of his recruits were ex-scouts. The unit grew quickly and in May 1933 H Company became a purely Jewish formation.

At its peak, the company had 120 men in three platoons. Men wore collar badges of the Star of David with SVC initials in the centre. Its motto reputedly was 'No Advance Without Security': a self-parodying pun on contemporary anti-Semitism. British War Office reports on the SVC said the company was made up of German Jews and might not be trustworthy if Britain found itself at war with Berlin. One of the few SVC men to die on active service, and probably the only one to be killed by another Volunteer, came from the Jewish company. In one of the most bizarre moments in SVC history, a Private Rapaport wandered into an area held by B Company when the corps had been called out to deal with unrest. A sentry ordered Rapaport to leave even though he was an SVC member in full uniform. Rapaport responded by daring the sentry to shoot him and was promptly killed.

An Army in Miniature

Specialist units were added to the SVC over the decades until it resembled a miniature version of a regular army. An *ad hoc* home guard or reserve unit was formed in 1889 from older men not up to serving in the main corps. Its role was to protect the families of Volunteers at strategic assembly points during emergencies. It evolved into a Reserve Company, nicknamed the

Shanghai Volunteer Corps, 1920

Parade of the SVC as reported by the *North China Herald*, 1 May 1920

Unit	Strength	Unit	Strength
Light Horse	39	American Company	78
Artillery	32	Portuguese Company	68
Engineers	24	Japanese Company	68
Machine Gun Company	16	Chinese Company	105
Maritime Company	18	Shanghai Scottish	44
A Company	47	Italian Company	22
B Company	21	1st Reserve Company	27
Customs Company	37		

Not all members attended.

'12 Bore Irregulars' because it included several hunters armed with shotguns. An engineering detachment was formed in 1890 with 30 men. This was followed in 1898 by a Naval Company recruited from merchant navy personnel to operate machine guns 'afloat or ashore'. A non-combatant General Service Company was formed around 1900, and for a few years it carried out logistic tasks, ambulance work and fire-fighting. A cadet company was formed with 78 pupils from the city's British school. It had a strength of 1,530 cadets by 1923 with some graduates later serving in the SVC.

Special units proliferated following the First World War as the SVC endeavoured to adopt recent advances in military technology despite some initial resistance in the higher echelons. Returning veterans of the Western Front were stunned that the SVC's leadership did not want to learn from their experience. Some older officers, who had spent the war in Shanghai, insisted the old ways were best and tried to block any changes. Angry veterans, many of whom had been officers in the war, refused to rejoin the SVC. A rival group called the 'Emergency Unit' was formed. Eventually, the old guard was moved aside and the veterans took over key SVC commands.

Horses gradually began to give way to motor engines and slabs of armour plating as the SVC slowly modernised after the war. The Light Horse acquired a few primitive armoured cars for members who could no longer ride because of war injuries, but still had a zest for shooting and itchy trigger fingers. An armoured car unit was created in 1921 as part of the machine-gun company. It was hived off as the separate Armoured Car Company with 10 vehicles in 1928. Non-British members were admitted only after a prolonged internal debate. Members wore black berets and uniforms modelled on the British Tank Corps.

An anti-aircraft unit was formed in 1932 after Japanese and Chinese planes damaged parts of the city. Company members were extremely enthusiastic even though the council refused to buy modern anti-aircraft guns because of the high cost. Instead, the Light Automatic (Air Defence) Company was armed with Lewis guns that were quite inadequate against modern aircraft. 'Not really Air Defence, but a M.G. Support Company,' a British Army memo admitted.[23] It tried to make up for its lack of suitable weapons with lavish uniforms modelled on the 'maternity' tunics of British First World War aviators. Winter and summer versions were worn and the men purchased a blue mess dress for social events. Monthly lunches and a private club located opposite Shanghai's cathedral gave the company a reputation for its lavish social life.

Modernisation proceeded with the creation of a Signals Company and a Transport Company in 1932. Efforts to strengthen the SVC further were hindered by a lack of specialists to handle the increasingly technical nature of modern weapons and warfare. Most businessmen and traders serving in the SVC were unable or unwilling to be mechanics or supply clerks. A solution was found by simply putting the council's engineering, electrical and maintenance personnel into SVC uniform as the Service Company to handle the corps' technical needs. It had a stock of 100,000 sandbags and 40 miles of barbed wire. Any heavy lifting and digging was done by the city Public Works Department's coolies.

Modernisation was expensive, however, and the city council made economies in other areas to meet the cost, including eliminating the artillery in 1936.

Riots and Wars

Emblazoned on the SVC's colours by 1938 were 25 'Battle Honours'. Each of the dates marked an occasion when the corps had been mobilised to defend the settlement. Only the 1854 clash with Chinese troops at Muddy Flat could justly be called a battle. Very few SVC Volunteers ever fired their weapons at anything except practice targets. SVC men were called out to guard the perimeter and assist regular troops based in the city whenever fighting from China's incessant civil wars and insurrections lapped around the Western enclave, but it was never attacked until Japan occupied it in 1941. Other mobilisations were responses to internal unrest. Shanghai's Chinese majority was never happy with Western rule, even if they benefited in some ways from the city's relative isolation and prosperity. Protests and

Mobilisations of the Shanghai Volunteer Corps

Battle of Muddy Flat 1854	Second Revolution 1915
Taiping Menace 1860–2	Rickshaw Coolie Strike 1915
Tientsin Massacre 1870	Rickshaw Coolie Strike 1918
Ningpo Joss House Riots 1874	Hawkers' Riot 1918
Yangtze Riots 1891	Anti-Japanese Riot 1918
Sino-Japanese War 1894	Kiangsu Chekiang War 1924
1896 Riot	Lunghwa Battle 1923
Wheelbarrow Riots 1897	Nanking Road Incident 1925
Joss House Riots 1898	Occupation of Shanghai by Nationalists 1927
Boxer Outbreak 1900	Sino-Japanese Clash 1932
Russo-Japanese War 1904–5	Sino-Japanese War 1937
Mixed Court Riots 1905	Anniversary Sino-Japanese Outbreak 1938
Chinese Revolution 1911	

strikes, demanding the return of Chinese control, regularly battered the settlement in the later years.

Early protests were often spontaneous eruptions triggered by seemingly trivial events that set off pent-up resentment and prejudices on both sides. Typical were the Ningpo Joss House Riots in 1874, when 'the Chinese registered their opposition to the creation of a road through a cemetery'. Desecration of Chinese graves prompted several clashes as the council took over land for development in the second half of the 19th century. 'You cannot hurt the feelings of a Chinaman more ... [than by desecrating] their dead,' a Volunteer wrote in the 1870s. Shanghai's Western rulers had no sympathy for anyone who disagreed with their definition of progress. A rise in city licence fees in 1897 sparked the Wheelbarrow Riots by infuriated coolies.

Far more serious were the Mixed Court Riots of 1905 over the authority of a local Chinese law court. Furious Chinese attacked a police station and set it ablaze. Volunteers rushed from businesses and homes to quell the bloody protests. 'The rush was so great, in fact, that most of them had no time for changing into their uniforms ... several volley's [*sic*] were fired with good effect,' a report commented. Contemporary photographs show Volunteers in civilian suits, bandoliers across their chests, patrolling the streets with bayonet-tipped rifles. Chinese corpses litter the background. A newspaper correspondent told American readers in 1911 that peppering Chinese protests with rifle fire was as natural as the change of the seasons:

'In most cases it is necessary to shed blood in the process. The excited Chinaman can be quietened by an object lesson. So a few volleys are fired into their ranks, they retreat into their houses and cellars, carrying their dead and wounded with them, and causing no further trouble until something precipitates another riot.'[24]

The council also reported that 'a gratifying result of the disturbance is the increased number of recruits now joining the corps'.

Widespread disturbances erupted in 1910 after city authorities cleared slums to prevent plague, as a report explained:

'Some of the more ignorant Chinese fiercely resented the steps the Council were taking to combat this disease. It was consequently necessary to mobilise the Volunteers and station them at strategic points to assist the Settlement police.'

While the clearance may have saved Chinese lives by preventing plague, it also left them without homes and livelihoods.

Shanghai's internal neutrality was tested in the First World War. Council leaders, determined to protect the city's vital trade, tried to make sure life went on normally as the settlement's protecting powers tore each other apart in Europe. British and German residents treated each other with frosty formality. The SVC German company and its small Austro-Hungarian unit dropped out of the corps' general activities, but did not disband. German Volunteers were mobilised in 1915 alongside other SVC men after sailors on a Chinese cruiser mutinied in the harbour – Europeans still stuck together in the face of a common threat in China. New enemies found it hard to abandon peacetime habits. A British Army colonel, who had been in command of the SVC, inspected the German company at its request when he left Shanghai at the end of his tour. The German company was not dissolved until 1917, when China joined the Allies and ended Berlin's extraterritorial rights. It turned out for the last time at a funeral of a member; the three volleys fired over the grave marked its own demise.

Most of the regular European military units based in Shanghai were called home. The SVC had to increase its strength, despite the loss of so many younger men to the war, as it took on greater responsibility for the settlement's security. Older residents and men who might not have been welcome in the past for social or racial reasons were enlisted to fill the depleted ranks. Many younger SVC men left to fight for their countries in Europe or other theatres. More than half the German company joined the regular forces defending German enclaves in China. Almost 100 members of A Company joined the British Army. All but one of the 25 A Company men killed on active service were officers, reflecting the high calibre of many SVC formations.

Peace saw veterans from both sides returning to Shanghai to resume their old lives. Business picked up and more Chinese poured into the settlement in search of jobs and security. Shanghai's wealth soared as the big business houses prospered in the 1920s. Western residents believed the good times would never end. Interest in volunteering dropped as residents told each other there would never be another war. Lieutenant-Colonel T. Trueman, who had commanded the SVC during the war, warned against the happy talk of global peace. China was in turmoil, he said, and Shanghai could not reduce its defences.

> 'The conditions here have not changed with the termination of the war in Europe and although we may hear of the reduction of army forces in other parts of the world, it is essential to maintain a striking force in Shanghai of such strength as to make it impossible for local disturbances to develop into riots which cause destruction of life and property.'[25]

Mobilisations of the SVC became ever more frequent to keep order in the settlement's increasingly turbulent streets. Strikes and demonstrations challenged Western control or protested the growing Japanese threat to China. All protests tended to be branded by the city authorities as 'communistic strikes and riots' and were dealt with harshly. Major riots in 1925 were suppressed bloodily by the SVC and the Shanghai police, setting off anti-Western protests across China. SVC men had a reputation for being quick to open fire on protesters and strikers. Westerners still had a lingering fear of being overwhelmed by a Chinese uprising. 'The foreign colony might even be wiped out of existence were it not able to take care of itself,' a journalist explained. However, J. E. March, who served in the Light Horse and the Machine Gun Troop, recalled that life in the SVC was still fun and the men enjoyed belonging to the force between the riots and other challenges.[26]

Sweeping change in China and the global drift to war began to erode the International Settlement's privileged isolation. Shanghai's security against anything more than limited internal unrest increasingly depended on the willingness of the Western powers to protect it. Armies of rival Chinese war lords clashed around the city in 1925. Battles involving some 70,000 Chinese troops with artillery and supporting aircraft raged on the city's boundary. More than 20,000 Chinese troops were killed or wounded in fighting that went on for weeks. Mobilising every man, the SVC could only muster 1,400 troops with virtually no heavy weapons. Shanghai was again threatened by Chinese forces in 1927. Western nations rushed some 40,000 troops, including a full British division, to the city. Such a massive show of force quelled the Chinese threat.

Japan's invasion of China posed a new danger. Japanese forces captured the Chinese-run sector of Shanghai in 1932 after heavy fighting between China's 19th Army and three Japanese divisions. Fighting spilled into the settlement and parts of the city were bombed. The defenders could do little except issue empty protests to the scornful Japanese military. Britain and other nations sent reinforcements, but the protecting powers were ever less willing to defend a tiny enclave on the other side of the world as the global situation deteriorated. China attempted to recapture its area of the city in 1937, and thousands of troops were killed in the fighting. Chinese planes attacking Japanese warships dropped four bombs in the heart of the International Settlement. At least 2,000 people were hurt.

Enrolment in the SVC jumped as the political situation deteriorated in the 1930s and worried Westerners signed up. The corps had enthusiastic, well-trained men, but was small and lacked modern weapons. Lieutenant-Colonel J. R. Wyndham, a regular British officer who inspected the corps, noted it was 'a formidable little force, well trained and admirably adopted to the purpose for which they existed'.[27] Its equipment was outdated, he added, and improvements were vital. Defence was already one of the settlement's largest expenses and the council was reluctant to spend more. A trickle of cast-off weapons and equipment from Britain and America could not make up for the lack of modern artillery and other heavy weapons.

While few in Shanghai would admit it, the International Settlement could no longer be defended against a major internal threat let alone an attack from outside. The SVC could never number more than a few thousand men even if every eligible resident enrolled. Calling up every able Westerner for military duty in an emergency, moreover, would soon bring the city to its knees by leaving nobody to run vital services. A rare admission of the SVC's weakness came in a 1936 letter from the municipal council to the local British consul-general:

> '. . . what could a mere handful of Volunteers do against a modern Chinese army in case of an attack upon the Settlement, and what would be the responsibility of the civil authority which put them in that position in the event of loss of life and injury?'[28]

Gone were the days when a few hardy Western amateurs could hold off the Asian hordes with a volley or two.

A 1930s' study highlighted the enormous problems of defending the enclave. Shanghai lacked natural defences or a protective hinterland. Its boundary was 11 miles long, 21 miles if the French concession was included. Shanghai had 1 million residents, of whom just 36,000 were Westerners. Any defence of the city could only take place in its streets with the civilian population exposed to withering artillery and air attack. Major-General Charles W. Gwynn, who studied Shanghai's defences, praised the SVC's training and efficiency. It could cope with minor disturbances, he wrote, not serious disorder or external attack. According to Gwynn Shanghai's wealth made the city a magnet for criminals and gangsters that the police and SVC struggled to control:

> 'The whole constitutes an extraordinarily mixed community of great wealth: a happy-hunting-ground for a mob intent on loot, and one in which the forces of law and order are beset with difficulties in exercising protective duties.'[29]

Defending Shanghai against a serious threat was far beyond the SVC's present and future capabilities, he concluded.

Petty politics and jealousy sometimes plagued Shanghai's tiny defence force even as the settlement's security crumbled. Scandal and farce enveloped the SVC in 1929 when Britain's ambassador in Peking told London he had received disturbing reports about the regular British officer commanding the SVC. Leading Shanghai residents claimed that Colonel Orpen-Palmer (who had earned the praise of the Chinese community) was a poor leader and there were doubts about his personal morality. His aide, Captain A. Sandels, had been evacuated 'as a medical case on account of alcoholism'.[30] Orpen-Palmer had allegedly ignored his aide's frequent public drunkenness. Foreign Office officials sent the complaint to the chief of British forces in China, Major-General J. W. Sandilands. His quixotic response was that the SVC should be commanded by a rising young officer who had energy and ideas. It would help if he was a good horseman, and a deft polo player to hold his own in Shanghai society, the general added.

Unimpressed, the Foreign Office pressed for an investigation into the complaints. It was aghast when Sandilands said he had shown the report to Orpen-Palmer. Army protocol, he added, required the colonel be given a chance to defend himself. Sandilands did not help by suggesting the whole matter was overblown, saying it was not as if Orpen-Palmer was a drunk or kept a couple of Chinese women. A trivial dispute over an obscure officer thus turned into a major spat involving the Foreign Office, the

Colonial Office and the Army Council. Foreign Office panjandrums claimed British prestige in Asia was at stake. The escalating row took on a hysterical tinge when the ambassador received a letter from Orpen-Palmer asking for a copy of his complaint. It seems that Sandilands had in fact told the colonel about the complaint without showing it to him. The military attaché in Peking had to reply that the letter was a confidential note to a crown minister and Orpen-Palmer had no right to see it. The ambassador was left trying to persuade his distraught aide that he had not betrayed a fellow officer.

Sandilands, a remarkably outspoken man, even for a general, next denounced the SVC as a relic of a lost age. He began a list of stinging complaints by rubbishing Shanghai's rulers as spoilt and lazy men, for whom military service was, at best, a light-hearted distraction. They presumed British help could be summoned with a mere flick of a finger. Shanghai needed a strong defence force, he continued, but its coddled residents refused to exert themselves. Even a superman would find it difficult to raise another hundred men for the corps. The SVC would never be credible unless military service was compulsory for all Western male residents. Sandilands concluded by stating that the affair proved how deluded the British government and the Army were in thinking they had any control over Shanghai and the SVC. The dispute eventually sputtered out with the diplomats making frosty remarks about the peculiarities of Army etiquette.

The Russian Regiment

Shanghai was crowded with thousands of White Russian refugees in the years after the Bolshevik Revolution. Most were desperately poor and looked down on by the British for supposedly besmirching white prestige by jostling for survival with the poorest Chinese. However, the municipal council turned to veterans of the White armies in 1927 to create a permanent unit to supplement the SVC. Business was suffering because SVC men were being constantly called from their desks to deal with riots and strikes. A permanent force was needed to help guard the settlement. Three hundred Russians were recruited for the new force. Many of the men had come on a little fleet of three decrepit merchant vessels that limped into Shanghai on 14 September 1923. They were packed with remnants of the Far Eastern Cossack Group, one of the last White Army formations to be driven from Russia.

Initially the new body was called the Russian Unit. N. Y. Foreman, a former captain in the Russian Imperial Navy, was the first commander.

He was assisted by a British Army adviser. Most of its officers were veterans of Russian Imperial Guard regiments. The unit was modelled from the outset on tsarist traditions – 'Shaping it in accordance with the best traditions of the Regular Russian Army'. It was renamed the Russian Detachment in 1928 before being expanded into 'C Battalion' or the Russian Regiment of the SVC with 16 officers and 412 other ranks. Full-time regulars made up the regiment's Nos. 1, 2 and 4 Companies and a headquarters detachment. Russian Volunteers of the SVC formed the battalion's No. 3 Company, but only served when the corps was mobilised. British Army inspectors rated the Russian troops as good as regular British infantry. 'They are a fine force and act as spearhead whilst the remainder of the corps is mobilising. With a British Officer to tell them what to do, they will go anywhere and do anything. Real tough nuts,' a British Army adviser informed London.[31]

A permanent force was invaluable as security in the settlement deteriorated. It was available at any time, unlike the Volunteers, who had to be summoned from work or home in emergencies and were not always free to respond. The Russian detachment had 20 trucks mounted with machine guns to rush them to emergencies. Its principal duties included aiding the police, riot duty, and guarding the city jail, store houses and other key facilities. It also provided a permanent honour guard at the council building. By 1931 the regiment's upkeep was costing more than the rest of the SVC.

Surviving photographs of the unit show a world conjured straight out of Russia's imperial past: Russian drill was used on the parade ground; Russian Orthodox priests in full robes blessed the men on parade; portraits of the slain Tsar Nicholas II and his empress adorned the officers' mess along with splendid icons; a Russian Orthodox church was built for the regiment; and its band played balalaikas and other traditional Russian instruments. Regimental colours featured the white, blue and red Imperial Russian tricolour emblazoned with 'Shanghai Russian Regiment' in a circlet around the Shanghai coat of arms. Each new recruit took an elaborate oath:

> 'Under the national [Russian] three-coloured standard, be a great Russian soldier, observe the foreign law that protects you, respect the authorities that care for you and serve faithfully for the glory of our regiment, and for the good of the community that you are called upon to protect. Develop a sacred love for your Colours, pay them their due respect and forever guarding their inviolability.'[32]

While Shanghai applauded the vigilance of its full-time troops, questions were asked in the House of Commons on 18 February 1929 about disturbing reports of 'Russian mercenaries' in British uniforms.[33] What, MPs demanded, did the government plan to do about it? Foreign Office officials sent an urgent query to the Shanghai consulate for details, but had to admit that the British government had no power over the settlement or its military forces. Part of the SVC on paper, the Russians were always a separate force with an alien ethos. These survivors of a brutal civil war, who had lost everything, were fervent nationalists who revered Russian autocracy and the Orthodox faith. They had little in common with the SVC's amiable weekend warriors.

The Final Years

By the mid-1930s, the SVC was an infantry brigade with British, American and Russian battalions and support units. On paper it was a tough, impressive force. 'It is almost completely self-contained, and is prepared at any moment to fight as, and undertake the duties of a brigade,' commanders asserted in 1934. Training standards were claimed to be high, the men committed and enthusiastic. Few doubted that the Volunteers were keen, had superb knowledge of the territory and a strong personal commitment to defend their families and livelihoods. In reality, the corps was still a puny collection of mostly part-time amateurs with a few machine guns and a handful of antiquated armoured cars. It could not defend the city, or even a part of it, against any serious threat.[†]

Shanghai's neutral status faltered as Anglo-American relations with Japan soured. London tried to appease Tokyo, and the Shanghai authorities handed over Chinese sought by the Japanese authorities. It made no difference. Japan wanted control of Shanghai to cement its hold over eastern China. The International Settlement would not go untouched if war came. Japanese officials used a mix of political tactics and terror to try to take control of the settlement. Tokyo demanded more council seats for the settlement's Japanese residents, with the aim of dominating the city government. British councillors made concessions as their control was gradually eroded. Japan gave nominal charge of the city's old Chinese sector to a pro-Tokyo puppet regime. Its rulers demanded an end to the international concessions in Shanghai and the rest of China. Puppet regime

† Britain's War Office reported plans in June 1935 to form a German company in the SVC, but nothing seems to have come of it. Several Nazi Party groups were active in Shanghai, including an SA detachment (TNA PRO WO 106/78).

Shanghai Volunteer Corps, 1938

Corps HQ – Permanent Staff
HQ Volunteer Staff

Corps Cavalry
Shanghai Light Horse   American Troop

Corps Troops
Shanghai Field Company   C Machine Gun Company
Armoured Car Company   Signals Company
Japanese Company   Chinese & Interpreter Companies
Transport Company   Chaplins
Medical Staff

A Battalion (British)	B Battalion (American)	C Battalion (Russian)
A Company	American Company	No. 1 Company
B Company	Portuguese Company	No. 2 Company
Shanghai Scottish	Philippine Company	No. 3 Company*
Jewish Company	American Machine Gun Company	No. 4 Company
Light Air Defence Company		** Volunteer*

Source: Kounin, Eighty-Five Years of the Shanghai Volunteer Corps.

forces clashed periodically with the Shanghai Police and the SVC. Key city and police officials were assassinated or fled for their lives as Japan and its proxies tried to destabilise the International Settlement. Japanese officials launched a propaganda campaign against the SVC. Japanese press articles denounced the force as British-dominated and criticised its high costs. The Russian Regiment was described as a useless make-work scheme for impoverished White Russians. A few deluded councillors, who refused to believe things would ever change, were muttering by the late 1930s that the SVC should disband because defence could be safely left to the Japanese.

Facing war with Japan, Britain concluded that Shanghai could not be defended. London, aware of its declining influence in Asia, wanted to improve its poor relations with China and had been distancing itself from Shanghai and the other concessions. Pleas from the settlement to guarantee its security were rebuffed. Britain's regular garrison of two infantry battalions was withdrawn in the middle of 1941. Britain's military presence was reduced to a solitary gunboat. America's Marine garrison left Shanghai in November 1941. When British troops left London urged all British residents to leave too but many people stayed on, refusing to believe that Japan would attack. Shanghai's own defence plans were quietly shelved.

Shanghai Volunteer Corps, 28 November 1941

Unit	Strength	Unit	Strength
Headquarters	50	A Infantry Battalion	350
Cavalry	160	B Infantry Battalion	190
		C Infantry Battalion	290

Membership by nationality/race:

British	460	Chinese	285
Russian	181	Portuguese	103
American	83	Filipino	81
Jewish	75	Miscellaneous	332
Japanese	110		

Source: PRO WO 106/2393. Japanese marked as 'not available'.

The Russian Regiment was merged with the municipal police. The SVC Japanese Company withdrew from the corps. In any case corps officials admitted it had been impossible to deploy the Chinese and Japanese companies together for some time. SVC units helped maintain law and order while the settlement waited for the Japanese. Even the most bellicose Shanghailander admitted resistance would only ensure the slaughter of the defenders and much of the population. SVC units stopped manning permanent defence posts on 20 November 1941. There would be no doomed resistance.

Shanghai was occupied within hours after Japan struck at Pearl Harbor and Hong Kong. The only resistance came from a British gunboat in the harbour. The SVC was not disbanded and helped maintain internal security for the Japanese. It took over police posts in February 1942. The council suspended all SVC training the same month, but the corps does not appear to have been disbanded until September when Volunteers were instructed to hand uniforms and equipment over to the Japanese. Perhaps the SVC Japanese Company eased dealings with the settlement's new masters. A few Volunteers asked the council for permission to keep their cap badges. Some officers were invited to a little ceremony in October 1942 to see the SVC's colours laid up in the council's committee room. Most Allied nationals were not interned until early 1943. They were allowed to stay in their homes in the meantime, pursuing hobbies and other pastimes because the war had halted all business, and they had no work. March, the long-standing SVC member, was only interned 15 months after the Japanese occupation. British officials in London and New Delhi received a message via the Swiss consulate in Shanghai from a British council official asking if he should stay in his post under the Japanese. Army commanders asked why young British men in Shanghai appeared to be making no effort to escape to join the British forces. 'British subjects, many of military age, living more or less normal lives, although good prospects of escape exist if effort made,' Field Marshal Wavell, the Viceroy in India, noted when reviewing the matter.[34] Questions about loyalty and possible treason were raised. Officials said the sight of British subjects working for the Japanese in Shanghai would further besmirch Britain's badly tattered image in the region. Whitehall concluded, after weeks of deliberation, that it was not treasonous to help keep essential services going.

In the end many SVC members were to emerge from prison camps after the war with virtually nothing. Their homes, possessions and bank accounts were swept away along with Shanghai's gilded epoch.

Chapter 12

PLUCKY OUTPOSTS

Tientsin and Other Volunteer Corps in China

A plethora of British self-defence forces sprang up in the treaty ports, cities and outposts across China where expatriates established themselves. They provided protection during the endemic wars and political unrest that gripped China through much of the 19th and early 20th centuries. Westerners were targets for nationalists and bandits, if for different reasons. The Volunteers' role was to shield the local Western community in emergencies until help could arrive in the form of a gunboat or regular troops. Little is known about many units; it is not even clear how many there were. Most of these motley groups comprised businessmen, engineers, traders and bank officials. Most forces had just a few dozen men. Some forces were purely or overwhelmingly British, others resembled the cosmopolitan ranks of the Shanghai Volunteer Corps. British officials encouraged the units: local consuls often kept a small store of rifles and ammunition to lend in emergencies. Army officials said the Volunteers reduced the number of regular troops that had to be kept in China to protect British subjects and interests, as a 1926 memo noted:

> 'These Local Defence Corps are ... small bodies formed in isolated British communities to meet the danger of anti-foreign riots or risings, or of attack by one of the numerous partisan armies at present maintained in China and supported largely by pillage.'[1]

Standards and training in most of the volunteer forces were indifferent. Regular British officers and NCOs were sometimes lent for a week or two to some units to try to teach the basics of shooting and forming ranks. A few of the larger formations had small mounted and artillery units and could field the equivalent of a small infantry company. Most forces were armed with just ex-army rifles and possibly a few elderly machine guns. Membership rose and fell depending on the number of Western residents and local political conditions. Some forces were formed in response to a specific threat and only lasted a year or two. Others endured for decades until they were disbanded at the start of the Second World War in Asia as

Britain rapidly withdrew from China. Some of the smaller forces were made up almost entirely of the employees of a Western company with an operation in some remote area. Uniforms and weapons were provided by the company and it was essentially a private corporate militia. All of the units were self-governing and unofficial. Some forces, well known for their strident anti-Chinese views, figured in a number of notorious incidents in the inter-war era that helped hasten the end of the treaty port system. A few diaries, photographs and faded clippings from the local Western press are often the only surviving trace of many units.[2]

The Tientsin Volunteer Corps was the second largest force after the Shanghai corps. It first appeared as a defence group organised hurriedly by British residents in the city south of Peking in the spring of 1898 as the Boxers swept through north China. A call for volunteers attracted 35 men and its strength soon rose to 100 members. Officers were elected and Captain C. H. Ross took command with Lieutenant J. Boyce Kup as adjutant. (This appears to be the same Ross who later raised the Hong Kong Volunteers' mounted unit and had seen service with the Shanghai force.) The corps was part of the small garrison of regular troops and civilian volunteers when Boxer and regular Chinese forces besieged Tientsin in 1900. Many of the Volunteers were vehemently anti-Chinese and probably were among the white residents who abused the British-led 1st Chinese Regiment, which helped defend the city (as described in the next chapter).

Tientsin British Municipal Volunteer Corps, 1926

Detachment	Officers	NCOs	Other Ranks
HQ	2	4	–
Infantry		10	40
Signals		2	7
Light Horse		5	19
Machine Gun		7	15

Source: PRO WO 106/5379.

Recognition of the unit's existence by the War Office came in 1902 along with a gift of surplus army weapons and equipment.[3] The British municipal council, which funded the corps, nonetheless insisted it was in sole charge of the force, a fact reflected in its formal name: The Tientsin British Municipal Council Volunteer Corps. Any European or American living in the British concession and paying local taxes was eligible for membership. An approving 1904 British Army report noted the force was made up of an infantry platoon and a small mounted infantry section called the Tientsin Light Horse.[4] Membership was put at three officers and 60 NCOs and privates. Members sported a lavish ceremonial uniform with a red tunic and black lambskin cap with a red bag or flap in the style of a hussar busby. Khaki was worn for more mundane activities.[5] It developed into a useful little force by the mid-1920s with two 2.75-inch guns, machine guns, a motor section with armoured trucks, and machine-gun and infantry platoons. British Army officers, noting its regular training and good equipment, rated the force highly.

Hankow's corps, which traced its roots to 1858, had about 150 members by the 1920s and could field an infantry company and small mounted infantry section. A significant force also existed in the British concession on Shameen Island at Canton. Its strength after the First World War was put at a weak infantry company with about a hundred men, although its armoury was said to have just 50 rifles and 10 machine guns. A 1929 War Office report, noting the force was assigned to man two concrete pill-boxes in emergencies, questioned the dependability of the businessmen who made up the unit: 'It is impossible to rely on their presence in case of trouble, as on such occasions the British firms in the Shameen are liable to close down, and order their employees to Hong Kong.'[6] Most other British volunteer units consisted of just a few dozen members. Those at Newchwang and Ningpo had 10 men apiece.

Most of the smaller units did not have uniforms or equipment, and relied on rifles held by the local British consul. Training for most minor units, on the rare occasions when it was held, rarely extended beyond a 'little elementary musketry'.[7] Typical was the Tongshan Rifle Club, made up of British and Belgian engineers and officials who were employed by the Kailan Mining Administration and the Peking–Mukden Railway in Tongshan. It had 26 members in 1926 and possessed 60 rifles of 1897 vintage. Members agreed it was not wise to hold parades or do any military drilling because of the unsettled political conditions.[8]

Chinese Nationalists singled out the treaty ports and their privileged Western residents after the First World War. Frequent strikes, protests and riots called for an end to the foreign concessions. After Shanghai's international police force shot and killed 12 people during a July 1925 demonstration protests over the killings spread rapidly to the other treaty ports. Rioters attempted to seize the Hankow defence force's armoury the following month. Men of the volunteer corps and sailors from two British warships shot and killed several of the protesters. J. E. March, a member of the Shanghai Volunteer Corps, who was visiting Hankow, turned out with

British Volunteer Defence Corps in China, 1920s/30s

Amoy	Kiukiang & Wuhu
Canton (Shameen)	Nanking
Changsha	Newchwang
Chefoo	Ningpo
Chengtu	Pagoda Island
Chinkiang	Shanghai
Foochow	Swatow
Hangchow	Tientsin
Hankow	Tsinanfu
Kailan Mining Administration (Tongshan)	Tsintso
Kianghchow	

Source: PRO WO 106/5379.

the local force.[9] He helped man barricades and saw the Volunteers and sailors fire at the protesters with Lewis guns and rifles. March found it all rather bracing, although he fretted that he was in civilian clothes and could not draw a uniform from the Hankow stores until the next day. Hankow Volunteers with armoured cars and machine guns later guarded the settlement with the help of Royal Marines from two British cruisers standing offshore.

Hankow was again the centre of trouble in 1927 when Chinese Nationalist forces demanded the return of the enclave. British women and children were evacuated as Royal Marines disarmed the Hankow defence force. March said the British consul had the Volunteers locked up to prevent them making trouble. The concession was returned to China and the Volunteer force disbanded. British residents across China were horrified when they learned that British troops had disarmed the Volunteers and surrendered Hankow. London was denounced for cowardly perfidy, while some British officials saw the Volunteer forces as reactionary hotheads.

London, conscious of its declining power and the rise of Japan, wanted to improve relations with China and was less and less willing to defend the treaty ports. British officials pushed local councils in some concessions to cede their monopoly on power. Tientsin's British enclave came under a new municipal council that shared power with Chinese officials. This meant the end of the Tientsin Volunteer Corps in 1931 because it had been organised by the now defunct British council. British residents boycotted a plan to replace the corps with a special constabulary because it would mean serving under a Chinese commander. A compromise was found with the formation of the Tientsin Emergency Corps. It was envisaged as a Sino-British force

under the new council and the local British consul with separate British and
Chinese infantry companies. By 1932 the British company had some 80
men with an infantry platoon and artillery and machine-gun sections. The
second company was never formed after fewer than a dozen Chinese
volunteered for the force. A civilian force, the Tientsin British Auxiliary
Corps, was formed in 1932 to help keep essential services running in
emergencies. It had 220 men and 60 women, with the latter volunteering
to be cooks, canteen workers and nurses.[10]

Tientsin's little military and civil defence forces never saw active service.
Japan moved to take over the enclave as its power spread across China. It
was blockaded from December 1938 to July 1939. London made
concessions and the regular British battalion was pulled out in 1941. The
local Volunteers were disbanded at the same time. Japanese forces occupied
Tientsin the same day they took Shanghai. It appears that the other British
volunteer forces in China had already collapsed or were soon disbanded.

Chapter 13

UNWANTED GUARDIANS

The 1st Chinese Regiment

FEW SOLDIERS HAVE BEEN SO REVILED and misunderstood as the men of the British Army's only regular Chinese regiment. Its men gave loyal and brave service. British generals praised their valour on the battlefield. American, Japanese and European troops were happy to fight alongside them. Other Chinese predictably despised them for serving a foreign power. And yet they were equally detested by many British soldiers and civilians. Contemporary British attitudes towards the Chinese were condescending or hostile. Popular imagination saw the Chinese as a pantomime mix of comic coolie and inscrutable fiend. Britons living and working in China often were among the country's harshest critics. Arming Chinese and putting them in British uniforms was denounced as madness. Such men, it was maintained, could neither fight nor be trusted.

*

A handful of British soldiers and officials with experience of China began toying in the 1870s with the idea of recruiting Chinese troops. Dreams of Chinese regiments to rival Britain's Indian and African armies enlivened their thoughts and discussions. General Gordon's exploits at the head of an imperial Chinese army were cited as proof of what a handful of Chinese troops could achieve under British command. Advocates of the tiny China school argued that Chinese troops could be employed anywhere in the world, even daring to suggest their use in India. An 1878 proposal to the Colonial Secretary, Sir Michael Hicks Beach, called for up to 20,000 Chinese soldiers of 'good physique for service in India, or, indeed, in any part of the world'.[1]

Hong Kong's military commanders were among those who welcomed the idea of using Chinese troops to man the colony's artillery defences. London was told that a senior officer in Hong Kong with China experience:

'...entertains a high opinion of their soldier like qualities. He thinks the Chinese we could recruit in Hong Kong would form native regiments more temperate, docile, and amenable to stricter discipline than any other native troops in her majesty's service.'[2]

India's military establishment was enraged by what it saw as a slur on the honour and paramountcy of the Indian Army. More temperate officials at the War Office in London questioned the scheme's practicality: China was not a British colony, its government was unlikely to welcome the recruiting of its citizens by a foreign army, and the men's loyalty would be strained if their families remained under Chinese control. Still, London was interested, suggesting it might be better to recruit Chinese in the Straits Settlements and not employ them in China. Mauritius was mentioned as a possible base. A memo agreed that 'no better troops could be found', but nobody seemed willing to make a decision so the matter went nowhere and was eventually shelved.

A Chinese regiment was not raised until 1896 when Britain acquired a naval base at Wei-hai-wei in northern China. Japan had briefly occupied the port in 1895 after one of its periodic clashes with China. Britain leased the Yellow Sea enclave from Peking as a summer station for the Royal Navy's China squadron. British forces took possession the day after Japanese troops pulled out. Britain was to use the facility until November 1940, when a new Japanese threat forced its abandonment. Its cool, bracing climate made the enclave a popular resort for British officials and businessmen escaping the searing summer temperatures of the interior.

A military force was naturally needed to protect the base. A British or Indian battalion would be expensive and require regular rotation so the old idea of Chinese troops was resurrected with plans to raise a regular infantry regiment of 1,000 men. It would be a British Army unit using Chinese as its working tongue. Advocates of Chinese soldiers finally had a chance to turn their ideas into a new pillar of imperial defence alongside Indian and African forces. Plans called for the unit to be named the 1st Battalion, Chinese Regiment, but this was changed almost immediately to the 1st Chinese Regiment.

Major Hamilton Bower, an Indian Army staff officer, was appointed to command the new unit with the local rank of lieutenant-colonel. War Office officials interested in a possible new stream of imperial soldiery encouraged the experiment. A special effort was made to select suitable officers. Most of the successful candidates came from the British forces rather than the Indian Army. British NCOs were to train the force until suitable Chinese soldiers had enough experience to take their place. It was recognised that a new system of training might have to be developed to blend Chinese culture and British Army traditions. An unusually large coterie of 25 officers was assigned to the regiment along with 27 European NCOs. Large numbers of capable and sympathetic trainers, however, could not overcome the problem of language. It was clear within days that the British instructors would struggle to learn even a smattering of Chinese. Bower had to depend on a German civilian, who served as his translator and secretary. Each company was given a Chinese civilian interpreter as a temporary solution, but language would be a perennial problem. Training was slow and confused. Each order had to be translated, causing lengthy pauses between a command and its execution. Translators struggled to understand the clipped jargon of British Army drill sergeants. Faulty translations caused frequent misunderstandings and occasional chaos, as described in a later account:

'The method would be somewhat as follows: The company (say four or six men at that time) would fall in for a parade. The Chinese interpreter pointing to the colour sergeant would say, "You see this great big white-looking man? Well, when he makes a loud shout you watch very carefully what he does, and you do just the same."'[3]

A contemporary magazine print depicts British officers being shadowed by Chinese translators in traditional long gowns and pigtails.

Recruiting was painfully slow in the first few months. Soldiering was reviled by most Chinese as just another form of the banditry that plagued the country. China's army was notorious for its harsh, degrading treatment of soldiers, where officers bullied their men and kept their pay, and could often attract only the worst kind of men. Local Chinese officials, angry over this latest foreign intrusion, tried to sabotage recruiting. Local people put up the most resistance because of fears they would never again see any son foolish enough to join. Wailing parents sometimes besieged the regimental depot to demand the return of their offspring. Eventually a handful of young peasants from surrounding villages was signed up. Recruiting rose as the first inductees sent back word of good conditions and regular pay. Peacetime soldiering for the British was an appealing alternative to back-breaking farm labour and frequent hunger.

Bower and his officers believed the key to making the regiment a success was teaching the men that military life, despite centuries of contrary Chinese tradition, was not a chance to extort money. Training had 'to try and instil into the men some notion however slight of ordinary honesty and upright behaviour in their dealings with those whom their positions may give them the opportunity to rob', an officer wrote.[4] Officers treated the men with exacting fairness to encourage them to handle others in the same way. It seemed to work and recruits began to come in from across northern China as word of the good conditions spread.

Regimental dress initially resembled Royal Navy kit: white shirts and trousers with red waist sashes, leather webbing and wide-brimmed straw hats. Bower then opted to follow Indian Army patterns. A blue *kurta* tunic, of the kind favoured by Indian irregular cavalry, with breeches was adopted for winter dress. Khaki uniform was used in the summer. A small turban incongruously topped the ensemble.

Wei-hai-wei was regarded as the ideal recruiting ground for the new regiment. British proponents of Chinese troops had their own version of the India Army's martial races concept. Southern Chinese were seen as weak, shifty and cowardly, echoing the Indian Army's view of southern Indians. Martial theorists extolled the tall, brawny men from the north as China's version of India's strapping Sikhs, Pathans and Punjabi Muslims. Delighted British recruiters praised the Wei-hai-wei men as excellent stock. 'They were quite a different type from the sallow Cantonese Chinaman one usually sees about the world,' explained one observer. 'There were mostly brown, almost red-cheeked men.'[5] The Indian Army preference for recruiting peasants was closely followed. It was argued that such men made the best soldiers because they were sturdy, simple and trusting. Village life had shielded recruits from the imagined evils of education and modernity that supposedly made Chinese and Indian city dwellers disrespectful and unmanageable. Peasants, while slow to learn, were 'more respectable, reliable and better behaved'.[6] The regiment was determined to shun men from the classes that traditionally provided soldiers in China. Such men were 'full of those vices which from time immemorial cause the Chinese soldier to be hated and despised by the respectable civilians of his nation,' a report claimed.[7] Efforts to keep such men out of the regiment were not very successful, probably because recruiting officers lacked the necessary language skills and understanding to screen recruits, and growing numbers of ex-Chinese army soldiers found their way into the ranks.

Training had not progressed far when the regiment faced the first test of its loyalty. Anti-Western groups inspired by the Boxer uprising appeared in some of the local villages in the spring of 1900. Reports came in of an armed mob assembling near the British base. Bower, an intelligent and energetic man, marched out with the regiment to meet it. Some officers were apprehensive about how the largely untrained men would fare. Many of the men had relatives and friends in the mob that confronted the regiment.

'[Officers] watched the men's faces, not without speculation – for it was the first time they had been called on to fight their own people, but the delighted smiles which broke on every [soldier's] face ... left no doubt as to their keenness in this emergency.'[8]

The crowd was easily disarmed and dispersed at bayonet point.

Far more serious trouble erupted a few weeks later when an Anglo-Chinese commission arrived to fix the boundary of the enclave. A survey party from the commission and its regimental escort were assailed by angry villagers. A relief force sent to rescue the survey party was attacked by armed Chinese. At least 20 protesters were killed when the relief force opened fire. A more serious attack the next day by thousands of Chinese armed with home-made cannon was beaten off with several rifle volleys. There was no further unrest and the border commission completed its work. British officials praised the regiment, pleased the experiment in recruiting Chinese troops had been vindicated so soon.

Higher authorities promptly demonstrated their confidence in the Chinese Regiment. Orders came for two of the regiment's eight companies to join an international force trying to reach Peking to relieve the Western embassies under siege by Boxer rebels. Even critics agreed the contingent fought well in the subsequent campaign. Most of the 200 men sent to the relief force were young, some less than 18, with virtually no military experience. Many had been in the regiment for only a few months or even weeks. There was no time to train the soldiers thoroughly or build cohesion and camaraderie. Profound language and cultural differences between officers and men still made even simple tasks and exchanges difficult. And now they were expected to fight against well-armed regular Chinese troops and fanatical Boxers.

A Chinese army was blocking the relief force of European, American and Japanese troops at Tientsin when the Wei-hai-wei contingent arrived. It was sent to capture Chinese positions near the city's European quarter. It next supported a British naval brigade attacking the Chinese-held arsenal. British commanders praised the contingent for defeating a Chinese flank attack during the action. More fighting followed as the allied force finally drove the Chinese troops from the city. The 1st Chinese Regiment earned further praise fighting alongside U.S. Marines, Japanese and Russian troops. Newly promoted Chinese NCOs were singled out for showing exemplary bravery, as a British officer recounted:

'I found a Chinese sergeant named Chi-dien-Kwei kneeling in the middle of the road, with bullets kicking up the dust all round him, and the men watching him from the huts. I yelled to him in Chinese to ask him what the devil he was doing ... he stood up quite calmly and saluted and explained that as he had been told to take up his half company in exactly the same manner that his officer had done, and since he did not know what that manner was, he had come out into the open to watch. Now that he had seen how they were to advance he could continue. It did not seem to have occurred to him that he was taking any unusual risk.'[9]

A cap badge depicting the main Tientsin city gate was approved for the regiment in recognition of its services.

British merchants and businessmen living in Tientsin were not happy that their rescuers included Chinese troops in British uniforms. The regiment was denigrated and some of its men insulted in the streets by Europeans. It was the start of a unique ordeal for the unit. Insults and abuse followed wherever its men ran into European civilians in subsequent months. Westerners were terrified and vengeful after a series of massacres of white missionaries and other civilians by Chinese forces. All Chinese were seen as blood-crazed fiends. Giving guns to Chinese was denounced as madness because, it was claimed, they would only turn them on Westerners.

Criticism also came from other British military units, which refused to treat the Chinese Regiment as an equal. Some of the regiment's officers believed the Indian Army contingent was behind the vilification of their men. 'There has been a good deal of prejudice against the regiment exhibited in one way and another, largely born of the conviction in many minds that Chinese are no good,' the *North China Daily News* commented. It tried to defend the regiment by insisting it was not like other Chinese. 'They fought with our troops, and on the side of civilization and humanity at a time when these abstractions have few friends among the Chinese.'[10]

Captain Arthur Barnes, one of the detachment's officers, later attempted to redeem the regiment's reputation by writing a book on its exploits during the Boxer Rebellion. He was particularly upset by the abuse aimed at the regiment by the British in China and at home.

'So many unkind things have been said about the Chinese Regiment, by people with no knowledge of the matter, that it has seemed advisable to place on record the doings of the regiment in the real hard fighting in Northwest China in 1900, as they actually occurred, in order to show that, though a regiment in its extreme infancy, fighting under alien officers and for an alien empire, against its own compatriots, its own Emperor, and its Imperial troops, it bore its part with the best, deserving none of the somewhat nasty things that have been put abroad about it.'[11]

While defending the regiment's military reputation, Barnes shared the general European view that the Chinese were an inferior race, even if he was clearly fond of his men. Barnes apparently never saw the need to ask why his men should want to serve Britain and inquire about their hopes and ideas. It made no more sense to question their motives than to ask why his favourite horse served so ably. He attributed the regiment's success 'simply and solely' to steady drilling.[12]

With Tientsin secure, the international force set out for Peking. British Indian forces reinforced the column and Barnes's detachment was relegated to a secondary role. It was sent to escort a Hong Kong–Singapore Artillery contingent. Chinese soldiers hauled the guns when the battery mules could not handle the loads in the searing heat. Boxer forces attacked the guns during the march and Chinese Regiment men had to guard the guns as they were rushed over a bridge under heavy fire. A drawing of the incident, a celebrated moment in the campaign, appeared in a leading London newspaper. Only the Indian gunners were depicted in the heroic sketch. The omission of the Chinese troops summed up British ambivalence about their newest soldiers, as Barnes remembered:

> 'No doubt it was thought that an Indian soldier, a more or less familiar feature in modern illustrated journalism, would look far more true to nature, and would be far more taking to the public eye than an unknown quantity like a man of the Chinese Regiment.'[13]

Barnes's little force arrived in the capital a few hours after the first troops reached the embattled legations in the middle of August. Most units rested after the exhausting running battle that made up the march to Peking. The Chinese Regiment men were instead ordered to clear the rotting human and animal corpses littering the city streets. It was terrible work amid the stench of decaying bodies, clouds of insects bloated with flesh and the intense heat of roaring pyres. A swift resumption of drilling and training followed. Barnes primly noted that while old units could be allowed a brief rest after a campaign, a regiment that had existed for little more than one year could not afford to relax. Barnes, a European sergeant and 10 Chinese privates marched in a Peking victory parade with other allied contingents. Long months of tedious guard duty passed before the contingent returned home in late October. Its achievements were praised by senior British commanders and finally drew approving comments from some newspapers.

*

All was not well in Wei-hai-wei when the veterans arrived. Desertion was rampant among the troops who had stayed at the depot during the Boxer campaign. It now spread to the returning force. A War Office report subsequently described the flight as a 'black record of desertions' that destroyed the regiment.[14] A separate report on the detachment that fought at Tientsin said, in rather understated tones, that the 'only drawback to its complete trustworthiness, training and efficiency is due to the frequency of desertion'.[15] Major-General A. R. Dorward, commander of British forces in China, reported in December 1901 that 805 men had deserted since the regiment's formation in 1899. A third of the deserters fled before the Boxer Rebellion and another third fled after the return of the veterans from Peking. It was a dismal report for a regiment numbering 1,000 or so, even if new recruits made good the losses from desertion. A War Office report said that many of the men left in Wei-hai-wei deserted out of fear the Boxers would inflict 'barbarous punishment' on their families.[16] Many men had received letters threatening them and their families.

It was a very different story with the men who returned from Peking. Many of them had acquired enough money and loot to be able to retire. Some had purchased valuable looted Chinese art and antiques for a few pennies from British and Indian soldiers who had no idea of their true value.

Barnes, who took command of the regiment, tried to defend his command, saying desertion had dropped from 30 per cent during the war to just 5 per cent when peace returned. He claimed that some men deserted because they had been left at Wei-hai-wei and not been allowed to fight. A campaign of slurs and insulting treatment, some from jealous rivals in other units, had undermined morale, he added.

General Dorward agreed that the regiment had fought well and endeavoured to save it. He called for a reorganisation of the unit along Indian Army lines.[17] Dorward believed the main problem was recruiting ex-Chinese imperial soldiers. Such men were habitual deserters, reputedly slinking away as soon as they had been paid for a month or two or to avoid having to settle gambling debts. Hundreds of ex-Chinese army soldiers had found their way into the ranks despite the ban on such men. Plans to rebuild the unit called for a purge of at least half of the regiment. Recruiting was to be confined to carefully selected peasant classes. Recruits and their families had to be thoroughly vetted in the same way as the best Indian regiments screened recruits. Officers must speak Chinese fluently, serve in the regiment for at least 10 years to build expertise, and be replaced as seldom as possible to build ties with the men. 'Working through interpreters is fatal,' Dorward rightly declared. British NCOs were to be dropped. Such men lacked the tact for what Dorward called the delicate work of moulding Orientals – 'of whom the Chinese are perhaps the most difficult'. Greater psychological sensitivity had to be tempered with strong discipline. Dorward sardonically observed that the regiment's founders had been naive. Men who deserted from the Chinese army were beheaded if caught. The maximum penalty for desertion in the Chinese Regiment was 28 days detention in a 'nice clean prison with plenty to eat and little to do – the only annoyance produced being probably by the amount of routine gone through to get there'. A civil servant reviewing Dorward's note hastily responded that the Army could not start lopping deserters' heads off.

Defenders of the regiment suspected the Indian Army was exacting revenge on an upstart rival. It was hinted that the Indians were jealous of the regiment's battle record. Such shrill outbursts were unjustified. There seem to have been no calls within the armed forces to scrap the regiment. Doubts about its future were coming from the government because there was no clear role for the unit. Plans to develop a major Navy base at Wei-hai-wei had been dropped, ending the need for a permanent garrison. Suggestions to move the regiment to Hong Kong were squashed by the governor, who said the unit could not be trusted. London said the expense of the regiment could only be justified if another colony would take it. Mauritius, Singapore and Esquimalt in Canada were considered and dismissed in turn for various reasons. Recruiting continued for a time, however, while the bureaucrats considered the regiment's future. Its strength rose to 1,300 men and there was talk of a second regiment. Recruits from across north China were attracted by the regiment's feats at Peking and likely rumours of the loot that was brought back.

Deliberations on the regiment's future dragged on for almost four years. Enlisting was halted in the meantime, and men started to leave. Peace was returning to China and there were more attractive opportunities for many men. Harvests were good and there was lucrative work available for coolies in Korea, Manchuria and even South Africa. It was finally decided to disband the regiment and end the experiment with Chinese soldiers after the War Office failed to find a colony willing to take it.

Some of the officers feared the men might mutiny if the regiment was disbanded overnight so it was agreed the force would be broken up gradually. Some 300 men were recruited for a British-controlled police force in Wei-hai-wei. A few men joined the Hong Kong Police. The rest were dismissed in batches of about 100 men a month after receiving three months' extra pay. A list of the men's addresses was kept in case it was decided at some future date that Chinese troops could play a part in the British Army after all.

Chapter 14

WRETCHES IN KHAKI

The Chinese Labour Corps

SOME 100,000 MEN of the Chinese Labour Corps (CLC) served with the British Army on the Western Front during the First World War. Paradox and contradiction colour almost every aspect of this largely forgotten corps' peculiar history. Britain maintained the Chinese were not soldiers, and yet they served in war zones where hundreds were killed and wounded. These ostensible civilians were led by British officers, wore uniforms and endured strict military discipline. CLC dead were buried in British military cemeteries and yet it never occurred to their British officers to explain to mere 'Chinamen' what the war was about. Even the few CLC officers who passionately defended their men blithely compared them to farm animals.

*

Britain was reluctant to use Chinese or other non-white auxiliaries in Europe. London feared the use of coloured labour in a European war would expose it to foreign and domestic criticism. Mounting casualties forced the British government to reconsider its initial objections. Manpower shortages were hobbling the war effort. Advocates argued that cheap and plentiful non-white labour from the British Empire and elsewhere would solve the growing lack of men. It would simultaneously free thousands of men in British labour units for front-line duties. France, which had suffered even greater casualties, began using Chinese labour in 1916 after rejecting protests from French trades unions. London finally decided to recruit coloured labour units after Paris said it would welcome them on French territory. British ministers, however, remained wary of using coloured labour at home. A plan to use imported workers on British docks was abandoned after trades unions threatened to strike in protest.

Approval was issued in mid-1916 to raise the CLC. Eventually some 200,000 labourers from China, India, Egypt, southern Africa, the West Indies, Malta, the Indian Ocean, and even 100 men from distant Fiji, served in British work formations on the Western Front. Many other labourers from various nations served in the Middle East and Africa. Chinese labourers made up almost half of the British foreign labour units in western Europe. A post-war evaluation of 'coloured labour' ranked the Chinese top, followed by the Fijians, (mixed-race) Cape Coloureds, South African blacks, Egyptians, West Indians and Indians. Reasons for the rankings were not given, but it was noted that some groups suffered more than others in the European winters. A British government pamphlet said of the CLC: 'It exists to select men capable of doing a hard and useful ten-hour day in France and thereby release "white" labour for the sterner business of fighting.'[1]

Germany protested as soon as its diplomats in China learned of the British plans. Berlin warned Peking that allowing its nationals to be recruited by the Allies would violate China's neutral status. German diplomats and agents in China tried to discourage recruiting and German representatives pressured and cajoled Chinese officials to oppose the British recruiting scheme. A covert German propaganda campaign distributed leaflets warning Chinese labourers they would be killed and maimed in Europe. It also played up traditional Chinese animosity to other races, as in a leaflet found by Allied censors:

> 'For 30 cents a day you will be expected to work near the trenches in France where day and night large German shells fall from the air to take your life, and where you will have to associate with African negroes, Annamese, Koreans and such other remnants of "dead" nations.'[2]

The vehement German opposition led British officials to see the CLC as a major setback for Berlin:

> '. . . the fact that we had commenced to employ Chinese could hardly fail to be a blow to the German General Staff who realise the practically inexhaustible nature of such a supply of human material.'[3]

British plans originally called for recruiting labourers in Hong Kong to maintain the façade of Chinese neutrality. The scheme floundered because of the British disdain for what one official described as the 'unsuitable qualities of the Southern as compared with the Northern Chinese'.[4] Southerners were derided by the British as weak, unreliable and far too clever. Northerners reputedly were sturdy, dependable peasants who implicitly obeyed European overseers. France used Chinese contractors to recruit its labour force. London insisted on using British representatives to run its scheme. T. C. Bourne, engineer-in-chief of the Pukow–Hsinyang

Railway, was put in charge of recruiting. A recruiting depot was established at the British enclave of Wei-hai-wei on China's north-east coast. The British government and private companies had acquired extensive recruiting experience in the area over the years. Thousands of men had been recruited for the South African gold mines and British officials had raised a short-lived military unit, the 1st Chinese Regiment, from local men, as has been seen. It was thought that veterans of the regiment could be used as foremen and police to supervise the CLC.

Recruiting was slow at first, even though there was nothing new about Western firms hiring Chinese labourers to work overseas. Armies of Chinese men had built railways and toiled in the gold fields of North America, Australia and South Africa. Poverty and lack of work in China meant men were willing to travel thousands of miles to work for years, often amid appalling conditions, in hope of returning home with a little money. However, most Chinese were apprehensive about serving in a war zone because of the risk of being killed or wounded and some worried that they would be forced to fight in the British Army once they got to Europe. British recruiters tried to assure the men that they would work only in safe areas. A clause was inserted in each man's contract stating: 'Not to be employed in military operations.'

Reports from early recruits of plentiful food, good conditions and prompt pay at the depot eventually brought in thousands of men. A second depot was opened in a former silk factory in the recently captured German enclave at Tsingtao. British officials claimed CLC pay rates were four times higher than those paid to labourers for comparable work in China. Dockers, machinists and other skilled men received higher pay levels. Many men opted to send 90 per cent of their pay home. British officials set up a secure system spanning northern China to get payment to the men's homes after some families complained that they had to travel long distances every month to receive the money.

A bureaucratic snit erupted when CLC recruiters discovered the Indian Army was running a rival scheme to recruit Chinese labour for East Africa and the Middle East. New Delhi had not told London about its efforts. Complaints about 'unauthorised' activity were answered by a counterblast from India that it was also entitled to recruit in China. One government report said there were 4,205 Chinese employed in Egypt by the Indian forces in early 1918.

Prospective recruits arriving in Wei-hai-wei underwent selection and processing. A medical exam weeded out those with tuberculosis, eye ailments, poor teeth, venereal disease and other conditions from a list of some 25 afflictions. Despondent rejects were sent back to their villages. Successful applicants were shorn of their traditional pigtails before being sent to a vast communal bath. Brown quilted uniforms and other equipment was provided for each recruit. Men wore small oval metal badges bearing the CLC's monogram on their hats. Labourers were issued with identity numbers. A metal bracelet with the number was riveted around each recruit's wrist to ensure it could not be removed. Fingerprints were taken by a former member of Scotland Yard. Each man signed a simple contract stating: 'By the terms of this contract . . . I the undersigned coolie recruited by the Wei-hai-wei Labour Bureau, declare myself to be a willing labourer.'[5] It was printed in English on the front and Chinese on the reverse and stipulated that the signer would work in dockyards, farms, mines, factories and other places. Food was plentiful to keep the men happy and docile while they waited for transport to France. Tables specified generous daily rations of rice, vegetables and fish. Each man received four ounces of meat twice a week. Regulations stipulated bones could not be counted as part of the meat ration's weight. Food shortages later caused protests in CLC units in France. Men slept in the depot's warehouses. Dozens of men lay squeezed together each night on wooden shelves once used to store goods. A British businessman was thanked by the War Office for generously providing facilities 'for the purpose of storing coolies in capacious depots'.[6] Officers insisted the Chinese found the sleeping arrangements cosy.

Training at the depot consisted of a little rudimentary drilling. Recruits were taught to stand in ranks and march in companies of about 500 men. Progress was slow at first. Not many of the officers spoke Chinese and almost none had military experience. Chinese were later hired as translators to solve the corps' chronic language problems. Most recruits could not see the point of drilling and treated it as a joke. It took days to teach the men just to stay in their places when a company was lined up on parade. One CLC officer claimed raw recruits had a habit of leaving their place in the ranks to chat with a friend in another row. The friend, seeing his approaching chum, would meet him half way. The two invariably lit cigarettes and began to chat. Men around them would join in, creating a gossiping knot in the middle of a company ostensibly standing at attention. In fact the training was probably designed mainly to fill the time until the men could be shipped to Europe. It provided no preparation for conditions in a war zone.

British officers commented on the habitual cheerfulness of the Chinese and their zest for games and jokes. It was taken as a sign of the men's childlike nature. A few, probably more perceptive, observers wondered if the men were making fun of the Westerners. Some worried that the men's taste for clowning would cause trouble with the hidebound regular British Army when they got to France.

Most British officers implicitly believed that beating was the only effective way to handle Chinese. Recruits were slapped, kicked and hit with the walking sticks officers carried. Some officers saw training as simply a matter of showing the Chinese who was in charge and routinely beat them. A few officers delighted in demonstrating how tough or cruel they were. Some officers competed to see who could break the most canes on the men's heads, backs, legs and shins. CLC officers boasted there was a shortage of walking sticks in Wei-hai-wei because so many had been broken on the recruits. In fact officers who got the best results from the men used tact and persuasion rather than their fists. These officers generally had a sense of humour, were interested in the men and did not take themselves too seriously. They were also a minority in the CLC officer corps. Chinese labourers revered kind officers, providing for their comfort and making them umbrellas and clothing as gifts. Whether it was the beatings or persuasion, the recruits learned to drill well enough in a few weeks. No other training was deemed necessary. The men already knew how to dig and carry vast loads after years of back-breaking work.

The CLC struggled throughout the war to find suitable officers. Initial plans called for men with extensive Chinese experience and a command of suitable dialects. The British community in China was small, however, and there were few eligible men with such skills. Many Britons habitually spent their careers in China without learning Chinese or acquired only a smattering. 'If a man, instead of going to the cricket ground or the tennis ground, or to the country club, or to the golf course, withdrew himself for the study of Chinese, people would shun him,' recalled a diplomat.[7] Moreover, very few members of the British community were willing to serve in a corps that was widely regarded as doubly inferior because it was a labour unit and Chinese. Most men with China experience who enlisted wanted to serve with combat units, and had the social background to obtain commissions in British or Indian regiments. Just one of the 25 members of a British company of the Shanghai Volunteer Corps who became officers in the British Army opted to join the CLC.

CLC officers were an odd mix of businessmen, traders, missionaries, engineers and journalists. Most were British along with a few Canadians, Americans and at least one Russian. Some were rough, self-made characters and not likely officer candidates. Many CLC officers, who were given commissions in the British Labour Corps, worried that they would not be seen as real officers because they commanded Chinese labourers. Some new officers spent the evenings at the recruiting depot memorising minute details of military etiquette because of their fears of being seen as uncouth upstarts. A proposal to give commissions to some of the Chinese translators was dropped because British CLC officers feared it would degrade their own status. A War Office memo said Chinese officers 'would not be received on a social equivalent' by their British colleagues in the corps.[8] Britons with any kind of Asian experience were being made officers as the force ballooned. A clergyman who spoke fluent Japanese, but not a word of Chinese, was put in charge of a company. Screening of applicants was notoriously poor. Some officers who claimed to speak fluent Chinese could only manage a few, mangled words. What came out of their mouths on the parade ground was gibberish to the Chinese recruits.

Some Westerners recruited in Asia agreed only to be 'escorting officers'. This meant they took command of a company at the depot and accompanied it on the long journey to Europe. The officers would then leave to join British or colonial units. It would be hard to imagine a worse system. An escorting officer would train a unit and travel thousands of miles with it halfway around the globe. Men got to know the officer, and, if he was a good or popular leader, formed strong bonds. On arriving in France, the very moment when the men most needed leaders they knew and trusted, the company would be turned over to a stranger, who invariably knew nothing about the men, their language or where they came from.

Men without any relevant qualifications were put in charge of newly arrived CLC units. J. M. Harrison, a private in the Royal Engineers, was persuaded to join the CLC after applying for a commission. Harrison left Oxford, where he was studying chemistry, to enlist in the Army. Because of his scientific education, he was sent to France without any military training to serve in one of the first poison gas companies. Harrison served on the Somme before requesting a commission. He was pressured to take an appointment with the CLC and put in charge of 500 labourers even though he spoke no Chinese and knew nothing about China. While an intelligent and conscientious man, Harrison admitted he found the Chinese strange and occasionally unnerving. Most of the CLC officers Harrison served with were even less qualified for such roles, although he did work for a while under a missionary who spoke some Chinese. He was happy when British NCOs were assigned to the company and he no longer had to deal directly with the men.[9]

A report by CLC headquarters in late 1917 denounced the increasingly poor quality of British officers and NCOs being assigned to the corps. Most could not speak Chinese and many were uncomfortable with the men or even afraid of them. British NCOs subjected the Chinese to 'rough handling and undue familiarity', and some were accused of stealing from the men or taking bribes.[10] The Army generally seemed to fear the Chinese and over-reacted to even minor problems, sometimes the report said, 'shooting those who are temporarily out of control', including the innocent. Such treatment diminished the CLC's usefulness, the report continued, warning that British prestige in China would be damaged when the men wrote home about how they were being treated. It reiterated that only suitably qualified candidates should be selected as CLC officers. Incongruously, it then suggested that the men should be given free calendars to improve morale. London agreed to recruit more Chinese-speaking missionaries to lead CLC units, presumably to boost communications and ensure a more caring regime. The War Office complained, however, that some British churches refused to release their missionaries from contracts in China to join the corps.

New CLC contingents often had to wait in China for months because of a drastic lack of shipping. Even when ships could be spared CLC companies faced long journeys. Most of the early drafts travelled to Europe via the Cape of Good Hope. Later drafts were sent via the west coast of Canada, crossing the continent by train to Halifax, where ships took them to Europe. Other detachments went via Canada, the Panama Canal, the Caribbean and across the Atlantic to Europe.

British authorities worried about the reaction in China if German submarines attacked ships transporting CLC companies to Europe. Recruiting was badly hit when 543 labourers were drowned after a submarine sank the French ship *Athos* in early 1917.

Recruits sometimes deserted before they could be sent to Europe and there were occasional mass break-outs. A CLC officer, who was at Wei-hai-wei when about 100 men bolted one night, said desertion was sometimes blamed on rumours spread by German agents about submarine attacks. Other officers said homesickness was the main reason for desertion.

Once it got to the front the CLC's main role was to help handle the mountains of supplies needed to maintain the British forces. CLC labourers were organised into companies of 500 men under the command of a British major or a captain. Four British lieutenants and nine British NCOs were also assigned to each unit. Chinese foremen or NCOs did most of the work of running the companies. Each company was issued with three bicycles for the officers, two if the commanding officer had a horse.

Work mostly involved very heavy labour, loading and unloading ships, trains, trucks and horse wagons. CLC units also built airfields, railway lines and other installations, repaired roads and did forestry work. Some CLC men did more skilled tasks, including repairing machinery. Others cleared up spent ammunition and shells. This was dangerous work that killed and injured many of the men assigned to it. CLC labourers routinely outdid British troops at moving heavy goods. Military officials cited an instance when 65 CLC men in eight hours moved 3,600 flour bags weighing 85 pounds each. It took 90 British troops nine hours to do the same work.

CLC detachments liked first to discuss among themselves the most efficient way to do a task. Contracts required the men to work a set 10 hours a day, up to seven days a week. The Chinese disliked the system and it caused protests and work slowdowns. Instead a task system was adopted that gave the men a set amount of work to do each day and left them free once it was done; this was popular and worked well. Some officers complained that the men would finish a day's work in a few hours so they could lounge around. According to Captain A. McCormick, a British Labour Corps officer:

> 'They were strong, healthy looking men, capable of enduring great physical exertion, and could work at an extraordinarily high pressure if they thought they could reduce the number of hours to be worked, to free them so that they could sit on their "hunkers" in little groups gambling.'[11]

Many British formations were reluctant to use CLC units because of a misguided belief that they were difficult to handle. As McCormick said this view seems to have depended mainly on traditional British prejudices:

> 'The truth is that these sturdy A class Chinamen could do a much heavier day's work – especially if kept to task work – and when well officered than the average [British] Labour Corps men could be expected to do. On the other hand the Labour Corps men were much more reliable, gave less trouble and usually the employer preferred to have a British Labour Company.'[12]

CLC labourers were under strict military discipline despite British Army insistence that the men were civilians. CLC men accused of crimes were tried by military courts and, if convicted, could be sent to a special military jail for Chinese prisoners or even face firing squads. At least five CLC men were executed: three for killing fellow Chinese and two for murdering French civilians. Chinese-style punishments were employed to punish minor infractions. Defaulters were made to stand for long periods with heavy wooden blocks locked around their necks. A man's crime was written on the block in Chinese characters. Daryl Klein, whose book on his time as a CLC officer was entitled *With the Chinks*, does not say if the slaps and kicks so liberally dealt out by officers in China continued in Europe but records indicate that the corps' behaviour and discipline were generally good with petty theft the most common crime. Massive recruiting and inadequate screening meant the formation included some 'professional criminals, riff-raff, agitators and undesirables', an Army report said.

CLC labourers sometimes protested over poor living conditions or food. Occasionally they would refuse to work and demand better treatment. Some protests were hastily and brutally suppressed by the Army such as the demonstrations by Chinese and Egyptian labourers in Boulogne in 1917. At least 25 protesters were jailed. The episode bore out complaints from senior CLC commanders that their men were treated far more harshly than British soldiers.

Scores of CLC men were killed or wounded in action even though its units normally operated well behind the front line. Most of the casualties were caused by German air and artillery attacks on the supply depots and other targets where the CLC was based. Chinese dock workers complained they were made to use air raid shelters that were inferior to those assigned to British personnel.

Little was done to prepare the Chinese for what they would face in Europe. There was no training to deal with air attacks or shelling. There was no combat training even though casualties were definitely expected – companies arriving in Europe were issued with a set of printed forms to report their losses. H. E. Cornwall, a British Army driver, saw German planes bomb CLC men at a camp near Dunkirk shortly after their arrival in France. 'For days after they were panic stricken and ran amok, scattering all over the country.'[13]

Harrison, the CLC officer, had a similar experience with a newly arrived company that was bombed by German aircraft while working at an ammunition depot. 'The Chinese fled into the woods and lived there from then on. They came in by day to work and scuttled back to the woods to sleep,' he said.[14]

CLC men almost invariably carried out their duties well despite being unprepared for conditions in the war zone. Some CLC men reportedly fought alongside British troops when the Germans broke through the Allied defences in 1918. Reports circulated of CLC men being given rifles and put into scratch units. Some CLC men reputedly fought with picks and shovels. CLC detachments sometimes stayed with British rearguards and helped to dig trenches and gun positions and a number of CLC work parties were taken prisoner. One detachment caught in a gas attack was said to have fought off German infantry after refusing to leave their wounded officer. Most of the men were killed before a relief force rescued the remnants of the unit. McCormick, the British Labour Corps officer, said there was a widespread story that when German shells landed on a CLC camp, 'They immediately squared accounts by attacking a German prisoners of war camp and killing several of the Bosche.'[15] It is difficult to confirm such reports. British reluctance to class the Chinese as combatants meant that accounts of their involvement in any fighting were played down or suppressed. CLC dead were buried nonetheless in the immaculate British war cemeteries in northern Europe. Most of the gravestones bear only the interred man's service number.

Britain never wanted the CLC to be seen as a combat unit. At first this was to attract recruits and avoid violating Chinese neutrality. London later maintained the position to dispel suggestions that China was an equal partner after Peking joined the Allies in 1917. Some Chinese officials wanted the force to be seen as China's contribution to the war effort. CLC officers were instructed to discourage any thoughts that the men were soldiers, as Klein recalled, alluding to Lord Kitchener's famous 1914 call for British recruits:

> 'And yet we are cautioned that it is not desirable to put too military a construction upon our duties. In other words, do not spread the notion amongst your men that they are going into the front-line trenches. Do not lead them to suppose they are China's first hundred thousand.'[16]

Some Allied officers believed the Chinese would make excellent soldiers. France's Marshal Ferdinand Foch said the Chinese were 'first-class workers who could be made into excellent soldiers, capable of exemplary bearing under modern artillery fire'.[17] Most British officers and soldiers had far less glowing views of the Chinese. Their attitudes had been shaped by the ghoulish caricatures of the Chinese as villains and buffoons in the popular literature and pantomime of the times, as Klein said:

> 'As children we were taught to believe that both Cain and coolies were murderers from the beginning; no coolie was to be trusted; he was a yellow dog, he would stick a knife into you in a dark alley on

a dark night. He was treacherous. Today we have outgrown this puerility.'[18]

But most British soldiers never abandoned such stereotypical images. Cornwall, the Army driver, said British soldiers regarded the Chinese as comical and would laugh or jeer whenever they saw CLC men. Even the defenders of the CLC did not see the Chinese as equals. Klein said the CLC man was 'a simple, jolly fellow . . . content with the very simplicities of life . . . he is extraordinarily happy; he grins and grins'. Even this most sympathetic of observers had no doubts that the Chinese were not fully developed human beings:

'The moral to be drawn is that nothing passes in the mind of a coolie . . . Nothing, that is, of a philosophic nature . . . His attitude towards existence is the attitude of a domesticated animal, and a very fine one too.'[19]

A sea of books, memoirs and diaries was left by soldiers and civilians from both sides in the war. Little if anything survives to show what the Chinese labourers thought of their experiences on the Western Front. Klein writes of a fellow officer who wanted to know why the men were willing to risk their lives in another country's war. He quietly summoned two Chinese sergeants to his cabin on the voyage to France. The first man was Tang Chi Chang, 27, a university graduate and a school teacher. Tang, who was married to another teacher, was a man of some importance at home. Some of the CLC officers laughed at him because he was a Christian and organised services for the men. Tang was asked why he abandoned a respectable, comfortable position to become a despised manual labourer. His answer was the desire to gain experience – presumably, of the wider world. Sen Shin Lin, 26, had deserted from the Chinese army to enlist in the CLC for its better conditions. His only fear was that he might be forced to serve in the British Army. Finally a labourer was called in. Lun Zun Chong, clearly frightened and tongue-tied, could only stammer that he enlisted to get money for his parents. Klein teased his fellow officer, asking what could he expect animals to say if you ask them questions.

About 2,000 CLC labourers died during the war, the majority from disease and other natural causes. Overall, the men of the CLC were perhaps not that badly handled by the standards of the war. And yet some of the British who served with the CLC sensed the Chinese should have been better treated. 'They have been of great service to us in this war,'

McCormick mused. 'I hope we treated them considerately and wisely, and left no seed likely to breed race hatred with us in the future.'[20]

Proposals to use Chinese labourers were floated in the early days of the Second World War. Plans called for assembling 30,000 Chinese recruits in France by August 1940 to support the British Expeditionary Force.[21] Elaborate planning followed as veteran CLC officers from the previous war were interviewed on how to structure the force. It was decided to recruit men in Hong Kong. London feared recruiting in China would bring demands from the Chinese government for aid against Japan. Reports of the planned formation appeared in Chinese newspapers along with claims that Japan might raise a similar unit for Germany. Extensive meetings were held in London as plans for the second CLC expanded to recruiting 50,000 men. Hong Kong was told to find suitable officers, and warned not to give commissions to White Russians or Chinese. The plan was shelved abruptly by the War Cabinet in January 1940. Ministers decided it was politically inexpedient to import foreign labour, even for a war zone, at a time when Britain still had 1 million unemployed.

Chapter 15

FLEETING GLORY

The Army of Burma

B ritish rule in Burma was brief and unhappy. The Burman majority, conscious of their long history as a regional power, particularly resented being treated as a part of India for much of the colonial period. India's civil service was equally uncomfortable with this alien addition to its domains. Civil servants posted to Burma usually had little interest in the country and hankered to get back to the centres of power in India to pursue their careers. Indian Army officers insisted Burmans[†] had no value as soldiers. British military policy was to use the hill tribes and other minorities – who despised the Burmans – and added another rich layer to the army's beloved concept of martial races.

Early Years

Indians, particularly Gurkhas and Sikhs, formed the backbone of the various forces Britain raised in Burma. Burmese were recruited for paramilitary forces starting in the 19th century, but no regular local troops were employed until the First World War when a major expansion of the Indian Army was needed to raise troops for the Middle East. A small force, the Burmese Pioneers, was raised as an initial step in late 1915. It was decided in September 1917 to turn the Pioneers into an infantry regiment. It became part of the Indian Army as the 70th Burma Rifles. A second regiment, the 85th Burma Rifles, was raised with predominately Indian volunteers from the Burma Military Police. (Two other groups were raised for war service in Europe: the Burma Mechanised Transport group, and a Labour Corps composed mostly of Chins.)

Four battalions with men from various races were raised for the 70th Burma Rifles in a few frantic months. Selection of the recruits was mostly entrusted to local chiefs and British district officers. Some chiefs saw it as a wonderful opportunity to rid their villages of petty criminals and

---

† British officials referred to the country's majority people as Burmans. Generally, the term Burmese was used to refer to all the colony's ethnic groups.

hoodlums. Many undesirables were forced to sign up and often deserted as soon as they could. 'The towns and villages were purged of all their worst and most dangerous elements,' wrote Major C. M. Enriquez, who later served with the Burma Rifles.[1] Some British district officers tried to block the recruiting, claiming it would inspire rebellion. Many recruits, even the willing, were unsuited to military life. They imagined they were embarking on a languid life of simple pleasure. Nothing in life had prepared them for the discipline and unyielding routine of army life:

> 'Probably not one man in a hundred has the haziest notion of what life in the Army will be. He will imagine that he will receive a uniform in which he can swagger about. In a few lessons he will learn all there is to learn, and after that there will be good pay and plenty of pleasant gambling, with successful amours with ladies in the nearest village. The reality comes as a rude and painful shock. He has never known any restraint to prepare him for discipline. He finds that everything requires the strictest attention, meticulous accuracy, and a severe concentration as he has never given to anything in his life. He sees before him weeks and months of drudgery.'[2]

Such recruits must have had even less understanding of what they would face in the deserts of the Persian Gulf and Sinai. There was no real training. Officers and NCOs struggled just to keep units intact and staunch the chronic desertion. British and native officers commanded the battalions on the same pattern as regular Indian Army regiments. Some of the British officers, recruited from local businessmen and settlers, were as dis-appointing as the feeblest Burmese recruits. Commanders complained that many officers were of poor quality, physically and intellectually, with little interest in their men or military life. Few of the officers made a serious effort to learn the local languages so that they could speak with the men or learn about Burmese ways.

Two of the 70th Burma Rifles battalions were shipped to India for training before being sent on to the Middle East. Burma lacked training facilities and sending the men overseas cut down on desertion. It was an extraordinary, often wrenching experience for young recruits rushed from isolated villages to the sprawling military cantonments of India and the war zones of the Middle East. British commanders in Egypt had no illusions about using such raw troops against the Turkish Army, and the men were kept in rear areas for more training. The 1st Battalion arrived at Suez in May 1918 and was sent up to Tel el Kebir. Much of the battalion's time was spent on training, with spells of guarding roads and Turkish POWs. Its war diary noted the men were keen and progress was rapid.[3] 'The Spirit of the Bayonet is now commencing to assert itself,' reads one note in the middle of 1918. Whatever its spirit, the battalion did not get a chance to fight. 'Armistice signed,' laconically recorded the war diary on 11 November 1918, adding that the men had been given the day off.

The 2nd Battalion's war was even less eventful. It arrived in Egypt after the fighting ended and was assigned to garrison duty.

Only the 85th with its military police veterans saw action, although against nationalist Kurds in Iraq after the war in 1919. It was raised in Mandalay in July 1917 and trained in India before being shipped to Basra. Its four companies were set up on class or racial lines like Indian Army regiments. Plans called for platoons of Sikhs, Punjabi Muslims, Gurkhas, Burmans, Karens and Kachins. Garwhalis and Kumaonis were enlisted when the quotas for Burmans and Karens were not met because of a lack of volunteers. The regiment numbered almost 1,500 officers and men by the end of the war. It suffered a steady trickle of deaths from disease in Iraq. The 85th did not return to Burma until 1920, while the 2nd Battalion of the 70th Burma Rifles did not see home until 1921.

The authorities decided to retain a Burmese unit in the Indian Army after the war. A 1920 reorganisation saw the amalgamation of the 70th and 85th into a single regiment as the 70th Burma Rifles. Burmans, Karens and Chins dominated the new formation. Two battalions of the regiment saw service in India during the 1920 Moplah Rising. It also provided the Indian Army's garrison battalion in Malaya. Efforts were made to improve recruiting standards to avoid the problems that plagued the regiment's early days. Enlistment was reorganised along traditional Indian Army lines. Recruiting parties made annual tours to view young men recommended by veterans and local notables, though some village chiefs still tried to force their more difficult delinquents on to the recruiters.

In 1921 the regiment was restructured into four battalions: 1st Battalion (1/70th Burma Rifles); 2nd Battalion (2/70th Burma Rifles); 3rd Battalion (Kachin Rifles); and 4th Battalion (Chin Rifles). Enriquez says the 3rd and 4th were replaced with mixed battalions around 1923 when it was decided to abolish single-class or -race units. The regiment became the 20th Burma Rifles as part of the 1922 reorganisation of the Indian Army, though records show it was not until 1924 that the unit took its intended form: 1/20th Burma Rifles; 2/20th Burma Rifles; 3/20th Burma Rifles; 10/20th Burma Rifles (depot and recruit battalion); and 11/20th Burma Rifles (Territorial battalion).

The inter-war years were the final golden moment in Britain's Asian empire despite rising nationalism and periodic unrest. British officials, settlers and soldiers imagined their world would glide serenely on for generations. Talk of Burmese independence was laughed off in British clubs and messes. Even the occasional uprisings and strikes that swept the country seemed part of the traditional colonial fabric. That the natives were 'restless' was part of the grand scheme, a welcome break from routine for the soldiers and police to show their stuff. A 1930 uprising, however, briefly shook British control. Saya San, a local mystic who proclaimed himself king, led a small ragtag army that was defeated without much difficulty by the Burma Military Police with the help of a Burma Rifles battalion, but revolts then flared in other parts of the country as Saya's followers waged a guerrilla campaign mixed with a strong dose of banditry. More than 10,000 British and Indian reinforcements were needed to crush the unrest in an arduous campaign in the jungles and hills that lasted some two years.

In 1925 the Army decided to remove Burmans from the 20th Burma Rifles. Future recruiting was to be confined to the Chins, Kachins and other minorities. The decision came without any warning and was 'a bombshell' to the regiment's officers, Enriquez said.[4] Doubts of Burman loyalty and ingrained prejudice appear to have been the main reason for the decision. The Indian Army had never been comfortable with recruiting from Burma's main ethnic group because it was seen as the main threat to British rule. Burman soldiers invariably were portrayed by the Army as slovenly, ill-disciplined and often corrupt. Colonial administrators preferred to bolster British rule by recruiting Karens and other minorities that were traditional rivals of the Burmans. Burma's hill peoples were eulogised as energetic, cheeky and plucky – pleasing local versions of Gurkhas and Sikhs. Enriquez, while conceding that Burmans had a strong military tradition, said they were not suited to peace-time soldiering. Recruiting Burmans could only have worked, he claimed, by enforcing the murderous discipline employed by medieval Burmese armies. Though he agreed with the decision, Enriquez still worried about its broader impact. 'I do sincerely regret the passing of the Burman from our ranks. In view of his overwhelming 8 million numerical predominance, it is surely a grave political error to have cast him out altogether,' he noted in his diary.[5] Perhaps, he mused, the Army had not handled Burmans in the right way.

Life in the new regiment possessed all the hallmarks of a sleepy backwater garrison with a little training and drilling in the mornings, sport in the afternoons and a busy social life for the officers. Battalions shuttled every few years between Rangoon, Maymyo and the solitary overseas posting in not very distant Malaya. Duty in Malaya was deemed somewhat more interesting: officers and men enjoyed the change of scenery. Active service consisted of sporadic spells helping the police deal with unrest and the occasional uprising. There was no chance of getting the Indian Army's most prestigious assignment, the North-West Frontier, where regiments had the best chance of seeing combat and earning laurels. Burma was too distant, the regiment too junior and too inferior socially for such service.

A picture of life in the 1920s and 1930s is captured in the aptly entitled *Peacock*, the regimental journal. Its pages are dominated by articles on sport, shooting and social life. It reads more like the publication of an exclusive golf or country club than a professional military journal. Editorially the tone is manly and crisp, befitting no-nonsense regular soldiers. Occasional articles on Burmese life, culture and crude anthropology show a fringe interest in their temporary home. Even rarer are articles on professional matters such as training and military operations. Guest articles by members of the Burma Military Police and Burma Territorial Force offer snapshots of other local units. Politics are never mentioned in the journal and there are no allusions to the darkening international scene. Bumbling cartoons and heavy-handed soldier's humour round out the fare. A rare hint of change in the wider world comes in an article by one of the first officers to fly home on long leave. It was a luxurious trip over almost two weeks, with stops each night to stay in local hotels or camps. Those who could afford it were urged to fly home, taking a map to keep track of the route and sights along the way. Life was clearly comfortable. Advertisements from leading shops in Rangoon and Mandalay fill page after page with the latest in imported European fashions, foods, jewellery, silverware and other luxuries. Its pages conjure up images of a cheerful, sunlit world seemingly destined to go on and on.

Separation and Building an Army

Burma became a separate colony on 1 April 1937. Administrative control, exerted from India since the country's creeping occupation in the 19th century, shifted to London. There had been strong Burmese pressure to make the change. It was widely believed the country was in thrall to Indian interests. Up to 1 million Indians had settled in Burma. Indian businessmen dominated large parts of the commercial sector, Indian labourers and peasants competed for work and land and Indians were common in the lower ranks of the civil service and the armed forces. Many Burmans believed their country was being swallowed up by Indian migrants. Anti-Indian sentiment was widespread, erupting in periodic riots that singled out Indians and Indian businesses. Chinese migrants were also attacked. More than 200 Indians were slaughtered in riots in Rangoon in 1930. Separation saw a Burman prime minister and cabinet assume limited responsibility for local affairs. A British governor and civil service, sheared from the Indian administration, retained the real power. Moderate Burman leaders saw the change as a step towards eventual independence. Younger radicals wanted an uprising to drive out the British.

A new army had to be created from almost nothing to defend the colony. Burma had been rated as a second-class military district under the Indian command system. That meant it was a military backwater with a small garrison and tiny command staff; but it could always call on India's great arsenal of men and equipment. That changed with separation. Indian reinforcements might still be available in emergencies, but military officials in Delhi were not going to help what they saw as a rival army. Delhi refused to allow Burma to go on recruiting in India and Nepal for the paramilitary units that made up the bulk of the Burmese forces. London did little to help and declined to add to the two British infantry battalions based in Burma. Rangoon was expected to create an army from its own slender resources. Major-General D. K. McLeod was handed the enormous task of building an independent defence force. McLeod, an energetic and conscientious man, had little to start with except the Burma Rifles. He was given just two or three staff officers to plan and build the new army. Logistics, engineer, ordnance, signals, medical and veterinary units had to be created overnight.

McLeod faced an almost impossible task. Burma was one of the largest British colonies. Its borders stretched for thousands of miles through some of the world's most difficult terrain; the Burman majority increasingly resented British rule and unrest was growing more frequent; truculent hill tribes in the so-called Backward Tracts were a constant irritant. McLeod and his advisers concluded that the only feasible role for the army was internal security and border control. Even that would be a major task. There were some 20 rebellions in the inter-war era; most were little more than local eruptions, but each had to be contained. A more serious 1938 revolt was only suppressed with the help of substantial British and Indian reinforcements. The few sketchy plans drawn up to defend against invasion were based on the garrison briefly delaying the attackers until imperial reinforcements arrived – not that anyone really imagined such a thing would ever happen. Burma sheltered behind friendly British, French and Chinese territory and the weak kingdom of Siam. Britain's mighty fortress at Singapore was held up as the colony's invincible shield.

The 20th Burma Rifles left the Indian Army to become the foundation of the Burma Army and was renamed as the Burma Rifles. The pleasant interludes of garrison duty in Malaya came to an end a short time later when the Federated Malay States formed its own military force. Plans to expand the regiment modestly were hurriedly revised after the start of the Second World War and it had ballooned to 14 battalions by early 1942. Most units were still forming or existed mostly on paper when they were thrown into the battle against the Japanese.

Burman politicians had demanded an end to the ban on Burman recruiting for the Burma Rifles. Reluctant military authorities acceded and made half-hearted efforts to increase the number of Burmans in the Army and paramilitary units. Several 'Burman gentlemen'[6] were given King's commissions as a sop to the new government. Many British officers, still scornful and distrustful of Burmans, disliked the change. Military commanders complained that few Burmans wanted to join the Army, and that the Burman politicians did nothing to encourage recruiting despite their demands for more Burman troops. Senior officers were still claiming in 1944 that Burmans were '. . . temperamentally unsuited to the discipline of a military career.'[7] In the event a few companies of Burmans were added to the Burma Rifles, mainly with war-time expansion in 1939.

However, large numbers of Burmans were recruited for the new Burma Territorial Force (BTF), a part-time reserve formation modelled on its Indian equivalent. It had some 3,300 men by 1941, of whom about 1,200 were Burmans. Kachins and Shans made up the rest of the force except for a few British, Indian and Chinese members. Guard duty was the force's main role, particularly at airfields, petrol and supply dumps. It could be mobilised in emergencies for service anywhere in Burma. Detachments were based around the country. Many of its men were farmers. 'A principal object of the Territorial Force was to give Burmans scope for serving their country,' an official history commented.[8] One BTF officer said it acted as a reserve to the Burma Army while the British and mixed-race Burma Auxiliary Force backed up the British Army.[9]

Burma's Paramilitaries: the BMP and BFF

Burma's oldest local military formation was the Burma Military Police (BMP). It was a colonial gendarmerie – with a very limited police role – and the main armed pillar of British rule. The force was the first line of defence or repression, depending on an observer's viewpoint, against intermittent revolts and unrest. BMP units also patrolled the remote jungles and frontiers, clashing with head-hunters, border raiders, and the occasional rogue elephant.

The force was mainly made up of Indian troops. Its origins dated back to the annexation of Upper Burma in the Third Burma War of 1885 when irregular Indian soldiers were recruited to help pacify the countryside and crush remnants of the royal Burmese army. These levies were formed into permanent formations as the BMP. (A separate force, the Burma Frontier Levies, existed briefly around this time to police the borders.) More than 50 BMP battalions were raised over the years, although only about 12 existed at any one time. Battalions were recruited for months or years as need dictated in various areas and then disbanded. Units were usually named after the region or location where they served, such as the Southern Shan States Battalion or the Ruby Mines Battalion. Each battalion had a mounted infantry detachment, often Sikhs, whose duties included providing the Governor's bodyguard

Life in the BMP sometimes resembled Victorian adventure books of dashing British officers imposing the rule of civilisation on savage tribes. BMP patrols stood watch over the frontiers and the Backward Tracts – regions that had not been brought under formal control. BMP detachments manning remote outposts often were the only sign of British rule. Frontier duty was adventurous, frequently uncomfortable, and occasionally deadly. Duties included suppressing head-hunting and slavery or chasing Chinese border raiders. Campaigns could be brutish and protracted: small BMP columns marched through jungles and hills for weeks and months, hunting elusive bands of recalcitrant tribesmen. Porters and camp followers frequently deserted or occasionally turned against the BMP soldiery. Ambushes, sometimes by arrow-firing tribesmen, were just one of the occupational hazards. BMP detachments fought back with tactics that rarely resembled popular notions of how English gentlemen behaved on the battlefield. Revolts were ended by burning villages, destroying livestock and crops, and rounding up women and children. Victory in these Lilliputian wars came with a bloody price. A campaign in the Chin Hills cost the BMP 29 dead and 26 wounded – a lopsided figure reflecting the difficulty of getting wounded men to medical help. Frontier campaigns continued well into the 1930s. Some of the most remote regions were still being explored on the eve of the Second World War though in truth most BMP battalions led less exciting, if more comfortable lives, in Rangoon, Mandalay and other large towns, supporting the civilian police and dealing with not infrequent riots, strikes and other unrest.

In the early years only Indian soldiers were recruited. Battalions were recruited from Gurkhas, Pathans, Garwhalis, Punjabi Muslims, Kumaonis and Dogras. The average age in BMP units tended to be above that of

Indian Army units because the men had to serve at least 15 years to earn a pension. Most battalions had just three British officers, usually seconded from the Indian Army: a major and two subalterns. Native officers and NCOs did most of the work of running the battalions. There were just some 50 British officers in 1934 when the force numbered close to 8,000 men. It was a challenging, rewarding life for young officers sent to command huge areas with tiny personal armies and very little oversight.

Non-Indians were recruited for the first time in 1909 when Chins were accepted in some units. Men of other hill tribes and a handful of Burmans were recruited by some battalions over the years. But the BMP remained a resolutely Indian force. It faced a crisis in 1937 when Burma became a separate colony. India's military authorities refused to allow the BMP to continue recruiting in their territory. BMP recruiters were forced to fall back on 'local' Gurkhas and Sikhs, descendants of men who had settled in the colony. Disgruntled BMP officers insisted these home-grown variants were inferior copies of the Indian originals.

British policy favoured using paramilitary forces for internal security because they could handle a broad array of tasks and were far cheaper to equip and run than army units, as a 1934 article in the journal of the Burma Rifles explained:

> 'The Burma Military Police is a semi-military force intended to perform at the cheapest possible cost as (a) frontier Watch and Ward duties (b) deal with minor insurrections amongst the less civilized hill tribes (c) and transport treasure (d) guard and transport long term prisoners to and from jails.'[10]

The last two functions were necessary because of the 'lack of trust-worthiness' of the civil police and a requirement that felons completing prison sentences be returned to their home districts.

The BMP was not organized or equipped to fight wars or serious insurrections. BMP battalions were armed with rifles and a few Lewis guns. Some urban detachments were armed with shotguns. Costs were kept to the bone-scraping minimum. Transport comprised mules, horses, river-boats, bicycles, elephants and a few lorries. The BMP did not have medical or supply services. Civilian hospitals and supply contractors were used to meet the force's needs. Each man was allowed to keep one cow and two goats to supplement his pay by selling milk.

BMP officers had a reputation for high social standards despite the corps' penurious existence. I. C. G Scott, a businessman posted to the BMP mounted detachment as a temporary officer in 1939, remembered a life of weekly drinks parties, ladies in long gowns and dressing for dinner each night. He recounted the following discussion with his commanding officer:

> 'I well remember Hughie [Lieutenant-Colonel Hugh Childers] saying to me once when we were discussing this. "I presume you take a bath and put on a clean shirt every evening before dining – do you?"
>
> "Yes sir," I said.
>
> 'Then why not put on the correct clothes after your bath? You will find that dinner tastes so much better when you are properly dressed."'[11]

Long years of often solitary duty in the bush saw BMP officers acquire a reputation for eccentricity. One officer recalled staying with a retired major who interrupted dinner by blazing away into the night with a gun. Returning to the meal, the host cheerfully explained it was necessary to scare off the local spirits. Drinking was heavy even by the liberal standards of colonial soldiers. Scott claimed to have served with an officer who drank a bottle of gin during the day and a bottle of whisky at night. The man took a supply mule loaded with spirits on exercises: one side carrying a crate of gin, the other a crate of whisky.

On separation from India the BMP was divided into two forces. Six battalions made up the new Burma Frontier Force (BFF) tasked with border protection. Three less well armed battalions remained in a rump BMP: two based in Rangoon and one in Mandalay, with detachments scattered across large parts of the country. By 1939 the force had 7,858 troopers. Most of the men were Indian with just 2,000 troopers recruited from various Burmese races. War saw rapid expansion, the BFF increasing to some 12,000 men by late 1941, while the three BMP battalions numbered about 4,300 men. Neither force was given adequate armaments to match its expanded military role. The Rangoon BMP battalions had just five Lewis guns, no field dressings and no grenades. Both battalions were short of everything from water bottles to uniforms.

War

Burma's governor declared the colony was at war with Germany as soon as hostilities began in 1939. Young British men fretted about getting home in time to serve before the predicted Allied victory. Burma's regular and Volunteer forces were put on a half-hearted war footing, though a few officials did fear Japan would use Britain's distraction in Europe to strike in the Far East. Not many of the British in Burma wanted to believe such

Battalions of The Burma Rifles, 1937–1942

1st Battalion	Regular battalion.
2nd Battalion	Regular battalion.
3rd Battalion	Regular battalion.
4th Battalion	Regular battalion.
5th Battalion	Formed 1 April 1940 from drafts of existing battalions and recruits.
6th Battalion	Formed 15 April 1940 from drafts of existing battalions and recruits.
7th Battalion	Formed 1 November 1940 from Burma Military Police and Burma Civil Police.
8th Battalion	Formed 1 October 1940 from Burma Frontier Force volunteers.
9th Battalion	Formed 24 July 1941 as reserve and advanced training unit, taking men from 10th Btn for additional preparation.
10th Battalion	Formed 1 July 1941 as a training battalion to prepare recruits for other battalions.
11th Battalion	Formed 1 April 1937. Burma Territorial Force battalion (included Rangoon University Training Corps).
12th Battalion	Formed 1 October 1937. Burma Territorial Force battalion.
13th Battalion (Shan States)	Formed 1 December 1939.
14th Battalion (Shan States)	Formed 15 May 1941.

warnings. The usual stories and jokes disparaging the Japanese as monkey-like throwbacks amused and comforted the settler classes. It was months before work began on preparations for a possible Japanese attack. Most of the settlers told each other it was just a precaution. Burma was too remote, they said, ever to be attacked.

Burma was less prepared for war than any of Britain's Far Eastern colonies in 1941. The colony's small military staff struggled to prepare its fledgling army to face a Japanese invasion. Work that should have taken years was ineptly shoehorned into a few months. Failure was inevitable. Army plans called for massive expansion of the Burma Rifles and the paramilitary forces. New battalions were created by lumping a few experienced and semi-experienced men with droves of raw recruits. Regular battalions were gutted for officers and NCOs to lead the new units. Such desperate and inadequate efforts only weakened the regular battalions without creating effective new units. Poorly armed frontier and military police units were turned into supposed front-line army formations with a stroke of a pen. Frontier Force drafts were 'just collections of men and officers drawn from various frontier battalions brought together in some central place, fitted out as well as possible and then sent into the line', a unit history recorded.[12]

Burma's little army had no concept of modern war. Regular and irregular forces were unprepared for the reality of aerial attacks, massed artillery and mechanised divisions. Experience of active service, for the few who had it, rarely went beyond chasing head-hunters in the Backward Tracts. Exercises of the Burma Rifles in the 1930s were based on hazy, 19th-century notions of warfare on India's North-West Frontier. Units still trained with officers trotting on chargers in front of steadily advancing bayoneted lines of infantry. Lieutenant-Colonel D. C. Herring, 1st Burma Rifles, wrote that the army still thought war was all about gallant last stands and forming squares to repulse enemy cavalry. Attempts at more realistic training were hamstrung by inexperience, incomprehension and incompetence. There was little training for the jungle or bush fighting that would dominate any Burma campaign.

A lack of British officers was one of many serious shortages. One BFF battalion had a single officer running its headquarters – a reserve subaltern who had seen less than a year in the military. Drafts of new officers from Britain and India virtually ended after the outbreak of war in Europe. Burma's small British population could provide only a trickle of suitable men for the newly established Army in Burma Reserve of Officers (ABRO). Graduates received a few months or weeks of training before assignment to Burma Rifles or paramilitary battalions. Few of them could speak the languages of the men they were leading. Many regular officers were elderly and sapped by years of peacetime soldiering. Many officers had no more idea of what to expect than the raw troops they led.

Burma's army also lacked the weapons and equipment to fight a serious war. Burma came at the end of the supply line at a time when Britain was desperately short of everything from aeroplanes to pistol bullets. What it did possess was often useless. Typical was the 3rd Frontier Force. Its 600 men had one machine gun for each platoon and a single mortar for the entire battalion. Bren guns were only received in July 1941 to replace the unit's First World War Lewis guns. A few units were given machine guns for the first time just weeks before the Japanese attack. A unit issued with Thompson submachine guns received just 400 rounds for each weapon. 7th Burma Rifles began the war with no transport and no modern signals equipment. Its mortar section had never fired a live round in training because it had no shells. Every unit was short of equipment of every kind. Some formations had maps dating from 1809, others lacked water bottles and uniforms.

New weapons rushed to Burma after the Japanese invasion went first to British and Indian battalions, with the Burmese units getting whatever was left. 4th Burma Rifles was ordered to give its heavy weapons to two Indian Army battalions that had lost theirs in a retreat. Senior commanders promised 4BR would not be sent into action until new heavy weapons were issued. It found itself in action 24 hours later without any replacement weapons. Morale was badly damaged by what the unit's war diary called 'a rebuff more severe than anything the enemy could administer'.[13] Some battle-shattered Burma Rifles units later claimed men had to share rifles.

Burma's colonial bureaucracy, which had sharply limited military spending in the inter-war years, did not change its miserly habits after the invasion. Governor Sir Reginald Dorman-Smith timidly asked London during the campaign for its views on giving native soldiers, who were fighting for the colony's existence, a modest pay rise. Equipment and supplies reaching Burma were sometimes useless or misused. One BFF column was designated a cyclist unit at the last moment. Men were solemnly given lessons on riding bicycles in the military style and then dispatched to a jungle region where the machines were useless. It set a pattern for what followed, as Colonel Herring described:

> 'It was pathetic. The troops were unsuitably clothed (still wearing shorts night and day, hot or cold) antiquated communications, flag, lamp or even helio (can you imagine it, helio for use in jungle country) supplies by motor transport tied to roads and generally no thought given to the jungle conditions in which the army must be expected to fight.'[14]

Disease decimated many units far more than Japanese firepower. Malaria, dysentery and other illnesses were rampant. Units were frequently at half strength because of sickness. There was a shortage of doctors and trained medical orderlies in most units. Medicine and field dressings were almost non-existent. Conditions were worst in the BFF and BMP, which had no integral medical services and were expected to rely on civilian hospitals. Scott of the BFF watched helplessly as many of his men were immobilized with malaria on the Siamese border. Quinine was not part of the regular supplies and appeals to the army for the vital medicine went unanswered. Scott wrote to a civilian chemist in Rangoon for quinine and paid for it with his own money. It took weeks for the medicine to arrive.

Burma's army had one other problem as it prepared to face one of the world's most powerful and ruthless militaries. British forces knew they would have to keep watch for a Burman revolt even as they fought the

Japanese. Colonial officials had claimed for years that the Burmans, while difficult, were essentially docile and pliant. Now they had to admit that large military forces would have to be assigned to internal security duty. It was one of the few times the local authorities proved to be right. Anti-British Burman forces entered the country with the Japanese Army and quickly attracted substantial support. Dorman-Smith complained to London that the Europeans deserved sympathy because they bore the '. . . double apprehension of enemy and possible local native reaction'.

Burmese units made up about half of the British forces defending the colony when the Japanese attacked. 1st Burma Division was the Burma Army's principal field force. Its 1st Burma Brigade guarded the eastern frontier, and 2nd Burma Brigade was concentrated around Moulmein in the south. Other Burma Army units were deployed on internal security duties, particularly in and around Rangoon. It was widely believed that the Japanese would be held in Malaya despite the increasingly bleak news from there. Some of the more arrogant or complacent settlers and their wives went on ridiculing the Japanese as freaks. Some turned their bile against the British forces, accusing them of needlessly disrupting the colony's peace-time routine.

The Frontier Force was organized into eight mobile columns, each with two or three infantry companies and a mounted detachment. Columns were designated FF1 to FF8. A few British patrols ventured a few miles into Siam after it was occupied by Japanese troops. Serious losses were allegedly inflicted on poorly armed Siamese gendarmerie before the patrols returned home.

British military planners had generally assumed that a major enemy force could not successfully attack Burma. Its eastern border was protected by jungle and hills and there were few roads on the Siam side. An attack from the south was deemed even less likely because of the swampy terrain though FF2 was sent over the southern border to destroy several bridges as a precaution. The ensuing failure heralded the disaster soon to envelop the British forces. Led by a veteran of the King's African Rifles, the force was decimated by Japanese ambushes as it blundered around the jungle. Its maps were out of date and one of the bridges did not even exist.

Showing their usual disregard for pre-war British military thinking, Japanese forces invaded Burma from the south and the east. Burma Rifles and Frontier Force units took the first major impact of the invasion. Frontier Force columns that tried to halt the Japanese in the east were flicked aside by the invaders. Most units scattered into the bush. Burma Rifles and FF units formed a major part of the garrison holding the long, narrow strip of Burmese territory jutting southward. 2nd Burma Brigade was based at Moulmein and included 3rd, 7th and 8th Burma Rifles with Burma Auxiliary Force troops and other units. Parts of 3rd and 6th Burma Rifles held the town of Tavoy to the south. British commanders confidently talked of using the force at Moulmein to halt the Japanese before going over to the offensive. First, however, Tavoy's defenders were swiftly pushed back to Moulmein. Next, efforts to hold a perimeter around Moulmein crumbled as soon as Japanese forces began to attack. Units tumbled back through the town to the jetties to escape across the river. Brigadier-General A. J. H. Bourke, commander of 2nd Brigade and an old Burma hand, was asked if his Burma Rifles could stand. He could only reply that he did not know.

The disaster at Moulmein was replicated again and again as the British began a withdrawal that swiftly became an unending retreat. Burma Army units sometimes fought well and held ground against fierce Japanese attacks. All too often they fell apart as the mostly untrained young soldiers were overwhelmed by crumbling morale, poor equipment, intermittent panic and unrelenting Japanese attacks. 1st Burma Division had some initial success in the doomed defence of Prome, although 5th Burma Rifles broke under a Japanese attack. The division never recovered from the mauling it suffered around the oil centre of Yenangyaung south of Mandalay. 1st Burma Brigade, with four Burma Rifle battalions, was left with fewer than 1,000 men or barely a quarter of its strength.

Some Burma Army officers believed their troops were misused from the outset. Lightly-armed units suited to irregular jungle and hill fighting were instead ordered to hold fixed positions against massive artillery and air attacks. 'Mobility, ambush, quick attack and withdrawal, hitting where least expected and never staying in one place for long' were the genius of the Burmese fighter, wrote J. D. Hedley of the 4th Burma Rifles.[15]

Many Burma Army battalions were reduced to the equivalent of a company or less by losses and desertions. Units broken by Japanese attacks often lacked the training or the will to escape and reassemble. Survivors just melted away or were rounded up by the Japanese. Commanders complained that great damage was done by constant orders splitting up battalions for company-size or smaller operations. It robbed units of cohesion, harmed morale and prevented officers from building up effective control. Units were also being constantly redeployed with long, exhausting marches from one location to another. Exhausted men would arrive at a new position after a long march and spend hours digging in, only to be told to head for another distant location with no explanation. FF3, for example, came under the orders of a different brigade practically every day over three weeks.

Some units did their best despite terrible odds. The 2nd Rangoon Battalion of the Burma Military Police fought at Prome even though it lacked heavy weapons and the men had no real military training. Other units collapsed before seeing combat. Several units assigned to internal security duties were deployed against looters in Rangoon and other towns as the Japanese approached. Seeing the British withdrawing, some of the men joined the rioters and took whatever they could grab. Others stayed loyal, helping to gun down scores of rioters. Burmese troops were often given the grisly task of helping to clear up after Japanese air raids, aiding wounded civilians and burying the dead. It was dispiriting and difficult work that further eroded morale.

Burma Army units were swiftly stigmatised with a reputation for running away that hung over the local forces throughout the campaign. Brigadier Bourke said Burma Rifles units had a daily desertion rate of 20 men by late February. Units that had not seen action were as badly hit as battalions that had. Depleted units were broken up, combined with the remnants of other formations and redeployed. The 9th and 10th Burma Rifles were 'wasted out' to strengthen other units; 6th Burma Rifles was reduced to a single company. Even pre-war regular units were affected: 3rd Burma Rifles was broken up because of internal unrest over conditions. Some commanders claimed desertion was confined mostly to the small number of Burman troops in the ranks. Others admitted that the hill tribesmen who made up most of the units were just as unreliable, and in fact several battalions of non-Burman troops collapsed or deserted without seeing action. Even the myopic Governor Dorman-Smith had to admit finally that decades of British rule had failed to win over the hearts of the Burmese people:

> 'It is definitely disappointing that after all our years of occupation of both Lower and to a lesser degree Upper Burma we have not been able to create the loyalty which is generally associated with our subject nations. But I fear that we must accept the fact that we have not repeat not induced among the masses that sort of loyalty which will withstand adversity.'

Burmese soldiers were in a far more difficult position than British and Indian troops as the imperial forces retreated. Native soldiers who had believed that British power was invincible were shattered by the rulers' swift collapse. Native troops lost their homes, belongings and even their savings in the British banks as things fell apart. Their faith in the British crumbled further as they watched some Europeans use their privileged status to get away. Many of the men grasped that the anti-British Burman nationalists would soon be in power. Anyone who fought for the British would face reprisals. A senior British officer wrote in a rare frank assessment:

> 'It has to be remembered in mitigation that the struggle against the invaders was hopeless from the beginning, that morale was very low, and that the indigenous personnel, in view of the certainty of Japanese occupation, were placed between the devil and the deep.'[16]

Many Burmese soldiers deserted to return home and protect their families when it became clear that the British were abandoning the colony. Several officers complained that no plans were made to evacuate the men's families while European women and children were taken to safety. Organised evacuation of families, they said later, would have given their men confidence to stay and fight. 'The treatment given to the families of the soldiers of the BFF was disgraceful,' wrote Lieutenant-Colonel Scott of the BFF.[17] Some Burmese and Indian soldiers lost families in Japanese air raids or on the long, deadly retreat by tens of thousands of civilians on foot to India. Subedar Makardhoj, an officer of FF3, lost 17 members of his family. Jemadar Mitrabahadur of the same unit lost his wife and six of seven children.

Desertion, demoralisation and disarray multiplied as the British retreated hundreds of miles to India. Units marched at night to avoid air attack and ambush, spending the days building positions that were abandoned at dusk to resume the retreat. Mordant humour sometimes blunted the bitterness of constantly running away. 'Orders were "beat it to the 12th mile." This was not good military phraseology and was later eclipsed by such orders as "Skin out",' recorded the war diary of the 4th Burma Rifles.[18]

Men were exhausted by the endless marching. Officers and NCOs of 4th Burma Rifles had to stay on their feet during breaks in night marches after the entire battalion fell asleep during one halt. Men wearied by weeks of fighting, digging and retreating stumbled on in a daze. Hallucinations were commonplace. Lieutenant-Colonel P. P. Abernethy of the Burma Rifles was standing next to a young officer who pointed out an enemy horseman 10 yards away. There was nothing there. 'Exhaustion and strange country produced the most uncanny effects on young soldiers. Bullock carts were reported as tanks, and stumps of trees became guns,' he recalled.[19]

Some Burmese civilians, particularly Burmans, became unfriendly and then hostile as the British forces collapsed. Bands of fleeing Indian refugees were attacked and many were murdered. Other refugees were helped and sheltered by villagers along the routes to the Indian frontier. Isolated bands of troops came under attack by gangs who wanted their weapons. Retreating troops even encountered occasional opposition from British officials. A Burma Rifles detachment ordered to destroy key facilities to stop them falling into Japanese hands was threatened with criminal prosecution by an officious district officer. An exhausted Frontier Force unit resting on government property was abused by a district commissioner for failing to get his prior permission.

Disintegration became rampant in Burma Army formations and other units as they trudged through the hills and jungle to India. More and more men slipped away with their rifles and equipment. The 11th Burma Rifles reached India with just three of its native soldiers. A British officer passing through a village saw a forlorn little group of 'five Colonels of Burma Rifles' who had lost all their men. Discipline cracked in some formations. Bands of retreating soldiers robbed villagers at gun-point, according to some reports. Others pushed aside civilians on the narrow tracks leading over the hills. British officers were among those putting their survival first, requisitioning supplies and transport for their private use. A few Burma Rifles men, captured earlier by the Japanese, returned to the ranks as spies during the retreat.

Bravery and loyalty were just as common during the retreat. Some loyal soldiers escorted their British officers to safety in India before returning to their homes. Many who went back were recruited into levies to fight the Japanese. Survivors complained of being snubbed by British and Indian Army officers when they reached India. They were criticised for running away and accused of not fighting. There was no sympathy for men whose homeland had been devastated and who had lost families and everything they ever owned. 'The fact does not seem to have been appreciated by many Indian Army and British Service officers who adversely criticized the regiment,' said a Burma Rifles report.[20]

Patchy records indicate that some 10,000 survivors of the Burma Rifles, BFF and BMP reached India. Most of those who got away were Indians and Gurkhas. Many Kachin, Chin and Karen soldiers returned to their native regions. Men willing to fight on were formed into the new Burma Regiment and the Burma Intelligence Corps. Both units were mostly Indian and Gurkha in composition. It had six line battalions, numbered 1 to 6, two garrison units, the 25th and 26th Battalions and a training unit designated as the 10th Battalion. Plans for a mounted infantry 7th Battalion were abandoned after a few months. Most of these units existed primarily on paper and were broken up and dissolved by early 1944. Several Burma Regiment and Burma Intelligence Corps units saw action when the imperial forces took the offensive after 1942. The Burma Rifles were re-formed in 1945 after Burma was retaken and formed part of the garrison until British rule ended a few years later.

Chapter 16

ANGLOS AND BURMANS

The Burma Auxiliary Force

V OLUNTEER UNITS WERE FIRST RAISED in Burma in the 19th century
for the usual auxiliary duties of aiding the regular forces in emergencies
and protecting the colony's small British community. The colony's four
Volunteer infantry battalions and an artillery unit traced their roots to the
second half of the 19th century. All were part of India's Volunteer forces
until Burma became a separate colony in 1937. The short-lived Burma
Auxiliary Force (BAF) was formed after the split and came under the new
Burma Army.

The Early Volunteers

Civil servants, planters, engineers and businessmen dominated the mostly
modest units in the early years. Standards were not overly demanding, and
the Volunteers cultivated the usual clubby conviviality. Training was random
and slipshod, a few hours once or twice a month, with an occasional camp
or field exercise. Burma's little force faced the same challenges as other
Volunteer formations in the Far East. The colony had few British residents
and only a limited number were willing to enlist. Many who did join left
after discovering like so many others that marching in the glaring sun did
not match their visions of military glory. Work, more pleasant pastimes and
frequent transfers further cut into recruiting and retention. Despite the
shortage, Burma was the last Far Eastern colony to drop a ban on
Volunteers who, in the language of the times, lacked European ancestry.
Mixed-race Volunteers had to prove one parent was white. Paradoxically,
Burma was more accepting of intermarriage than most British colonies and
Anglo-Burman Eurasians did not face the discrimination endured by
Anglo-Indians in India. In the end numerous Anglo-Burmans served in the
Volunteers, particularly in the years before the Second World War.

Moulmein in southern Burma appears to have raised the first Volunteer
unit. Its motto, '*Primus in Burma*', declared its seniority. Starting life as a
local defence detachment, the force became the Moulmein Volunteer
Artillery Corps in 1885. W. G. St. Clair, the energetic journalist who later

galvanised the Singapore Volunteers, saw early service with the force. It is not clear if the artillery role was abandoned when the force was renamed two years later as the Moulmein Volunteer Rifle Corps. It was reduced to a single company in 1889 because of a lack of recruits. Recruiting later improved and it was reconstituted as the 14th Tenasserim Volunteer Rifles in 1917, becoming the Tenasserim Volunteer Rifles in the Indian Auxiliary Force in 1920.

A loosely organised Volunteer force was formed in Rangoon around 1860 after the British annexation. The unit did not assume a permanent structure and start to flourish until 1877. A civilian, Mr H. Krauss, served as commandant until it was decided regular military experience was needed to improve standards. Major Evanson, who was serving as a local magistrate, was appointed commander with a Captain Cuthert of the 89th Regiment as adjutant. Cadet companies were formed in 1878 at the city's two European schools. There were enough men by 1879 to form a new unit, the Rangoon Volunteer Artillery, which by 1892 was helping man forts protecting the port. The Rangoon Engineer Volunteers was formed in 1892 as a submarine mining detachment. It was turned into an electrical engineer company in 1902 and manned searchlights in the river forts. A mounted infantry company was formed in 1885 at Akyab on the coast some 250 miles north-west of Rangoon. It took part that year in mopping-up operations in Upper Burma during the Third Burma War. Records describe it as the first 'outstation company', suggesting similar units were formed as part of the Rangoon battalion.

Rangoon's infantry unit became the 18th Rangoon Volunteer Rifles in 1917 and then the Rangoon Volunteer Rifles as part of the Indian Auxiliary Force in 1920. A detachment of the Rangoon Artillery saw service in the Middle East during World War I as part of an Indian Volunteer force. Rangoon's infantry and artillery were Burma's pre-eminent Volunteer units as befitted the colony's largest and richest city. Various sub-units were established over the years, including a highland company and an armoured car detachment.

Far less exalted was the Burma Railway Volunteer unit. It was established in 1879 as the Rangoon Irrawaddy State Railway Volunteers. Its officers were railway company officials and many of the rank-and-file were Eurasians. The unit went through various transformations, becoming the Burma State Railway Volunteer Corps in 1884, the Burma Railway Volunteer Corps in 1899, the 21st Burma Railway Volunteer Corps in 1917 and the Burma Railway Volunteer Corps in 1920. Working as train crews meant men were often away and it was hard to assemble large numbers at any one time even though it was a big battalion. Its duties mostly consisted of guarding key installations, primarily the railways, during unrest.

Northern Burma was covered by the far-flung Upper Burma Volunteer Rifles formed in 1886. Battalion headquarters was at Maymyo with tiny detachments dotted around the isolated settlements of the north. Such dispersion made it difficult to assemble more than a few men at a time and bedevilled training. It became the 34th Upper Burma Volunteer Rifles in the 1917 Indian realignment and the Upper Burma Battalion in 1920.

Burma Auxiliary Force, 1937–1941

Burma took responsibility for its own defence and internal security in 1937. The five Burmese units of the Indian Auxiliary Force were amalgamated into the new Burma Auxiliary Force as the Rangoon Field Brigade (Royal Artillery); Rangoon Battalion; Burma Railways Battalion; Tenasserim Battalion; and Upper Burma Battalion.

Volunteer soldiering was not popular in the inter-war era. Officials complained that many young British men working and living in the colony shirked military service. A War Office report on the Rangoon Battalion said Europeans showed little or no interest in the force.[1] Most Britons believed the colony did not face a threat and saw no need to spend their evenings and weekends drilling with the local BAF detachment. A better response came from Eurasians. A pre-war report shows the BAF had 2,108 Europeans, Anglo-Burmans, Anglo-Indians, Sino-Burmans and a single Burman. BAF officers were predominantly British. A few mixed-race Volunteers were given war-time commissions in the BAF and the Burma Naval Reserve. Some recalled being snubbed by British colleagues.

BAF forces were mobilised in September 1939 when Burma followed Britain in declaring war on Germany. The BAF was even less ready for war than the colony's paltry regular forces. Training was still haphazard, few men had any serious military experience, and weapons and equipment were old and scanty. Still, nobody in Burma imagined there was any chance of fighting the Germans on the approaches to Rangoon or Mandalay. Young whites fretted about getting back to Britain to enlist as older men reminisced about service during the last war. Four hundred men of Rangoon's BAF battalion were called out to guard oil refineries, government buildings and other key facilities. They alternated spells of guard duty with civilian jobs over the coming months. British Army units took over most of the guard duties in mid-1940 except for a single BAF company that was employed full-time. Battalion records said this gave jobs to many jobless or poorly paid men in the battalion. Most were probably

Burma Auxiliary Force, Strength 1941

	Officers		Other Ranks	
	Active	Supernumerary	Active	Reserve
Rangoon Field Brigade, RA	30	4	553	126
Tenasserim Battalion	6	–	221	63
Rangoon Battalion	25	2	634	291
Anti-Aircraft MG Battalion	6	–	155	–
Burma Railways Battalion	22	–	426	140
Upper Burma Battalion	17	4	449	131

Plus a small detachment of regular British officers and NCOs as trainers.

Burma Auxiliary Force, Ethnic Composition 1941

Burman	362	Karen	171
Kachin	5	Chin	2
Shan	1	Indian	73
British/Mixed-Race	2,372		

Source: PRO WO 106/3656.

mixed-race soldiers since there were few unemployed or poor whites in the colony.

Burma began frantic efforts in 1940 to prepare for a possible Japanese attack. New legislation required British men in the colony to do some form of military service. BAF numbers did not soar despite the legislation. Civil defence and other auxiliary units competed with the BAF for the limited number of available men. Many men were given exemptions because they held key government and civil positions. Nor was recruiting boosted by a decision to open BAF units to all races. A 30 April 1941 report shows an increase of just 265 white and mixed-race BAF volunteers since 1939 along with 614 new Burmese and Indian recruits. The first figure was not broken down, but it appears that at least half were mixed-race. The very modest intake of 614 Burmese and Indian volunteers suggests the BAF did not make much effort to recruit non-whites.

BAF units were also depleted when scores of men were selected as officers and transferred to regular units. Key men were snapped up, such as George Riffin, regimental sergeant-major of the Rangoon Battalion, who became a captain in the Burma Rifles.

Last-minute efforts to train and equip the BAF battalions for war were sketchy and often futile. The driblets of equipment that reached the Burma Army went mostly to the regular units. BAF formations were given vague promises of getting the regulars' dilapidated equipment. Rangoon's

Volunteer artillery unit had four World War I-era field guns. It was assigned to guard the approaches to the port after the start of war in 1939. Equally threadbare were the regiment's four vintage armoured cars. Troopers joked that the vehicles had seen service in Palestine during the last war. Others, like Captain Bruce Kinloch, failed to see any humour in sending men to fight in rusting death traps:

> 'It was here that I saw some of the armoured cars that were being used. Relics of the last war or before. Many men were killed in them before they were destroyed, and someone deserved to be shot for sending men into action in them.'[2]

Efforts to boost training were stymied because many Volunteers could not be spared from their civilian posts except in emergencies. Government officials had to run the country and prepare war plans, while engineers and planters were needed to keep producing oil, metals and other vital war supplies. Just 130 men were available when an intensive 65-day training session was held for the Volunteers in 1941.

The BAF's modest artillery and armoured units were transferred to the Burma Army on the eve of the Japanese invasion. Rangoon's Volunteer gunners provided the men for several artillery units. The 5th Field Battery, BAF, was formed for mobile service. BAF gunners also manned two 6-inch guns that arrived to defend Rangoon's port. An anti-aircraft machine-gun battery was equipped with Browning machine guns from American supplies intended for China, and helped defend Mingaladon air base outside the city. It was replaced by the 1st Heavy Anti-Aircraft Regiment, BAF. The regiment started training without guns, only receiving 3.7-inch and Bofors 40-mm cannon after Japanese forces crossed the frontier. Its 1st Heavy Anti-Aircraft Battery was armed with 3.7-inch guns and the 3rd Light Anti-Aircraft Battery with the Bofors.

The Japanese Attack

Anti-aircraft gunners of the Rangoon BAF battalion were the first Volunteers to see action when Japanese planes attacked Mingaladon airfield on 23 December 1941. They claimed to have downed two Japanese aircraft over the next few weeks. Rangoon's infantry battalion was mobilised to help wounded civilians and clear wreckage after air raids pulverised parts of the city. In the following weeks they distributed food, helped maintain essential services and assisted reinforcements disembarking at the city docks.

Most BAF units were assigned to internal security duty at the start of the war. Auxiliaries guarded roads and bridges, provided security against

Burma Auxiliary Force, 1941

Rangoon Field Brigade, RA
    Coast Defence Battery   (2 x 6-inch guns 4 x electric lights)
    5th Field Battery   (4 x 18-pounder guns)
    Fortress Company, RE
    Wireless Section
    Motor Transport
    Signals
    Anti-Aircraft Machine Gun Battery   (20 Lewis guns)
    Replaced by:

1st Heavy Anti-Aircraft Regiment   (4 x 3.7-inch guns, 4 x Bofors 40-mm)

Tenasserim Battalion
    HQ
    1 Rifle company
    1 Machine-gun section
    1 Light motor patrol

Rangoon Battalion
    3 Rifle companies
    1 Machine-gun platoon
    1 Armoured car section

Burma Railways Battalion
    HQ
    3 Rifle companies

Upper Burma Battalion
    HQ
    3 Rifle companies (less two platoons)
    5 Motor patrols

Source: PRO AIR 2/2690.

airborne attacks and protected troop and supply convoys. Some units could do little with the handfuls of men they could muster. The Upper Burma Battalion, with some 500 men, was supposed to guard key facilities in an area the size of England. Its platoons and subsections were scattered up to 300 miles apart.

Men of the Tenasserim Battalion, the smallest BAF unit, were the first Volunteers to clash with Japanese troops. It had some 200 men in two small companies based at Moulmein and Tavoy in the far south. A January 1941 War Office memo had expressed concern that the unit was much smaller than other BAF battalions but efforts to strengthen the force saw only a modest increase. Tenasserim's Volunteers, nonetheless, earned a good record

Burma Auxiliary Force, Dispositions 1941

Akyab	Detachment, Rangoon Battalion
Chauk	D Company, Upper Burma Battalion
Lanywa	Detachment, D Company, Upper Burma Battalion
Lashio	Demolition Squad, Upper Burma Battalion
Nasam Falls	Detachment, C Company, Upper Burma Battalion
Namtu	C Company, Upper Burma Battalion
Yenangyaung	D Company, Upper Burma Battalion
Rangoon	Rangoon Field Brigade, RA
	1st Heavy Anti-Aircraft Regiment
	Rangoon Battalion
	Railways Battalion (*but would have been scattered all over the country*)
Moulmein	Tenasserim Battalion
Tavoy	1 company, Tenasserim Battalion

Source: PRO CAB 44/325.

in a campaign that tarnished the reputations of many regular units. Many of the Tenasserim Volunteers were engineers at the mines dotting the province. They used civilian telephone lines to provide a stream of intelligence in the first hours and days after Japanese forces crossed the border. Its detachments hit Japanese columns with running attacks and used the miners' skill with explosives to block roads. When regular troops abandoned Tavoy without a serious fight after it was encircled, the local Tenasserim company fought on in the bush, blowing up three bridges to delay the Japanese advance. Some of its men only got back to the British lines days later. The other Tenasserim BAF company took part in the brief defence of Moulmein, its survivors escaping when the regular garrison pulled back across the Salween River.

Rangoon's armoured car section were the next Volunteers to see action. Its four cars – *Snipe, Kestrel, Eagle* and *Hawk* – had been caught in the air raids on Mingaladon airfield. Three of the cars were damaged and had to be repaired before the unit was sent to the front in early February. *Eagle* and *Hawk* were assigned to take a Gurkha officer with an important message to Martaban near Moulmein. The little party ran into Japanese troops. Both cars were damaged and most of the crew members wounded before pulling back. *Eagle* and *Hawk* were salvaged, but had to be abandoned several weeks later in Mandalay as beyond repair. *Snipe* and *Kestrel* formed part of the main rearguard when British forces were driven from Thaton in mid-February. *Snipe* was lost after toppling into a bomb crater in the retreat to the Sittang River. *Kestrel* and the remnants of the armoured car detachment reached the Sittang bridge. Setting up camp, the men were breakfasting as the two surviving officers went to find local headquarters. Japanese infantry rushed the camp and several of the armoured car unit were injured as machine-gun fire raked the position. The Volunteers could not get to *Kestrel* and only escaped after abandoning the vehicle. Survivors of the section eventually reached Mandalay.

The BAF's anti-aircraft gunners saw regular action during the campaign, helping to defend bridges and other vital points during the long retreat north. Two of the BAF field battery's 18-pounders, deployed as anti-tank guns, fought in the catastrophic defeat at the Sittang. Survivors of the Rangoon BAF battalion, by now numbering no more than the equivalent of a single company, left with the regular forces when the city was abandoned.

A belated decision was made to mobilise the Burma Railways Battalion in late January as the railway system fell apart. By then many railway workers and some managers had abandoned their posts or slumped into despondency as Japanese attacks ravaged the network. Perversely, the battalion had not been embodied at the start of the war because the administration said railway staff could not be spared from such essential duties. The belated decision to mobilise the battalion predictably made little difference. The unit appears not to have played any significant part in the campaign.

Some Anglo-Burman and Anglo-Indian Volunteers were torn between staying in the ranks or leaving to protect their families as the British forces retreated. Such men had much to fear from a Japanese victory. Eurasians were seen by the Japanese and their Burman allies as staunch supporters of British rule and likely targets for reprisal. There was no systematic attempt to evacuate dependents of mixed-race BAF men along with the families of European Volunteers.

Remnants of the BAF forces reached Mandalay, where they regrouped and tried to find new equipment and supplies. A 23 March 1942 directive merged the Rangoon, Tenasserim and Upper Burma Battalions into a composite unit. Each battalion had only enough men to form a single company apiece in the new Burma Battalion, BAF. It was assigned to guard duty in Mandalay and helped organise Europeans being evacuated to India. It also operated river ferries whose civilian crews had fled. BAF men handled one of the larger river boats ironically named the SS *Japan*. Refugees, regular troops and supplies were shuttled up-river to overland escape routes to India. Inexperienced BAF men pressed into service as crew occasionally ran vessels on to sandbanks or collided with other boats.

What was left of the composite battalion left Mandalay on 23 April on a ferry towing two barges. Some 2,000 troops, many from the Burma Rifles, were crammed into the vessels. Abandoning the steamer when it could go no further, the remnants of the BAF battalion began an overland trek to India from Katha on 2 May, most of its men reaching the frontier later that month.

BAF detachments destroyed oil wells, mines and other vital facilities as the British Army retreated through northern Burma. Lieutenant G. H. Cooper of D Company of the Upper Burma Battalion, an oil engineer in civilian life, helped destroy oil fields at Chauk.

> 'As an officer of the BAF I was in charge. We boarded the steamer just after the tank farm on the foreshore had been "fired". Six 1-million gallon tanks of oil! We had heard that the Japs were very close to Chauk and were moving by road and river. Burning oil was floating down river so that must have put paid to a lot of boats.'[3]

Anti-aircraft crews of the BAF destroyed their weapons on 1 May when the retreating army found its heavy equipment could go no further over the jungle tracks. Cooper, leading a small column, performed one of the BAF's last official actions in Burma. He met a Captain West of the Burma Frontier Force, who was organizing Chin guerrillas in the frontier region. West had very few weapons to arm his men. 'I realized the remnants of the BAF would not require arms any longer so I promptly gave all there was going. He [West] was delighted,' Cooper later wrote. In a poignant little ceremony, Cooper prepared a receipt for 37 rifles, three pistols, 22 bayonets and some 3,000 rounds of ammunition. West solemnly signed the chit and then stood watching by the roadside as the bedraggled BAF remnant marched away.

Initial plans called for preserving the BAF after its survivors reached India. There was talk of forming a field battery, a coastal battery, an anti-aircraft battalion and a depot from the survivors.[4] A snap decision was then made to disband the force. Surviving records gave no explanation for the ruling. A lack of men may have been the main reason. Volunteers who wanted to stay in the military and met the necessary standards were posted to new units. Other men were returned to civilian life.

Chapter 17

CHEERFUL WARRIORS

Fiji Military Forces

THE NECKLACE OF ISLAND COLONIES stretching across the south Pacific rarely troubled the thoughts of Britain's colonial strategists. These remote specks had been acquired almost as an imperial afterthought. Most were too isolated and too small to have any real value. There was little besides palm trees, modest trade based on copra and other marginal products and, in later years, one or two relay stations for undersea telegraph cables. London saw no need to base regular forces in the region. Occasional flag-waving patrols by the Royal Navy were judged sufficient. A handful of Lilliputian armed constabularies and territorial military units guarded the larger island groups. They were expected to handle internal stability and, in theory, repel invasion. Most had little to do and life generally meandered on quietly for year after year. Only Fiji's police and volunteer defence force numbered more than a few dozen men. Military planners believed the only possible threat, if war ever touched the region, would be a maritime raider. Local forces were instructed to loose off a few rifle volleys, enough to vindicate British prestige, if a hostile ship ever loomed over the horizon. No one imagined these beguiling backwaters would witness some of the bloodiest battles of the Second World War.

Some of the islands had acquired a murderous reputation in the early years of Western exploration. Warrior cultures dominated many islands and there was a long history of conflict. Stories of cannibalism enthralled and terrified 19th-century Western audiences, as an official account of the Fiji Islands noted:

> 'The early Fijian was undoubtedly a ruthless savage, a stark fighter whose pastime seemed to be war. In this he spared neither woman nor child and, in the treacherous methods resorted to for over-coming an enemy, he showed diabolical cunning. As a cannibal he took first place in the world's history . . .'[1]

The Early Decades

Britain reluctantly took control of Fiji in 1874. Speculators with powerful friends in Australia and New Zealand, missionaries who had converted thousands of Fijians, and local Royal Navy officers made up an unlikely alliance pressing for annexation. All claimed that the Fiji islands faced catastrophe if the local tribes were allowed to go on running their own affairs. There was little interest in Fiji after it was taken over, however. An 1882 Royal Commission concluded that the islands were too remote and unimportant to justify a regular garrison. It singled out the United States and Panama as the only possible threats, but said they were so far away that there was no need to construct coastal batteries or other defences.

A volunteer defence force, the Fiji Volunteers, was raised in 1899 to repel invasion and quell local disturbances. Fiji's governor controlled the force with the power to call it out in emergencies. It was organised as an infantry battalion with a small headquarters detachment and four companies. Companies consisted of a captain, 2 lieutenants, 7 NCOs and 40 privates. Five officers, including the commandant, and 2 NCOs made up the HQ detachment. The force came under the Army Act when it was mobilised. Men who failed to report for mobilisation could be classified as deserters.

Initially membership was confined to whites: 'a condition of enlistment was that all candidates should be of pure European descent'.[2] This rule was revoked in 1903 and the unit opened to Fijians.[3] A report by the Imperial Defence Committee noted that local Europeans generally opposed the change.[4] Volunteers could resign by giving 14 days' notice in writing. Men aged 18–45 were eligible to join the force. A cadet company enlisted boys aged 14–18. Prospective cadets needed permission from their parents to join the force.

Internal security rested primarily on the Fijian Armed Constabulary. This was a military unit rather than a police force. It was made up of European officers and Fijian officers and men. The force had two companies with a total strength of 5 European officers and a European sergeant-major, 5 Fijian lieutenants and 2 Fijian chaplains along with 100 Fijian constables. All of the Fijian officers and chaplains were hereditary chiefs. The force was formed in the early years of British rule when it was used to suppress cannibal tribes and briefly reached a strength of 1,400 men. Lieutenant L. P. Knollys of the British Army's 32nd Light Infantry commanded the force when it saw fierce fighting in 1876. Detachments subdued and disarmed the truculent cannibals after storming a series of stockades and fortified caves. A constabulary detachment was subsequently based in the

Fijian Forces, 1902				
	Establishment		*Strength*	
	Officers	*Other Ranks*	*Officers*	*Other Ranks*
Volunteer Infantry	17	183	16	158
Fijian Armed Constabulary	13	109	13	109

Source: PRO CAB 9/6/1.

interior of the main island of Viti Levu to keep an eye on the 'wild highland tribes'.[5] It spent much of its time building roads, bridges and telegraph lines. Service in the unit was evidently popular and constables could not serve more than four years. Its men wore a white version of the traditional native *sulu* or long skirt and blue tunics with a red cummerbund. British officers compared the outfit to the kilts of highland regiments. A constabulary contingent marched in Edward VII's coronation parade in London.

London reluctantly reconsidered the question of Fiji's defences in 1902. A trans-Pacific telegraph cable under construction was to have an important relay station in Suva. Imperial officials conceded that an enemy raid to cut the cable in any future war could make Suva a target. A report said the Volunteers were not impressive and most did not attend the weekly drills.[6] Against that, the committee noted, the cost of providing artillery and regular troops to guard Suva would be prohibitive. Official parsimony won out. London concluded that the Volunteers and constabulary had enough rifles to put up some kind of defence if Suva was ever attacked. It suggested forming rifle clubs for local Europeans to create a modest reserve force. Despite these suggestions a defence review in 1912 found Fiji's defences had dwindled in the intervening decade. The only good news appeared to be the creation of rifle clubs at Suva, Navua and Rewa. Members used surplus army rifles and a free annual issue of ammunition.

Fiji's tiny British community responded to the coming of the First World War with a patriotic fervour that equalled any part of the Empire. A regulation was passed making all European men aged 18–45 liable for service in the defence force. A German cruiser squadron was active in the southern Pacific, and there were hurried efforts to bolster Suva's flimsy defences. Many young white men left in the first weeks of the conflict to join the British, Australian or New Zealand forces. The local administration decided to organise contingents of Volunteers for the British forces and oversee their travel arrangements. A first batch with 56 men and a single officer left for Britain on 31 December 1914. Hundreds of Fijian Europeans

Fiji Defence Force, 1930

Headquarters
    3 European officers *(1 professional)*
    1 European warrant officer *(1 professional)*
    2 native NCOs

European Company
    Establishment   5 officers, 200 European and 'half-caste' ORs
    Actual strength   86

Fijian Regiment
    Establishment   5 officers, 200 native other ranks
    Actual strength   100 approx.

Source: PRO CAB 9/20.

served in Europe and the Middle East: 131 were killed in action or died from other causes on active service. About 100 settlers became officers in the British and colonial forces.

Fiji's Melanesian majority also offered to form a fighting force for the British Army. Local officials eventually said that the offer had to be regretfully declined. Britain was reluctant to use non-white troops in Europe. A small labour force of about 100 men was eventually recruited for service in Europe. It was rated highly by British commanders for its enthusiasm and efficiency.

A modest effort was made to expand Fiji's defences after the war. There was not a great deal of local interest. Thoughts of another war ever reaching the south Pacific seemed improbable. A 1921 ordinance cleared the way to expand the Volunteers, but the new Fiji Defence Force (FDF) was not created until two years later. By 1925 it comprised a small headquarters and three rifle companies. British Army officers and NCOs were sent on temporary assignment to train the corps. One company was exclusively European while the other two were described as a mix of European, non-European and native – presumably to cover mixed-race and Indian recruits as well as Fijian natives. Most of the European volunteers were businessmen, labourers and mechanics. Men who completed three years' service were eligible to join a reserve force for emergency service.

By 1930 the FDF had a small headquarters run by a regular officer and a warrant officer on temporary secondment. A separate Melanesian company had been formed. Men were required to attend 48 weekly training drills each year. Few of the Volunteers were meeting the requirement, and local officials wanted to reduce it to 36 drills a year. Volunteers were given rifle, Vickers and Lewis gun training. There was a drastic shortage of equipment, and much of what the force possessed was worn out and close to useless. Local commanders estimated that only half of the force could be equipped if it was mobilised for active service. A report also complained that the men in the Fijian native company were of poor quality. It said the 'better sort of native' was not ready to serve just for honour and glory. It suggested a more showy uniform might attract better recruits.[7] The only high point was the defence force band, whose 35 members gave popular Sunday evening concerts. London, noting that coastal artillery could not be built in Fiji because of the 1927 Washington Naval Treaty, concluded the force was adequate to face any likely threat despite its poor standards.

FDF membership by 1934 was 11 officers and 261 men and recruiting improved in the late 1930s as the darkening global political situation touched even remote Fiji. Enlistment in the FDF rose to 527 men on the eve of the war. An Indian platoon was formed for the first time. It was hardly an impressive turn-out for a colony with a population in 1940 of 110,000 Fijians, an equal number of Indians (who had been brought in by the British as labourers) and 5,000 Europeans. London had shown a rare spark of interest after a 1936 report noted that advances in air power meant Fiji might be developed as a base. Nothing came of it and defence officials in the imperial capital admitted the FDF was not up to much except guarding Suva against the old threat of a seaborne raiding party.[8]

The Second World War

Fiji was determined not to be left out of the Empire's war effort when conflict swept across Europe in 1939.[9] 'Small as we are we must pull our weight,' proclaimed the *Fiji Times and Herald*. Compulsory military training for all European males aged 18–36 was adopted a month before the start of the war. Work began on turning the FDF into a regular infantry battalion for overseas service. The new 1st Battalion was to consist of a headquarters, three rifle companies, a machine-gun platoon and a small signals detachment. It would consist mostly of Melanesian troops under European and Melanesian officers. Plans for a second battalion followed in October 1939 made up of the territorial companies that had been raised in different parts of the islands. A July 1940 order that all men aged 18–36 undergo three month courses of military training applied only to Europeans but a growing number of Melanesians nonetheless volunteered to serve. Indian recruiting was much more modest, although there were enough men to form a separate Indian company for the first time. It was attached to FDF headquarters. Many white and mixed-race men left Fiji at the start of

Fiji Defence Force, December 1940

Force Headquarters	
Suva Battery	
1st Battalion	3 Regular companies, 2 Territorial companies
2nd Battalion	Territorial
Reserve Motor Transport Section	Regular
Natabua Training Camp	
Ordnance Section	Regular
Pay and Records Section	Regular
Force Armoury	Regular

Source: Howlett, The History of the Fiji Military Forces.

the war to enlist in Britain, Australia and New Zealand. A ban was then imposed because officials feared the exodus was hurting local industry and leaving the FDF short of potential officers and NCOs.

Fiji's little army was amateurish and unimpressive despite the recruits' enthusiasm. Regular British officers complained that the men were still civilians despite all the efforts to turn them into soldiers. Major C. W. Free, a regular staff officer, claimed the force was mostly a ceremonial and social organisation. Free told London there was little discipline and most of the men imagined they were doing the Empire a favour. European recruits, he claimed, were preoccupied with business and social matters and reluctant to put military needs first. Fijian soldiers were castigated as virtually useless. Free demanded they be put under European NCOs. His dyspeptic report ended with the assertion that the force lacked any spirit or sense of service and sacrifice '. . . and from top to bottom does not realise that an order is an order'.[10] Free said the only solution was to form a permanent company of Europeans as the backbone of the defences and indeed a reserve company of ex-servicemen was formed in early 1940.

The 1st Battalion's first regular rifle company was assembled in May 1940. Two more regular companies were formed in September. The battalion also had two part-time Territorial companies. It was decided the 2nd Battalion would be a Territorial force whose members continued their civilian jobs and trained at nights and on weekends. A Home Guard had been formed in September 1940, incorporating most of the existing reserve company, and eventually numbered some 600 men. New Zealand provided instructors for FDF formations. Units had little equipment and even fewer weapons in the early years of the war. Fiji was far down the list for vital supplies in the years before the Japanese attack. Spare parts were cannibalised from a First World War German machine gun that had been a prize exhibit in Suva's museum. Native Fijian soldiers wore improvised khaki uniforms of a shirt, sandals and *sulu* skirts with serrated edges. The men were allowed to keep their long bushy hairstyles because there were no helmets. Conditions improved when Fiji became an advance base for New Zealand forces which began to arrive in October 1940 for training and garrison duty. Fijian forces now came under New Zealand command.

A coastal artillery unit was also formed to defend Suva. A New Zealand warship paid a flying visit to deliver two 4.7-inch naval guns. Fijians loved to recount in later years how the two large guns were nonchalantly carried ashore by a pair of sailors: both were wooden dummies. The battery was a fake. The dummies were replaced a few months later by guns reputedly stripped from Hong Kong's defences. Five batteries with 6-inch and 4.7-inch guns and anti-aircraft guns were eventually installed around Suva and other strategic points. The 1st Heavy Regiment, Fiji Artillery, was formed in October 1940 to help man the growing coastal defences. New Zealand officers and NCOs dominated the unit. Fijian natives were used only as ammunition carriers at first. Later they were added to gun crews and given other responsibilities. The regiment eventually became a hotchpotch of Pacific nations with men from Fiji, New Zealand, Australia, Britain, Canada, China, Tonga, British Samoa, the Solomon Islands, the Gilbert and Ellice Islands plus one American Samoan and a solitary Free French volunteer.

Training continued in 1941 as Fijian and New Zealand commanders strove to turn the FDF into a fighting force. Local administrators had ambitious ideas about raising a full brigade for service in Europe or North Africa. They were eager to boost Fiji's standing by making an outsized military contribution to the imperial war effort. A major step came in July when the 1st Battalion became a purely regular unit. Its two territorial companies were assigned to the 2nd (Territorial) Battalion.

A growing number of Fijian troops were now enlisting in the FDF. Improvements in supplies saw the first issue of khaki battledress and boots to native troops in September 1940. Almost 50 local tailors were employed to produce uniforms for the ballooning FDF. However, Fijians struggled to adapt to Western footwear that had a crippling effect on men used to going barefoot or wearing sandals.

Everything changed with the start of the war in Asia in December 1941. Fiji was threatened as Japanese forces over-ran south-east Asia and surged southwards. Rapid expansion of the FDF to defend the islands against invasion followed. Another regular infantry battalion was formed and became the 3rd Battalion. Three commando or guerrilla forces were created to operate behind enemy lines if the Japanese landed. The Fijian and New Zealand commandos were trained in jungle warfare and sabotage. The three units – Southern Independent Commando, Western Independent Commando and Eastern Independent Commando – were given specific areas of operation. Western Independent Commando was disbanded in late 1942 and some of its men shifted to the newly-formed Northern Independent Commando, which was initially set up as a mounted force. Weapons and virtually everything else the FDF required still had to be imported.

Huge changes came with the arrival in May 1942 of U.S. troops. Fiji became a major logistical centre for the planned American offensive in the south-west Pacific. Fleets of cargo ships delivered mountains of equipment for the U.S. Army's 37th Division. A Fijian labour battalion was formed in October to handle the spiralling congestion in Suva's docks. A second labour battalion was created at the end of 1942. Recruits for the FDF infantry battalions also found themselves toiling on the jetties. U.S. forces took responsibility for the defence of Fiji and the New Zealand 3rd Division was withdrawn, though several small New Zealand administrative and support units remained to provide the FDF with medical and technical services. American commanders expected the Fijians to adopt their ways. Local officials, aware of London's desire to appease the Americans and of British weakness in the Pacific, worked hard to ensure cordial cooperation.

Local colonial officials and the islands' traditional chiefs still had dreams of a Fijian brigade operating in a major theatre. A third regular battalion was formed in October 1942 and designated 4th (Regular) Battalion. This cleared the way for the formation on 1 November of the long-anticipated Fiji Infantry Brigade Group. 1st Field Battery, Fiji Artillery Regiment, was formed the same month to provide an artillery arm. It was equipped with 25-pounder field guns. More improvements came when the 4th Battalion received 12 Bren gun carriers.

Fiji officials lobbied for the FDF to be employed against the Japanese. The troops, some of whom had been training since 1939, were fed up with endless guard duty and labour details but American military commanders were reluctant to use the Fijians. American commanders said sending the Fijians to the front line would mean using U.S. units to garrison Fiji. They also had concerns about the fighting qualities of the FDF and there was reluctance to use non-white troops in combat. (The U.S. armed forces were still racially segregated at the time and combat units were almost exclusively

Fiji Military Forces, December 1942

Fiji Infantry Brigade Group
1st Battalion, Fiji Infantry Regiment
3rd Battalion, Fiji Infantry Regiment
4th Battalion, Fiji Infantry Regiment
1st Field Battery, Fiji Artillery Regiment
1st Field Company, Fiji Corps of Engineers
1st Brigade Section, Fiji Corps of Signals

Eastern Independent Commando

Southern Independent Commando

Northern Independent Commando

1st Composite Company, Fiji Army Service Corps
1st Reserve Motor Transport Company, Fiji Army Service Corps
1st Bearer Company, Fiji Medical Corps
36th Light Aid Detachment, New Zealand Ordnance Corps
Fiji Military Forces, School of Instruction

Administrative Headquarters and Base Details
Administrative Headquarters

1st Heavy Battery, Fiji Artillery Regiment

2nd (Territorial) Battalion, Fiji Infantry Regiment

1st Battalion, Fiji Labour Corps

2nd Battalion, Fiji Labour Corps

Base Training Depot
Fiji Provost Corps
Fiji Ordnance Corps
Fiji Home Guard
Fiji Bridge Guards

Source: Howlett, The History of the Fiji Military Forces.

white.) Some U.S. officers, however, had been impressed by the Fijians who had helped train American forces in jungle warfare. It was decided to send a small Fijian guerrilla force to the Solomon Islands as an experiment. A force of 8 New Zealand officers and NCOs and 22 Fijian natives left for Guadalcanal in late December 1942. All of the Fijians were made lance-corporals or corporals to raise their pay to 2 shillings a day. The force patrolled behind Japanese lines and gathered intelligence. A series of clashes with Japanese troops proved the Fijians' excellent fighting skills. Solomon Island native irregulars were recruited and trained by the force.

U.S. commanders were delighted with the Fijian's performance. Fiji Governor Philip Mitchell boasted to London that the U.S. Marine Corps had praised the Fijians as 'the finest type of native in this part of the world'. He added that: 'Even hard types of Southern officers had to admit that for native people they were "Tops" which is a great tribute.'[11] Mitchell, who campaigned tirelessly for the FDF, followed up with a message in June 1943 reporting that the U.S. Navy wanted to use more Fijian troops, but the U.S. Army was ambivalent. Army resistance, he explained, reflected '. . . their great dislike of their own Negro troops, with which, in their minds, they certainly associated Fijians to some extent. U.S. Negro troops that I have seen seem to me to be lamentable.'[12]

Fiji's colonial administrators played up the success of the guerrillas in the Solomons with a publicity campaign to boost the image of the FDF. Several American correspondents wrote admiring articles and the Fijians attracted attention at the highest levels. Winston Churchill sent a note suggesting the Fijians be used in Burma or elsewhere after hearing of the Solomon success. Officials in Suva suddenly worried that they had been too successful. A note circulated within the Fiji government suggesting the publicity campaign had 'got rather out of hand . . . wise to pipe it down for we do not yet really know what quality the Fijian is'.[13]

The sudden caution did not diminish the efforts to get the Fijian brigade deployed as a unit. Mitchell opposed individual battalions or units being deployed. He argued the Fijians would be most effective as an independent force under their own commanders. Most of his efforts focused on getting the brigade sent to Burma. London did not share the enthusiasm emanating from government headquarters in Suva. A slate of reasons was cited to show the plan was not feasible, including a lack of shipping, language problems and the potential strain on the Indian government of having to deal with a brigade of Melanesian warriors. It was a duel that lasted to the end of the war.

A 1943 proposal to send the whole Fijian brigade with a New Zealand force to New Caledonia was blocked because U.S. commanders did not want to take over the defence of Fiji. Officials in 1944 discussed using the Fijians to garrison British Pacific islands liberated by the Americans. The idea was dropped after objections that it would be a waste of excellent combat troops. (A subsequent proposal to use West Indian troops also went nowhere.) London offered the Fijian brigade to the Australian Army in 1945 on condition the Australians took over garrisoning the Solomons. Canberra countered it would accept the Fijians if Australian forces did not have to garrison the Solomons. Mitchell's adamant pursuit of the dream of a Fijian brigade on the battlefield probably frustrated chances of the FDF seeing more action.

London did agree to one fillip at the end of 1942. A proposal from Suva to change the name of the FDF to the Fiji Military Forces (FMF) was approved. The proud governor said the change was justified because the old name's emphasis on defence no longer did justice to the Fijian military capability.

Although never deployed as a brigade, some Fijian units saw significant action. FMF spirits soared when the United States asked for Fijian reinforcements for the Solomons. A mixed force of infantry and commandos was readied. A new unit, 1st Commando, Fiji Guerrillas, was formed for the assignment with 39 New Zealanders and 135 Fijians. A Tongan platoon with 28 men was added to its strength. The 1st Infantry Battalion and the new commando group left for the Solomons in April 1943, where they joined up with the existing Fiji guerrilla detachment. 1st Commando was used for patrol and intelligence work on New Georgia. A series of clashes with Japanese forces cost the commandos 11 dead and 20 wounded. A detachment of Solomon Islanders was added to the commando, which operated in a babble of English, Fijian, Tongan and Pidgin English. U.S. forces called them the South Pacific Scouts because of their reputed aversion to the term commando. The 2nd Commando was formed when the three regional commando forces were disbanded and many of the men joined the new regular formation. 2nd Commando arrived on Guadalcanal in November 1943. 1st Commando, decimated by malaria and other diseases, returned home to Fiji in December 1943; 2nd Commando returned home after a few months and both commando units were disbanded in April 1944. It appears the regular Fijian battalions, which had since proved their value, made the commandos superfluous.

The 1st Battalion was not used for several months after reaching the Solomons. Its commanding officer insisted it must be used as a full unit and not broken up into detachments. Finally it was sent in October 1943 to clear Kolombangara Island of Japanese forces only to find it had been abandoned. The battalion joined the Bougainville Task Force at the end of December 1943. It established a remote jungle base behind Japanese lines and sent patrols out to gather intelligence. Encroaching Japanese troops eventually forced the abandonment of the base. The battalion split up and escaped through thick jungle to the American lines. Parts of the battalion saw bitter fighting during subsequent Japanese attacks on the Allied beachhead, and it was in almost continuous action until June 1944. It returned to Fiji in August 1944.

The 3rd Battalion arrived in the Solomons in March 1944. With it was the 1st Docks Company, newly formed from the two Fiji Labour Corps battalions, to clear supplies from the beaches. 3rd Battalion saw its first action during an amphibious landing with U.S. troops. The 3rd Battalion returned to Fiji in September 1944. It and the 1st Battalion suffered badly from malaria and other diseases during their time in the Solomons.

Corporal Sefanaia Sukanaivalu won the Victoria Cross, Britain's highest award for battlefield heroism, during the fighting on Bougainville. He rescued two Fijians who were wounded in an attack on a Japanese machine-gun post. Sukanaivalu was then hit and left sprawled in front of the enemy position. His men ignored Sukanaivalu's orders to pull back and tried repeatedly to reach him despite the intense enemy fire. Realising his men would not abandon him despite the risk to their own lives, the corporal sacrificed himself by staggering to his knees and was cut to pieces by the machine-gun fire. The VC citation said Sukanaivalu's selfless act saved his unit from annihilation. His body was recovered months later and buried in a British military cemetery.

Fiji's defences began to be dismantled in 1943 as it became clear the Japanese drive had been blunted. The Home Guard was disbanded at the end of 1943. 2nd Battalion, the Territorial reserve force, ended training in early 1944. Most of the coastal artillery was mothballed, and the gunners transferred to the infantry battalions. The war was far from finished, however, and FMF leaders and their civilian masters still wanted to see a Fijian brigade in action after the successes of the Solomons. A major training effort was launched in early 1945 to ready the three regular infantry battalions for more operations. Even the field battery was converted to infantry. New recruits replaced Solomon veterans worn out by disease and exhaustion. Fiji colonial officials again pressed London to use the brigade in Burma. Talks were still going on when Japan surrendered in August 1945. 1st Docks Company, which had returned to Fiji in February 1945, was the last Fijian unit to see overseas service.

Demobilisation of the FMF was announced on 1 September 1945. By the end of December only a handful of administrative and guard units were still in uniform. Their main role was winding up FMF paperwork and guarding the massive U.S. supply dumps waiting to be shipped home. Most of the units were put under the new 5th Battalion which had been formed to handle the winding up. It was disbanded in March 1946 except for a company that was retained for a few months.

A Question of Race

The FMF earned an excellent reputation in a theatre that saw some of the most savage fighting of the war. Fijians were hailed as some of the best jungle troops in the world. About 11,000 men served in the FMF during the war, and it numbered 8,513 regulars and reservists at its peak in August 1943. Melanesians made up three-quarters of the force and overwhelmingly dominated the lower ranks. Fiji's military prided itself on the racial equality in its units. Or at least the Europeans who wrote about the force during and immediately after the war did. Experiences and views of non-whites were not widely recorded. White Fijians dominated the officer and NCO corps but about 20 per cent of the officers were Melanesian, a high ratio by contemporary standards in British colonial units. Most Melanesian officers were lieutenants, however, and there was only one Melanesian lieutenant-colonel and a single major. (Hundreds of white New Zealand officers and NCOs were attached to the FMF as instructors and leaders.) The three regular infantry battalions were composed predominantly of Melanesian privates under mostly white officers. It is not clear if there were any white privates in their ranks. Separate white companies existed in the territorial 2nd Battalion while the Home Guard was mostly European.

Fiji does not appear to have suffered from the worst forms of racism that permeated some British colonies in 1939. Colonial officials were mindful that British rule rested largely on the consent of the Melanesians. Major expansion of the Fijian military forces came after the governor sought, and won, the support of the traditional chiefs for the war effort. Some of the pressure to use the FMF as a brigade in combat and earn the maximum prestige for Fiji probably came from the chiefs. The paternal official view of ordinary Fijian soldiers was as 'sensitive, but intelligent children'.[14] At least some white Fijians clung to the biases that dominated the rest of the Empire. New Zealand army trainers complained that most Melanesians were subservient towards whites, and it initially hindered efforts to turn them into soldiers. Melanesian labour troops were startled when white New Zealand soldiers first worked beside them unloading ships and digging latrines. Some of the New Zealanders predicted the position of the white settlers would be shaken by the war.

Emblematic of the racial contradictions was the life of Lieutenant-Colonel Sir Ratu Lala Sukuna, the FMF's highest-ranking Melanesian officer, and architect of Fijian independence. He was a senior chief by birth and sat on the colonial Legislative Council. Sukuna was a trailblazer throughout his life. He was the first Fijian to breach the tacit British ban on university education for Melanesians, eventually graduating from Oxford University and earning a second degree in law. Sukuna served with the French Foreign Legion in the First World War after being turned down by the British military. He was wounded and received the Croix de Guerre.

Later in the war he served in the tiny Fijian labour corps on the Western Front with the British forces. Sukuna was a driving force for the build-up of the FMF and acted as the force's chief recruiter. He believed that Fijians would not be respected until they proved themselves on the battlefield. Aiding Britain, he believed, would be a major step toward emancipation.

Fiji had a second major racial group in the descendants of Indian labourers imported by the British to work in the sugar fields. By 1940 the Indians were as numerous as the Melanesians. Indians had branched out into business and the professions, and there were demands for scarce agricultural land from Indian farmers. Many Melanesians were increasingly worried by the swelling Indian numbers and the resulting tustle over land and political influence, a tension that still rankles in Fijian politics. British officials had doubts about the Indians' loyalty during the war. FMF units were deployed to counter labour unrest among Indian sugar workers.

Indians did not play a significant role in Fiji's military forces, in part because they were not particularly welcomed by the British or the Melanesians. The FDF had a small Indian company in the 1930s. An Indian Reserve Motor Transport Section was formed in 1940 with one European officer and 36 Indians. An Indian construction unit existed for a year in the Labour Corps' second battalion. A solitary Indian platoon in the 2nd Infantry Battalion was disbanded at its own request after protesting differences in pay between Europeans and non-Europeans. London received a request in 1944 to allow about 30 Indian members of the FMF to enlist in the Indian Army as a unit under the sole Fijian Indian officer. London said it would be impossible to reinforce such a tiny unit and it was unlikely the Indian Army would agree to accept it. The men were told they could volunteer as individuals for the Indian forces.[15]

Towards Independence and Beyond

Fiji's defences were reduced to a token presence after the end of the war. A 1947 report[16] gave the FMF strength as 6 officers and 72 other ranks, mostly administrators and a band. Interest in regional defence revived with the onset of the Cold War. An ambitious 1949 plan envisaged creating two artillery regiments, two infantry battalions and support units. A permanent force of 20 officers and 200 men and a territorial reserve of 100 officers and 2,000 men was planned. Work on the force continued steadily over the next few years and Fiji possessed an impressive little army when independence came in 1970.

Chapter 18

DISTANT SPECKS

The Solomon Islands and Other Outposts

A SCATTERING OF TINY MILITARY and paramilitary police units guarded a few of Britain's other South Pacific outposts. A 1913 defence review of the Western Pacific decided the region would be a backwater in any likely war except for the remote chance of maritime raids.[1] Officials admitted the islands would be virtually defenceless if an enemy ship ever appeared. The Imperial Defence Committee, nonetheless, said the handfuls of local settlers and police would be expected to put up enough resistance to vindicate British pride. Islands were instructed to destroy their coal stocks and fire a few rifle volleys.

The sprawling Solomon Islands had the only significant forces besides Fiji. An armed constabulary was structured on a 1915 ordinance that defined its role as defending law and order, internal stability and defence against external aggression.[2] By 1925 it had 3 British officers and 150 native constables in detachments on eight islands. It was far too small to cover such an enormous area.

Plans were drawn up in the 1920s for a Volunteer unit to be called the Solomon Islands Defence Force (SIDF). It was not established until 1939. The SIDF was composed of a handful of British officials and settlers with some Melanesians, and does not appear to have existed as a meaningful force. It was decided to disband the unit in February 1942 as it became clear that the Solomons faced a Japanese invasion and any resistance would be suicidal. Dissolution was still underway when Japanese troops landed.

Natives were later recruited as porters for U.S. forces during the Battle of Guadalcanal and the subsequent fighting in the Solomon Islands chain. Porters were organised under British officers as the Solomon Islands Labour Corps. A few men joined the Fiji Guerrillas and fought behind Japanese lines. Some accounts refer to the local detachment as the Solomon Island Scouts. American and British commanders decided Solomon Islanders were not effective as soldiers outside of their islands and they were not employed elsewhere. Some Solomon Islanders worked and fought for the Japanese.

Some of the smallest military and police units in the British Empire guarded the far-flung Gilbert and Ellice Islands. The Gilbert and Ellice Islands Armed Constabulary ostensibly was the first line of defence against external attack. It had a strength of 5 British officers and 45 native constables. A 1917 ordinance provided for creation of the volunteer Ocean Island Defence Force on the main British island in the Gilberts.[3] It was a European force. By 1924 it had a nominal strength of 1 officer and 23 other ranks. Ocean and Nauru islands were attacked by the German Auxiliary cruisers *Orion* and *Komet* in December 1940. The Ocean Island Defence Force was disbanded in March 1942 as Japanese forces swept across the Pacific. Officials recognised it could not offer any meaningful resistance. There was no fighting when Japanese forces took Ocean Island in August 1942.

A 1918 ordinance provided for the creation of a part-time defence force on Fanning Island in the Line Islands. It had not been formed by 1925 and there is no indication that it advanced beyond a plan on paper.

Tonga, an independent island kingdom under British protection, aligned itself with London in 1939 when war erupted in Europe. The Tonga Defence Force and a home guard were formed with the enthusiastic support of the ruling dynasty and much of the population. Three infantry companies had been formed by 1941 and there were plans for a fourth company to make up a battalion of 450 men. New Zealand officers and NCOs arrived in mid-1941 to train and help lead the force. A rather sour New Zealand Army report said the force was likely to produce good native troops if stiffened with white men.[4] A platoon of Tongans under a Tongan officer served with the Fijian guerrillas in the Solomons. Demobilisation of the Tonga Defence Force began in February 1944 once it became clear that Japan no longer posed any threat to the island.

NOTES

Chapter 1: *Forgotten Regiments (pages 1–13)*

1. Quoted in Wasserstein, *Secret War in Shanghai*, p. 12.

Chapter 2: *In Oriente Primus (pages 14–47)*

1. Winsley, *A History of the Singapore Volunteer Corps 1854–1937*, p 2.
2. Accounts suggest there were some 18,000 men in the British Volunteer forces in Malaya and Singapore in 1941 comprising the various military Volunteer forces, para-military police reservists and the local service corps.
3. Quoted in Winsley, p. 3.
4. Winsley, p. 3.
5. Winsley, p. 4.
6. Winsley, p. 132.
7. Winsley, p. 5.
8. Winsley, p. 13.
9. Winsley, p. 20.
10. Winsley, p. 27.
11. Annual Inspection of Penang Volunteers 1902, National Archives (TNA): Public Pecord Office (PRO) CAB 9/5/15.
12. Report on the Penang Volunteers 1907–1909', TNA: PRO CAB 9/5/15.
13. Report on Malay States Volunteer Rifles 1911–1912, TNA: PRO CAB 9/5/15.
14. Report on Malay States Volunteer Rifles 1912, TNA: PRO CAB 9/5/15.
15. *Ibid.*
16. Papers of Malcolm Bond Shelley, National Army Museum, London (NAM).
17. *Ibid.*
18. *Ibid.*
19. *Ibid.*
20. 1921 unidentified press clipping, Imperial War Museum, London (IWM).
21. Straits Settlements Volunteer Force Year Book 1938/39, IWM.
22. Straits Settlement Volunteer Force Annual Report 1925, TNA: PRO CAB 9/19/54.
23. *Straits Times*, 14 October 1924.
24. Undated newspaper advertisement, IWM.
25. Straits Settlements Volunteer Force Annual Report 1930, TNA: PRO CAB 9/19/54.
26. Straits Settlements Volunteer Force Year Book, 1938/39.
27. Straits Settlements Annual Report 1925.
28. Papers of Charles Kinahan, IWM.
29. Papers of W. M. Innes-Ker, IWM.
30. Author interview with Tom Evans, 20 March 2009.

31. Straits Settlements Volunteer Force Annual Report 1930, TNA: PRO CAB 9/19/54.
32. Papers of C. Thornton, IWM.
33. Papers of R. A. Middleton, IWM.
34. Evans interview.
35. Papers of G. E. D. Lewis, IWM.
36. Papers of I. A. McDonald, IWM.
37. Papers of R. M. Hoops, IWM.
38. Papers of Charles Kinahan, IWM.
39. McDonald papers.
40. Papers of S. J. Littledyke, IWM.
41. Papers of T. H. Evans, IWM.
42. Brigadier R. G. Moir, 'Notes on the Malayan Campaign', TNA: PRO CAB 106/156.
43. Hoops papers.
44. Middleton papers.
45. Papers of C. H. Lee, IWM.
46. Papers of H. A. Porter, IWM.
47. Thornton papers.
48. Moir, 'Notes on the Malayan Campaign'.
49. Papers of Donald Webber, IWM.
50. Papers of C. W. S Seed, IWM.
51. Papers of J. R. Hodgson, IWM.
52. Evans interview.
53. Evans interview.
54. Evans papers.
55. Papers of James Taylor Rea, IWM.
56. Papers of J. K. Gale, IWM.
57. Papers of L. V. Taylor, IWM.
58. Papers of Guy Turner, IWM.
59. Littledyke papers.
60. Evans interview.
61. Taylor papers.
62. Thornton papers.
63. Gale papers.
64. Hill, *Diversion in Malaya*, p. 62.
65. Middleton papers.
66. Evans papers.
67. Kinahan papers.
68. Killing of Chinese of SSVF in Singapore Aug. 1945 – Feb. 1946, TNA: PRO WO 325/30.

Chapter 3: Forlorn Hope (pages 48–49)

1. Author interview with Tom Evans, 20 March 2009.
2. Papers of I. A. McDonald, IWM.
3. Bill Cranston, the leading expert on Malay military badges, describes the badge as a violet-coloured circle with an inverted triangle in the centre. The legend 'Dalforce' runs across the badge.
4. Woodburn Kirby, *The War Against Japan*. Vol. 1, *The Loss of Singapore*, p. 364.
5. McDonald papers.

Chapter 4: *A Sultan's Toy (pages 50–56)*

1. The main sources for the early history of the Guides are the various annual reports on the regiment contained in TNA: PRO CAB 9 and Singh, *History of Malay States Guides.*
2. 'Malay States Guides Report 1903, TNA: PRO CAB 9.
3. 'Malay States Guides Report 1911, TNA: PRO CAB 9.
4. 'Malay States Guides Report 1904/05, TNA: PRO CAB 9.
5. TNA: PRO WO 106.

Chapter 5: *Loyal and True (pages 57–64)*

1. Papers of G. H. Kelling, IWM.
2. Ramli, *History of the Malay Regiment 1933–1942*, p. 7.
3. Cameron, *Our Tropical Possessions in Malayan India.*
4. Britain took over some Malay troops serving in Dutch colonial units at the start of the 19th century, notably the Ceylon Rifle Regiment, but it was later disbanded.
5. Quoted in Ramli, p. 18.
6. Quoted in Ramli, p. 9.
7. *The Malay Regiment 1933–1947*, p. 3.
8. Ramli, p. 8.
9. Sheppard, *Beginning and Growth of the Royal Malay Regiment.*
10. Sheppard.
11. Sheppard.
12. Sheppard.
13. Papers of J. K. Gale, IWM.
14. Papers of Lieutenant Alastair MacKenzie, IWM.
15. *Ibid.*
16. *Ibid.*
17. According to Ramli the executed officers were Lieutenant Mohammed Ariffin bin Haji Sulaiman, Lieutenant Abdul bin Judin, Lieutenant Ibrahim bin Sidek, Lieutenant Abdullah bin Saat and Lieutenant Abbas bin Mohammed Said of the Straits Settlements Volunteer Force attached to 2nd Battalion, Malay Regiment.

Chapter 6: *White Rajas (pages 65–66)*

1. Much of this account is drawn from *History of the Sarawak Rangers. The White Rajahs* by S. Runciman was also consulted.
2. The Ceylon Rifles was a unit composed of Malays that served the Dutch when they held that island. It was taken over by the British along with the territory only to be later disbanded.

Chapter 7: *Second to None (pages 67–98)*

1. This section consulted, in part, Reports of the Imperial Defence Committee, TNA: PRO CAB 9; Bruce, *Second To None*; Hong Kong Museum of Coastal Defence, *Serving Hong Kong*; and Hayes, *A Short History of the Military Volunteers in Hong Kong.*
2. Bickers, *Britain in China*, p. 73.
3. TNA: PRO CAB 9/5/15.
4. Quoted in Bruce, p. 31.
5. Quoted in Bruce, p. 66.
6. Report on Hong Kong Volunteers 1909–10, TNA: PRO CAB 9/5/15.
7. Report to Colonial Defence Committee May 1902, TNA: PRO CAB 9/5/15.

8. Report on Hong Kong Volunteers 1907–08, TNA: PRO CAB 9/5/15.
9. Report on Hong Kong Volunteers 1909–10.
10. Report on Hong Kong Volunteers 1912–13, TNA: PRO CAB 9/5/15.
11. Report on Hong Kong Volunteer Defence Corps 1918–19, TNA: PRO CAB 9/5/54.
12. *Ibid.*
13. Report on Hong Kong Volunteer Defence Corps 1934–35, TNA: PRO CAB 9/19/54.
14. *Ibid.*
15. Report on Hong Kong Volunteer Defence Corps 1935–36, TNA: PRO CAB 9/19/54.
16. Report on HKVDC 1934–35.
17. TNA: PRO FO 228/4081 Dossier 94A-B.
18. Report on Hong Kong Volunteers 1905–06, TNA: PRO CAB 9/5/15.
19. TNA: PRO WO 106/78.
20. Report on HKVDC 1934–35.
21. Report on HKVDC 1935–36.
22. *South China Morning Post*, 6 August 1998.
23. Report on HKVDC 1935–36.
24. *South China Morning Post*, September 1995.
25. Yearbooks of the Hong Kong Volunteer Defence Corps. Various years. IWM
26. Hong Kong Legislative Council Minutes, 27 July 1939, PRO.
27. TNA: PRO CO 129/540/1.
28. TNA: PRO CO 129/557/7.
29. Report on Hong Kong Volunteer Defence Corps 1927–29, TNA: PRO CAB 9/19/54.
30. Report on Hong Kong Volunteer Defence Corps 1932, TNA: PRO CAB 9/20/46.
31. Report on HKVDC 1935–36.
32. Report on HKVDC 1939, TNA: PRO CAB 9/19/54; and *Sunday Morning Post*, Hong Kong.
33. Secret Report on the HKVDC 1940–41, TNA: PRO S/56/1999.
34. Hewitt, *Children of the Empire*, p. 82.
35. Secret Report on the HKVDC 1940–41.
36. The account of the HKVDC's role in the battle for Hong Kong is based on surviving British records and Anon., *A Record of the Actions of the Hong Kong Volunteer Defence Corps in the Battle for Hong Kong December 1941.*
37. War Record No. 1 Company HKVDC, TNA: PRO WO 172/1693.
38. *Ibid.*
39. Private papers.
40. Private papers.
41. *London Gazette*, 27 January 1948.
42. *Gunner*, November 1946.
43. Hong Kong Company War Diary, 1 Jan 1944 – 31 December 1944, TNA: PRO WO 30.
44. TNA: PRO WO 32/12688, WO 32/11452.

Chapter 8: *Our Very Own (pages 99–106)*

1. Chapple, Field Marshal Sir John, 'Notes on the Hong Kong Regiment', NAM 7712-2-4.
2. *Ibid.*
3. *Ibid.*
4. *Ibid.*

5. *Ibid.*
6. TNA: PRO WO 32-6721.
7. *Ibid.*
8. *China Mail*, 25 June 1892.
9. *Ibid.*
10. TNA: PRO WO 30/103.
11. *Ibid.*
12. *China Mail*, 25 June 1892.
13. *Hong Kong Daily Press*, 30 July 1892.
14. *Ibid.*
15. Undated press clipping, NAM.
16. TNA: PRO WO 30/104.
17. TNA: PRO WO 30/103.

Chapter 9: *Sober Gunners (pages 107–129)*

1. Much of this chapter is based on the Crowe papers, a collection of official HKSRA records and documents held by the Royal Artillery Museum, Woolwich.
2. HKSRA Disbandment, Notes by Lieutenant-Colonel M. E. S. Laws, Crowe papers.
3. *South China Morning Post*, 1905 supplement.
4. *Free Press*, undated article.
5. Crowe papers.
6. *Ibid.*
7. *Ibid.*
8. Wildey, Brigadier-General Alec, 'History of Anti-Aircraft Units of HKSRA, 1937–1943', in the Crowe papers.
9. Crowe papers.
10. *Ibid.*
11. *Ibid.*
12. *Ibid.*
13. *Ibid.*
14. War Diary, 1st Hong Kong Regiment, HKSRA, Crowe papers.
15. *Ibid.*
16. *Ibid.*
17. *Ibid.*
18. *Ibid.*
19. *Ibid.*
20. *Ibid.*
21. The account of the exercise is in Wildey.
22. *Ibid.*
23. *Ibid.*
24. War Diary, 1st Hong Kong Regiment.
25. Rubin, *Murder, Mutiny and the Military.*

Chapter 10: *Ghost Formations (pages 130–132)*

1. *Hongkong Telegraph*, 14 October 1896.
2. TNA: PRO WO 106/2427, WO 32/2520.
3. Rollo, *The Guns & Gunners of Hong Kong*, pp 112–13.
4. TNA: PRO CAB 106/88.
5. TNA PRO WO 106/2427.
6. *Ibid.*
7. *Ibid.*

Chapter 11: *To Our Respective Nations (pages 133–161)*

1. Quoted in Kounin, *Eighty-Five Years of the Shanghai Volunteer Corps*, p. 8
2. Kounin, p. 11.
3. *North China Herald*, 30 April 1853.
4. Kounin, p. 144.
5. Kounin, p. 147.
6. TNA: PRO FO/228/4081, Dossier 94A-B.
7. Kounin, p. 27.
8. Private collection.
9. Kounin, p. 24.
10. Kounin, p. 50.
11. Kounin, p. 31.
12. Kounin, p. 33.
13. *Town and Sportsman*, October 1934, Shanghai.
14. Kounin, p. 198.
15. A Company SVC Mih-Ho-Loong Rifles 1870 to 1930, undated pamphlet, NAM.
16. Kounin, p. 161.
17. *New York Times*, 12 November 1911.
18. Kounin, p. 184.
19. TNA: PRO CAB 9/19/54.
20. TNA: PRO WO106/78.
21. Papers of H. B. H. Orpen-Palmer, NAM.
22. Quoted in Kounin, p. 236.
23. TNA: PRO WO/106/78.
24. *New York Times*, 12 November 1911.
25. Quoted in Kounin, p. 80.
26. Papers of J. E. March, IWM.
27. TNA: PRO WO/106/81.
28. *Ibid.*
29. Gwynn, *Imperial Policing*, p. 190.
30. TNA: PRO FO/228/4081, Dossier 94A-B.
31. TNA: PRO WO/106/78.
32. Quoted in Kounin, p. 242.
33. TNA PRO WO 106/78.
34. TNA: PRO WO/106.

Chapter 12: *Plucky Outposts (pages 162–166)*

1. TNA PRO WO 106/5379.
2. Clayton, *The British Empire as a Superpower 1919–39*, pp. 185–211. Bickers, Robert, *Britain in China, passim.*
3. TNA PRO WO 106/5379.
4. TNA PRO WO 106/5379.
5. Annand, A. McK., 'The Tientsin Volunteer Corps in the Boxer Rising 1900', *Journal of the Society for Army Historical Research*, December 1958.
6. TNA PRO WO 106/5379.
7. *Ibid.*
8. *Ibid.*
9. Papers of Captain. J. E. March, IWM.
10. TNA PRO WO 106/5379.

Chapter 13: **Unwanted Guardians** (pages 167–176)

1. TNA: PRO WO 32/67/94.
2. *Ibid.*
3. *Iron Duke*, Vol. IX No. 26, October 1933.
4. TNA PRO WO 32/67/94.
5. *Iron Duke, ibid.*
6. TNA PRO WO 32/67/94.
7. *Ibid.*
8. *Iron Duke, ibid.*
9. *Ibid.*
10. *North China Daily News*, 1 September 1900.
11. Barnes, *On Active Service with the Chinese Regiment*, p. xi.
12. Barnes, p. xiv.
13. Barnes, p. 69.
14. TNA: PRO WO 32/67/94.
15. *Ibid.*
16. *Ibid.*
17. *Ibid.*

Chapter 14: **Wretches in Khaki** (pages 177–188)

1. *The Story of the Chinese Labour Corps*, Preface.
2. German government pamphlet.
3. Quoted in Summerskill, *China on the Western Front*, p. 58.
4. TNA: PRO WO 106.
5. Example in IWM.
6. TNA: PRO WO 106.
7. Quoted in Summerskill.
8. Quoted in Summerskill, p.169.
9. Papers of J. M. Harrison, IWM.
10. TNA: PRO WO 106.
11. Papers of Captain A. McCormick, IWM.
12. *Ibid.*
13. Papers of H. E. Cornwall, IWM.
14. Harrison papers.
15. McCormick papers.
16. Klein, *With the Chinks*.
17. Xu Quoqi, 'The Great War and China', *Journal of Modern History*, vol. 72 No. 1, January 2008.
18. Klein, *With the Chinks*.
19. *Ibid.*
20. McCormick papers.
21. TNA: PRO FO 371/23537, FO 371/24653.

Chapter 15: **Fleeting Glory** (pages 189–207)

1. Enriquez, Major C. M., 'Story of the Burma Rifles', Typescript account in 'Burma Rifles', Documents of Major E. H. Cooke, NAM 7302-44.
2. Enriquez.
3. TNA: PRO WO 95/4732.
4. Enriquez.
5. Enriquez.
6. TNA: PRO WO 106/3656.
7. TNA: PRO CAB 44/324.

8. TNA: PRO CAB 44/208.
9. *Peacock*, December 1934.
10 *Ibid.*
11. Papers of I. C. G. Scott, IWM.
12. TNA: PRO WO 106/3675.
13. TNA: PRO WO 172/977.
14. Papers of D. C. Herring, IWM.
15. Papers of J. D. Hedley, IWM.
16. Enriquez.
17. Scott papers.
18. TNA: PRO WO172/977.
19. TNA: PRO WO172/974.
20. TNA: PRO WO 172/974.

Chapter 16: *Anglos and Burmans (pages 208–216)*
1. TNA: PRO WO172/310.
2. Quoted in Draper, *Dawns Like Thunder*, p. 71.
3. Papers of G. H. Cooper, IWM.
4. TNA: PRO FO 643/10.

Chapter 17: *Cheerful Warriors (pages 217–230)*
1. *The Colony of Fiji*, p. 22.
2. *Land Forces of the British Colonies and Protectorates* (1905), p. 189.
3. Fijian is used to this day to denote the islands' Melanesian population. Indian and other citizens are not covered by the term.
4. TNA: PRO CAB 9/19.
5. *Land Forces* (1905), p. 191.
6. TNA: PRO CAB 9/6/1.
7. TNA: PRO CAB 9/20.
8. *Ibid.*
9. Howlett, *The History of the Fiji Military Forces 1939-45*, was consulted for the period covering the Second World War.
10. TNA: PRO CO 83/232/7.
11. TNA: PRO CO 820/50/18.
12. TNA: PRO WO 208/3098.
13. TNA: PRO CAB 9/21.
14. Larson, *Pacific Commandos*, p. 23.
15. TNA: PRO CAB 9/21.
16. TNA: PRO CO 537/3575.

Chapter 18: *Distant Waters (pages 231–232)*
1. TNA: PRO CAB 9/19.
2. *Land Forces of the British Dominions, Colonies, Protectorates and Mandated Territories* (1925), p. 68.
3. *Land Forces* (1925), and TNA: PRO CAB 9/19.
4. TNA: PRO WO 106/3404.

SELECT BIBLIOGRAPHY

The Colony of Fiji, Government Printer, Suva, 1931

History of Coastal Defence, HMSO, London, 1948

History of the Sarawak Rangers, Malaysian Armed Forces College, 1981

Land Forces of the British Colonies and Protectorates, HMSO, London, 1905

Land Forces of the British Dominions, Colonies, Protectorates and Mandated Territories, HMSO, London, 1925

Land Forces of the British Dominions, Colonies, Protectorates and Mandated Territories, HMSO, London, 1934

The Malay Regiment 1933–1947, Department of Public Relations, Malayan Union, 1947

Serving Hong Kong: The Hong Kong Volunteers. Hong Kong Museum of Coastal Defence, Hong Kong, 2004

The Story of the Chinese Labour Corps, HMSO, London, 1918

Anonymous, *A Record of the Actions of the Hong Kong Volunteer Defence Corps in the Battle for Hong Kong, December 1941*, Ye Olde Printerie, Hong Kong, 1955

Barnes, A. A. S., *On Active Service with the Chinese Regiment*, Grant Richards, London, 1902

Barnett, Correlli, *Britain and Her Army*, Allan Lane, London, 1970

Bayly, Christopher, and Tim Harper, *Forgotten Armies*, Allen Lane, London, 2004

Bickers, Robert, *Britain in China*, Manchester University Press, 1999

Bruce, Philip, *Second To None*, Oxford University Press, 1991

Cameron, John, *Our Tropical Possessions in Malayan India*, London, 1865

Chandler, David, *et al.*, *The Oxford Illustrated History of the British Army*, Oxford, 1994

Clayton, Anthony, *The British Empire as a Superpower 1919–39*, Palgrave, Basingstoke, 1986

Draper, Alfred, *Dawns Like Thunder*, Leo Cooper, London, 1987

Farrell, Brian P., *The Defence and Fall of Singapore 1940–1942*, Tempus, Stroud, 2006

FitzGerald, C. P. A., *Concise History of East Asia*, Penguin, London, 1978

Ford, James Allan, *The Brave White Flag*, Hodder and Stoughton, London, 1961

Frank, Bennis M., 'The Jewish Company of the Shanghai Volunteer Corps', paper given at a conference 'China and the Jewish Diaspora', 1992; available at www.sino-judaic.org/pointseast/seder (accessed June 2009)

Gwynn, Charles, *Imperial Policing*, Macmillan, London, 1939

Frei, Henry, *Guns of February*, Singapore University Press, Singapore, 2004

Hayes, James, *A Short History of the Military Volunteers in Hong Kong*

Hewitt, Anthony, *Children of the Empire*, Kangaroo Press, Kenthurst, 1995

Hill, Anthony, *Diversion in Malaya*, Collins, London, 1948

Hirofumi, Hayashi, 'Japanese Treatment of Chinese Prisoners 1931–1945', *Nature-People-Society*, No. 26, January 1999, Kanto Gakuin University

Howlett, Lieutenant R. A., *The History of the Fiji Military Forces 1939–45*, Government Printer, Fiji, 1948

James, Lawrence, *The Rise and Fall of the British Empire*, Little, Brown, London, 1994

Jackson, Ashley, *The British Empire and the Second World War*, Hambledon Continuum, London, 2006

Klein, Daryl, *With the Chinks*, John Lane, London, 1919

Kounin, I. I., *Eighy-Five Years of the Shanghai Volunteer Corps*, Cosmopolitan Press, Shanghai, 1938

Larson, Colin R., *Pacific Commandos*, A. H. and A. W. Reed, Wellington, 1946

Latimer, Jon, *Burma: The Forgotten War*, John Murray, London, 2004

Lindsay, Oliver, *The Lasting Honour*, Hamish Hamilton, London, 1978

Lunt, James, *Imperial Sunset*, Macdonald, London, 1981

——, *The Retreat from Burma*, Collins, London, 1986

Mason, Philip, *A Matter of Honour*, Purnell Book Services, London, 1974

Maxwell, George, *Civil Defence of Malaya*, Hutchinson, London, 1946

Moore, William, *The Thin Yellow Line*, Leo Cooper, London, 1974

Murfett, Malcolm H., *et. al.*, *Between Two Oceans*, Oxford University Press, 1999

Priday, H. E. L., *The War from Coconut Square*, A. H. & A. W. Reed, Wellington, 1945

Ramli, Dol, *History of the Malay Regiment 1933–1942*, Singapore, 1955

Rollo, Denis, *The Guns & Gunners of Hong Kong*, Corporate Communications, Hong Kong, 1991

Rubin, Gerry R., *Murder, Mutiny and the Military*, Francis Boutle Publishers, London, 2005

Runciman, S., *The White Rajahs*, Cambridge University Press, 1960

Sheppard, Dato Haji Mubin, *Beginning and Growth of the Royal Malay Regiment*, Malaysia, 1968

Singh, Inder, *History of Malay States Guides*, Penang

Smith, Colin, *Singapore Burning*, Viking, London, 2005

Summerskill, Michael, *China on the Western Front*, Privately published, London, 1982

Tarling, Nicholas, *The Cambridge History of Southeast Asia*, Volume 2, Cambridge University Press, 1992

Thompson, Peter, *The Battle for Singapore*, Portrait Books, London, 2006

Wasserstein, Bernard, *Secret War in Shanghai*, Profile Books, London, 1998

Winsley, T. M., *A History of the Singapore Volunteer Corps 1854–1937*, Government Printing Office, Singapore, 1938

Woodburn Kirby, Major-General S., *The War Against Japan*, Vol. 1 *The Loss of Singapore*, Naval & Military Press, 2004

——, *Singapore: The Chain of Disaster*. Cassell, London, 1971

INDEX